The Way It Was

The Other Side of Huntsville's History

By

Tom Carney

Huntsville, Alabama

Old Huntsville
HISTORY AND STORIES OF THE TENNESSEE VALLEY

Copyright © 2018 Cathey Carney

Old Huntsville, Inc.
716 East Clinton Ave
Huntsville, AL 35801

CBA Publishing Services, LLC
cbapub.com
editor@cbapub.com

Editing and layout by Christine M. Brown
Cover design by Anna Talyn

All rights reserved. No part of this book may be reproduced in any form or by any electronic means including storage and retrieval systems—except in the case of brief quotation embodied in critical articles and reviews—without express written consent from its author, except provided by the Unites State of America copyright law.

First Edition 1994
Second Edition 2018

ISBN-13: 978-1726417402
ISBN-10: 1726417409

This book is dedicated to my grandfather,
Oscar Thomas Frazier,
who always wanted to be a writer.
This is the book he would have written.

End of an Era

General John,

I'll leave the weeping to the

women.

We understand each other,

you and I.

We are of the same blood.

What we cannot change

we accept.

Death limits all of us.

But still Grandfather,

there are times

I'd like to share

some wine with you.

                    John Crow

Contents

	Introduction	1
	Preface	2
1.	To Cross the Hogohegee	4
2.	The Salt Seller: The Story of John Gunter	6
3.	The Pioneers	13
4.	John Hunt	17
5.	Huntsville's First Hanging	26
6.	The Battle of Huntsville	29
7.	Horse Race at the Green Bottom Inn	33
8.	Monument to a Swindler	35
9.	Three Months to Live	43
10.	First Bathtub in America	47
11.	Sally Carter	49
12.	Scandal on Randolph Avenue	53
13.	The Indian Creek Canal	59
14.	Blood Kin	61
15.	The Forgotten Hero	62
16.	James Bierney, Presidential Candidate	68
17.	The French Settler	71
18.	The Man with No Name	74
19.	Mystery Lady of Keel Mountain	77
20.	A Man Named Sam	81
21.	The Black Widow	87
22.	The Last Gathering	91
23.	War Comes to North Alabama	92
24.	Frank Gurley: Fugitive in Gray	97
25.	Court Martial of the Mad Cossack	104
26.	A Love Story	111
27.	A War Letter	114

28. A Captured Flag	115
29. Black Confederates	117
30. The Last Surrender	119
31. Blood Bill Quantrell	121
32. Was McCoy Really Quantrell?	130
33. A Successful Man	131
34. The Rebel Yankee	135
35. "Devil" Monroe	137
36. Frank and Jesse James Ride Again	146
37. Days of the Ku Klux Klan	152
38. Howard Weeden	157
39. The Sleeping Preacher	160
40. The Monte Sano Railroad	167
41. Underground Dancehall	169
42. A Letter Home	173
43. The Wrong War	175
44. Uncle Matt	176
45. A Bitter Legacy	178
46. Huntsville's Stone Warrior	179
47. Alabama Birdman	182
48. Royalty in North Alabama	184
49. Legend of Lily Flagg	188
50. UFO's Sighted in 1910	191
51. Watercress Capital of the World	193
52. Simp McGhee	195
53. La' Overture Toussaint	200
54. The Judge Lawler Murder	202
55. The Life and Time of J. Emory Pierce	207
56. The Mill Strike	214
57. Obsessed Love	220
58. Moonshine, The Law, and Sugar Tits	229
59. Feeding the Kids	237
60. The Russel Erskine Hotel	239
61. Get a Real Job	243

62. Army Birdmen Lose Their Way 245
63. The Courthouse 248
64. The Futility of Man 251
65. King of the Snuffdippers' Ball 254
66. The Last Soldier 261
67. Huntsville Hospitality 266
68. The Keller Automobile 268
69. Delivering the Mail 271
70. Suicide 273
71. The Bon Air Restaurant 275
72. The Last Slave 276
73. Vance Morris and the Alabama Playboys 279
74. The Man Who Would be Sheriff 284
75. The Birth of Huntsville 289
76. A Tale of Two Friends 292
77. An Old Man and His Violin 295
78. Earthquake 297
79. The Church with its Own Beer Cooler 298
80. The Parkway 300
81. Tombstone for a Monkey 301
82. Clinton Avenue Archaeology 303
83. Music Appreciation 305
84. The Governor Goes to Breakfast 307
85. Account Paid 309

ABLE'S SENATE,

ADJOINING CITY SPRING.

J. LE ABLES, - - - - Proprietor.

This popular place of amusement is kept open all hours of the day and night, for the accommodation of gentlemen. This establishment is provided with Jenny Lind Billiard, Bowling, and Oyster Saloons, Restaurant, Bar, etc., all fitted up in good style.

Families supplied with Fresh Pickled Oysters, Fresh Fish, Venison, and Wild Game of all kinds, during the season.

Introduction

In writing this book, I have included eleven stories written by other authors. *Old Huntsville* owes a large debt of gratitude to these people, for without their dedication and research much of our past would have been lost.

I have purposely listed the names of these authors at the beginning of the book, rather than with the individual stories, as their contributions have far exceeded any single article.

Cathey Carney

Clarence Scott

Billy Joe Cooley

Fred Simpson

Tom Kenny

Mike Kenny

Charles Rice

Ken Owens

John Cross

James Record

Preface

Several years ago, I wrote a short, nostalgic story about the closing of Bragg's Grocery on Hurricane Creek. It was about people, most of whom are long dead, who had traded at the store.

I had forgotten the story until late one afternoon when a strange car pulled into my driveway. An elderly, well-dressed woman got out and walked over to where I was standing.

After I introduced myself, she asked, "Please, my mother is in the car, could you say something to her?" The lady went on to explain that in the story I had mentioned her father, who had been dead for almost fifty years.

Walking over to the car, I introduced myself to the old woman sitting there. Her face was wrinkled from almost a century of living and on her left hand was a worn wedding ring that must have been almost as old as its owner. In her other hand she clutched a copy of the story I had written.

Slowly she turned her head to look at me and, after glancing again at the story, said in a low, soft voice, "Someone remembered ... someone remembered his name."

I spent almost an hour talking to the old lady that day. She regaled me with tales about the Huntsville of her youth and the people she had known. She told me about dancing to the fiddle of Monte Sano Crowder and about working at Redstone Arsenal during the Second War when she would go home every day with yellow skin, a result of the chemicals with which she worked.

I listened as she described growing up in a mill village where preachers and bootleggers rubbed elbows at the local speakeasy. It was obvious that she enjoyed remembering.

Unfortunately, her body was weaker than her memory and soon her daughter had to take her home.

The memory of that old lady stayed in my mind for a long time. "A life of stories," I thought, "and when she dies, they will be gone forever."

For the next several years collecting these stories became an obsession. Literally thousands of hours were spent talking to senior citizens and searching through old newspapers and manuscripts.

During this time, I was confronted with many questions. Are ghost stories part of our history? Does a whimsical story about a neighbourhood bar fit into a book about our city's history?

In the final analysis, the answer had to be yes. All of these stories helped to make our city special.

Old Huntsville Magazine makes no pretence of this being a literary work. That endeavor is best left to the scholars. I also leave to the historians the task of quibbling over people's middle initials, the exact date of some long ago occurrence and the thousand other trivialities about which they seem to be concerned.

My sole intention is to try and preserve that part of our rich heritage which has been ignored for far too long.

Tom Carney
1994

Chapter 1

To Cross the Hogohegee

He moved silently and quickly through the autumn foliage near the big spring. The Alabama forest formed a canopy that kept the normally thick undergrowth down and made it easier to move. Still, his senses were alert for any noise, smell, or movement that could mean danger or death. John Ditto had come too far from Virginia to end his quest through carelessness.

The year was 1802 and the world was changing rapidly. Across the ocean Napoleon was solidifying his conquest of Italy, and Beethoven and Hayden were busy composing new masterpieces. In America, Thomas Jefferson was president of the New Republic and Ditto was looking for a place to camp on a site that would later become downtown Huntsville, Alabama.

He built himself a comfortable campsite consisting of a lean-to shack against a bluff near the big spring. He had cool, clean water and the surrounding countryside abounded in game. For most men this would have been enough to make them stay.

John didn't tarry long, though. He had a mission. Like so many other frontiersmen of this era, John had moved into the new territory looking for a new life and fortune. And find it he did. Traveling south, he located the big bend of the Hogohegee River and at a place called Chickasaw Fields, below the lower point of an island, John found the place he had sought. Making friends with the Indians, Ditto soon established a thriving trading post. Another incentive to settle here was the burgeoning keel-boat traffic from the up-river settlements enroute to New Orleans.

The river was good to John. In 1807 he built a gunwale type flatboat propelled by sweep oars that he used as a ferry to transport settlers across the Hogohegee. He also set up a boat yard where he built shallow draught boats for use over the treacherous shoals down-river. Andrew Jackson with his small army of volunteers used the ferry in 1813 enroute to fight the Creeks during the great Redstick Indian uprising.

The Hogohegee later became the Tennessee River. Chickasaw Island eventually became known as Hobb's Island and Ditto's Landing was the focal point for the town of Huntsville's transportation network. The infant town's great highway was the river and Ditto's Landing was its port.

John Ditto was one of the forerunners of that romantic, boisterous, and sometimes dangerous period of the 19th century Southern frontier movement. His contemporaries were men like Jim Bowie, Davy Crockett, and Mike Fink. It would be for others to build the settlement into a thriving and prosperous city. But they couldn't have done it without men like John Ditto and a place called Ditto's Landing.

Chapter 2

The Salt Seller: The Story of John Gunter

Most accounts claim John Gunter was born in Scotland and emigrated to America at an early age. During the Revolutionary war he sided with the British and afterwards was forced to flee because of his Loyalist sentiments.

Instead of heading north, to Canada, as most Loyalists did, Gunter travelled south into what was known at the time as the "Great Indian Nations." Much evidence suggests that he was a salt trader, possibly buying the salt in Knoxville and traveling the length of the Tennessee River trading with the Indians.

Around 1785 Gunter's travels brought him into North Alabama to a small Indian village named Creek Path, the site of present day Guntersville.

The Chief of the small settlement was Bushyhead, a Cherokee of the Paint Clan. Bushyhead and his group of followers had backed the British in the Revolutionary War and they too had been forced to flee southward at the end of hostilities.

The Cherokees depended on trade with the whites for essentials such as salt and gunpowder, so John Gunter was probably tolerated, if not exactly welcomed, when he first appeared at their village. Legend has it that Gunter was already fluent in the Cherokee language.

Chief Bushyhead, though at first probably considering Gunter a necessary evil, soon warmed to the quiet and unassuming young man. The Chief spent days patiently relating Indian lore and teaching Gunter the ways of the Cherokees.

"Land," Bushyhead would tell Gunter, "is the mother and father of all Indians. It belongs to everyone but belongs to no one."

If the chief seemed to place great emphasis on land, he had good cause. As the white settlers moved into North Carolina, Virginia, and Tennessee the Cherokees had been pushed farther south until now they resided at the very southern fringes of what had once been vast tribal lands.

Finally, the day came when John Gunter was no longer considered a visitor. For all practical purposes, he had become a Cherokee. He wore his hair long like the Indians, spoke their language and had adapted to their customs. The Indians had begun to trust the young man and literally considered him as one of their own.

Bushyhead, while realizing his tribe was dependent on the whites for trade, never the less wanted to keep contact to a minimum. The perfect solution seemed to be to make Gunter their agent in dealing with the whites. After much consultation with the council, the chief signed a treaty with Gunter which said, "As long as the grass grows green and the waters flow, the Indians can have salt."

To seal the treaty, Bushyhead gave his fifteen year old (some sources say 13) daughter, Ghegoheli, to the 35 year old Gunter as a wife. Later, Gunter Anglicized his wife's name to Catherine, or Katy.

The next twenty years were to prove an idyllic time for the Gunters. They built a large two-story house near Big Spring Creek where they raised seven children. A nearby warehouse contained the hides and ginseng he received in trade with the Indians. The only contact with whites were periodic trips to Tennessee to trade, or an occasional flatboat that might drift down the Tennessee River.

Within a few years Creek Path, or Gunter's Landing as it

was known to the whites, became an important trading post. Indians from throughout North Alabama would travel to the settlement to trade for salt or gunpowder, while the occasional white traveling through the Indian Nation would find it a convenient place to stop and obtain supplies.

Gunter became recognized as a leader in the tribe, often being called upon to settle disputes with neighboring tribes. When Chief Bushyhead died, Gunter became, for all practical purposes, the leader of the Creek Path settlement.

However, content the scene may have been, Gunter probably realized it was a false illusion that could not continue forever. He had travelled throughout the "white" world and knew it was simply a matter of time before the whites began moving into the Valley.

His prophecy proved true in the early 1800s when he received word of a white, John Ditto, settling at Ditto's Landing. A few years later he heard of a settlement at Hunt's Spring, followed soon by whites taking up land at the nearby Muscle Shoals. When some of the young warriors wanted to take up arms against the settlers, Gunter preached caution, saying there were too many of them and any conflict would end in disaster for the Cherokees. Instead, he urged a peaceful coexistence. "The Federal Government," he said, "has promised that we can keep our lands."

In preparation for the inevitable, Gunter had raised his children in both worlds. They were fluent in both the English and Cherokee languages and easily fit into either society. As one contemporary said, "They looked white but thought Indian."

Gunter and his family prospered. Like many other Cherokee families, they were slave holders and had vast amounts of acreage under cultivation. By 1810, Gunter was known as one of the wealthiest men in the Valley. Much of his success was in being able to be both Indian and white without taking sides. Regardless of Gunter's reluctance to take sides, he was forced to in 1813 when the Creeks waged war on the whites who had settled on their lands. General Andrew Jackson and Davy Crockett had camped nearby, and while waiting for their supplies to catch up, raised a regiment of Cherokees to help fight the Creeks.

Though the Creeks were traditional enemies of the Cherokees, there was still a reluctance on the part of the Creek Path Indians to fight on the side of the white man. Gunter, however, probably realizing that Jackson could be a powerful ally for the Cherokees, urged his tribesmen to join the campaign. Over 200 Cherokees, finally enlisted, with Gunter's son, Edward, serving as Major.

If Gunter thought that having an ally such as Andrew Jackson would solve the Cherokees' problems, he was soon mistaken. Under increasing pressure from white settlers, the Cherokees, in 1819, were forced to cede their lands north of the Tennessee River. Edward and John Jr., two of Gunter's sons, were instrumental in the treaty which caused an uproar throughout the Indian Nation.

The Cherokee Nation, at this time, consisted of two factions. One faction, led in part by the Gunters, believed that peaceful coexistence was the Cherokees' only hope, while the other side was adamant against giving up any land.

The Indians' concept of land ownership was something the whites could not understand. Where a white could purchase and sell land at will, the Cherokees believed the land belonged to the Indians and could not be sold. While an Indian might farm or live on some land, it never actually belonged to him, but to the tribe. Unfortunately, if an Indian sold the land to a white man, the white man's law recognized the sale as legal.

Even so, a few individual Indians, having become accustomed to white ways, had begun to sell the land they lived on. The Gunters, led by their father, though not agreeing with the treaty, realized the Nation could not contest the sales successfully in a federal court, so they urged the Indians to accept it.

Reluctantly, the tribe agreed to do so.

The Indian Nation had always been a sore point with most of the white settlers who resented having a "foreign nation," with its own laws, in their midst. In an effort to break up the tribal lands, the federal government offered the Indians "reserves" of land. By leaving the reservation, an Indian could take ownership of a piece of land to which he had free title. This proved attractive to many Indians who wanted to live like the whites.

At the same time, the federal government began pressuring the Indians to migrate west to the new Indian territory (present-day Oklahoma).

Land sales by Indians to whites had reached a point in 1825 where the Cherokee Council was forced to enact special legislation forbidding Indians from selling land.

Regardless of the law, some Indians continued to sell land. In 1828, as a last resort, the Cherokee Council met and passed the "Blood Law," which stated that any Indian that sold land to whites could be put to death. Edward and John Gunter, Jr., were again delegates to the convention.

Numerous Indians, though no one knows how many, were executed under this law. This served to infuriate many Indians who thought the whites should be the ones put to death. Time and time again, Gunter preached restraint to the young warriors who wanted to make war against the whites for taking their land.

Still fighting for peaceful coexistence, Gunter sent his youngest son, John, to the new Indian territory to observe firsthand the conditions there. Hopefully, he thought, it would be a place where the Indians could live in peace.

John's report to his father was devastating. The Indian territory consisted of barren lands over which intertribal warfare had broken out and the whites were subjecting the Indians to more laws which had the effect of making them second-class citizens.

At about the same time Gunter's daughter, Martha, met and married Hugh Henry. According to custom, Martha received land from the tribe to farm and live on. A short while later her husband sold the land, which was his right under white law.

This was the crushing blow to John Gunter. He was too much of a white man to take vengeance on his daughter's husband, but too much of an Indian to ignore it. He banned his daughter from ever stepping foot in his house as long as she was still married to Henry. The fact Henry was not killed by the Cherokees was probably due to the respect they had for Gunter.

John Gunter was an old man by now. He had preached peaceful coexistence with the whites and had raised his sons to be leading figures in the Cherokee Nation only to see the white man break all of his promises. Where once he had hoped the Indians could migrate to another land and once again be a powerful tribe, Gunter realized now it was all a pretence on the government's part.

Sensing his days were numbered, John Gunter had his will drawn up, a move highly unusual for an Indian. By using the white man's law, Gunter hoped to insure his family's future. The will stated that the land left by Gunter could not be sold or used by anyone except his family and though he left much property to his daughter Martha, it was stipulated that she would not receive it as long as she was married to Hugh Henry. To make sure his will would be enforced he named four of the leading Cherokee chiefs as his executors.

Ever since he had arrived at Creek Path (today Guntersville) almost a half century earlier, Gunter and his wife had often walked to a nearby hill where they would sit for hours watching the lazy river wind itself through the valley. They had watched the history of the South travel down the river. First there were Indian canoes, then crude log rafts followed by keelboats and steamboats. They had watched the peaceful little village next to the river grow from nothing into a bustling community of almost 800 Indians, with two stores and a ferry. Where once boats called at Gunter's Landing with supplies of salt and trading goods, the cargo they carried now was much more tragic.

It was the time of the Indian Removal, and Gunter's Landing had become a major shipping point for the Indians being sent west.

Tales still abound about Gunter, old and crippled with age, walking among the imprisoned Indians offering help and solace when help was too late. It is said that Gunter once again let his hair grow long and began dressing in the Indian fashion.

Shortly before his death on August 28, 1835, John Gunter suffered a stroke. While lying on his deathbed a group of young Indians visited him, asking for advice.

"I'm too old to give advice," he said.

When pressed about what he would do if he was younger, a fiery look came into the old man's eyes as he remembered his youth and all that he had seen. "I'd be a warrior," he finally replied, "and fight for my land."

Three months after his death the treaty of New Echota was signed, forcing all the remaining Indians at Guntersville into exile in Oklahoma. John Gunter's will was never executed.

From a population of 800, Gunter's Landing had dwindled to less than 200 people by the end of the Indian Removal.

Chapter 3

The Pioneers

The following account of Huntsville's early days was written in the late 1800s by Judge Thomas J. Taylor, a probate judge of Madison County from 1886 until 1894.

As more settlers moved into what we know today as Madison County they were greeted by a vast untamed wilderness. From the year 1805 to 1809 transportation of supplies of all kinds was laborious and difficult and what few supplies did come into the county were often so expensive as to be out of the reach of the common settler. Forced to do without many of these necessities, the pioneers had to improvise.

During the first year, far from other settlements, they had to bring corn and salt on pack horses through the wilderness. The first settlers in Madison County had no mills for bread nearer than the neighbourhood of Winchester. In those days this involved a tedious journey, and frequently the settlers would be without bread or salt for many days, subsisting on jerked venison. The first priority for every new settler, after building a shelter, was to plant and cultivate a corn patch and raise corn for bread. There were no mills convenient for the first two or three years, and each family constructed a hominy mortar by burning or digging out a large bowl in the end of a large piece of hard, tough timber, in which they pounded their corn by the use of a large pestle worked by a sweep. Many families living at a great distance from mills subsisted for many years on bread pounded in these mortars.

Clean wood ashes were easily procured, and after they raised a corn crop, lye-hominy was a favorite substitute for bread. Bread from wheat flour was seldom seen, as the roads to Tennessee and Virginia were not yet opened. For many years little or no wheat was raised in the county. When the county had largely increased in population, flour was brought down the Tennessee River in considerable quantity, and Ditto's Landing was the rendezvous for the flatboats that supplied the area. A flour inspector was appointed at the landing to inspect, grade, and stamp the flour offered for sale.

Parched corn was the portable food of the explorer and hunter, on which, together with the game found in the forest, they were able to live for long periods of time during their hunting and exploring excursions. They had great abundance of meat and a variety of fish, flesh or fowl, but were frequently without salt, which first was brought from Nashville on flat-boats, then over the roads in wagons. After boats were used in carrying cotton down the Paint Rock and Flint rivers, salt was frequently brought back, though it was hard work propelling the loaded boats against the current.

Iron was scarce and expensive, and many of the first houses built did not have a particle of iron used in their construction. The doors swung on wooden hinges and were fastened, if fastened at all, with wooden locks. The floors of the rooms were dirt or made of puncheons; the boards were laid on the roof and held fast by weight poles laid on each course, the lowest pole pegged down and the others separated and kept in position by timber pieces between them.

The settlers dug their bread trays and turned bowls and tableware out of the buckeye, basswood, and other soft timber, but some of the more pretentious made a display of pewter table service. China and Delphware were not in use, and the neat housewives scoured their pewter plates until they shone like silver and set them edgewise on shelves. The tinkers, pliers of a profession now obsolete, travelled from house to house, repaired and mended the family pewter, and received in payment a little money and a great deal of barter in the way of family supplies.

At first, they depended on game for a supply of meat which was shot or trapped, and in every family were two or three good steel traps. In hunting, the old-fashioned long rifle with flint lock was the universal weapon and as lead was essential they never wasted it and generally managed to keep a supply. Powder was also scarce and dear, but the settlers, when they could not buy it, were equal to the emergency. Sulphur was easily procured, and they constructed hoppers in the mountain caves and made saltpetre. They burned willow for charcoal and made gunpowder. Though it may not have been as good and reliable as that made at the present time, yet it answered their purpose. These men were expert in the use of the rifle, and it was not considered an extraordinary feat to bring down a deer at full speed at a distance of seventy-five or eighty yards.

When our forefathers located in this county, they depended largely on dressed buckskin for clothing. From it they made covering for their beds, garments of every description, moccasins, sacks, and hunting pouches, and it was cut into thongs for sewing purposes and twisted into ropes. Many of the families had flax wheels, and with the flax, made cloth from it of excellent quality. Cotton was soon introduced, patches were planted for spinning purposes, and the old spinning wheel and cards, the loom and winding-blades and reel soon became common in every settler's house.

As there were no gins to clean the cotton, the family in the long winter evenings would pile it before the fire and all hands would clear it of the seed by picking them out with their fingers. In this way they would prepare enough of the snowy fabric for a year's supply for the wheels and looms of the family. Suspended from pegs inserted in the walls of the room were usually to be seen bunches of "shanks" of homespun thread ready for warping, bars, and loom. The cloth made from this material was of a coarse nature and well-suited to the rough wear to which it was exposed.

From the bark of various forest trees and by the use of copperas and indigo the cloth was dyed in a variety of colors. Calico was almost unknown and was worth fifty cents a yard, much too expensive for the average settler.

House furniture was of the rudest character. Shelves were used for cupboards; their dining tables were made of puncheons. Their cabins were without glass in the windows, and cooking utensils were few in number. Tallow and rosin and beeswax furnished them light. First, they used bear's grease in their lamps, which were homemade, but when cattle became common they had moulded or dipped tallow candles with a cotton wick.

In summer they retired early and seldom used a light except in sickness. In some places they would construct a cotton wick measuring fifteen or twenty feet long, dip it in beeswax and rosin and wind it round a corn cob, making a taper that lasted for a long time. In those primitive times houses were generally small and families generally large, and they generally managed to divide sleeping spaces when it was time to retire by the use of curtains of buckskin. The little children were stowed randomly about on pallets on the floor, while the larger boys would normally sleep in the loft.

Such were the lives of our ancestors, apparently full of privation and hardships, yet they were a cheerful and contented lot who managed to carve their homes out of the wilderness and leave a great legacy behind them.

Chapter 4

John Hunt

For well over a hundred years, John Hunt, the founder of Huntsville, has been shrouded in mystery. Where did he come from? Where and when did he die? Was he the illiterate backwoodsman that history has made him out to be? John Hunt was born in 1750 in Fincastle County, Virginia, to parents of Irish and Dutch descent. His family had migrated to America in 1635 and after living in New Jersey and Maryland moved to Virginia around 1730. The family appears to have been fairly prosperous. In 1752, records show that a man by the name of Thomas Foster was appointed constable in the home of John Hunt, Sr.

Among the families living in Fincastle County were the Acklins, Holbrooks, and the Larkins. Many of these families would later play prominent roles in the early development of Huntsville.

In 1769 John Hunt married the daughter of William Holbrook, a close friend of his father. The following year the Holbrook family moved to Hawkins County, North Carolina, and John moved with them. Within a few years the Larkins, and Acklin families had joined with them in the new settlement.

With the advent of the Revolutionary War many of the settlers took up arms to fight for their new country. Many historians would later contend that John Hunt served as a captain during the war. This mistaken claim would later lead to confusion in trying to establish Hunt's early years. In fact,

Hunt's only military service consisted of several months enlistment as a private under Captain Charles Polk of the Company of Light Horses, in Salisbury District, North Carolina.

Although John did not see much service, records seem to indicate that his father was a member of the Colonial army while his uncle served as a Colonel in the British army.

Short service periods of a few months were common in North Carolina as the settlers had crops and Indians to deal with and could not be gone for long periods of time.

At the end of his short military career, Hunt returned to his home in Hawkins County. Young John and his wife probably lost several children at childbirth, as it was not until eight years after their marriage that they had their first recorded child.

In 1779, John Hunt was appointed a lieutenant in the state militia, serving as a paymaster.

As the young community grew in size, the North Carolina government began to realize the need for some type of civic jurisdiction. John Hunt had established himself as a leader of the community and in 1786 was appointed the first sheriff of Hawkins County. It was required at that time for a sheriff to post a bond as a prerequisite to taking office. The bond, in the amount of "1000 pounds current money" signed by John Hunt and four sureties, can still be seen at the North Carolina Archives, located in Raleigh.

In 1789, when North Carolina voted to ratify the Constitution, John Hunt was a delegate at the convention.

One year later, in 1790, when North Carolina ceded the lands west of the Allegheny Mountains, John Hunt was made a captain of the militia by William Blount, the newly appointed governor of the territory. The duties of a captain in the militia and a sheriff had many similarities in the sense that they were both charged with keeping the peace, and as Hunt's term of sheriff had just expired, he was a logical choice. As he was also the first and only sheriff at the time, he was probably the only choice.

Everyone living in the territory had heard stories about the new, rich land lying across the Clinch River. This was Indian land and supposedly protected from settlement by the treaties with the federal government. Many families, ignoring the treaties, began to move into the new lands.

John Hunt, along with the Acklins and Larkins, moved across the river in the mid-1790s into an area known as the Powell River Valley. Years later this community would become known as Tazewell, Tennessee, and John Hunt would be recognized as the founder.

Many stories have been written about the romantic frontiersmen who were bitten with wanderlust. Legends have us believe that the early pioneers kept moving to escape the confines of civilization, constantly moving to see what lay over the next mountain range.

Nothing could be further from the truth. In reality, greed was the motivating factor.

In Tennessee, Alabama, Georgia, and many other states, vast areas had been set aside as Indian territories. Although these areas were supposedly protected by federal law, it did not prevent "squatters" from settling. These squatters knew that it would only be a matter of time before the government recognized their rights and then they could gain possession of large tracts by simply paying a registration fee. If they settled on the right land, with a little luck, they could become wealthy.

Basically, it was a get-rich-quick scheme that worked for many people.

The other alternative was to wait until the lands had been "opened" for settlement and bid for them at auction. Few pioneers could afford to acquire prime land in this manner.

John Hunt had carved a respectable homestead out of the wilderness when he learned, to his dismay, in 1797, that president John Adams had sent 800 federal troops to evict the settlers. In an attempt to stall his eviction, and probably using his title of Captain in the Tennessee State Militia to help his cause, he wrote the newly-elected governor, John Sevier, asking for help.

On November 25, 1797, Governor Sevier wrote Hunt:

"Yours of yesterday I am honored with and am sincerely sorry for your embarrassed situation, and would I, to God, I had it in my power to render you relief. You may assure yourself that everything will be done for you that is possible for me, but it is in the president's own power to do whatever he may think best on this very important and alarming occasion. I hope in three or four weeks to hear from Congress and whether or not anything is likely to be done in your favor. In the meantime, I earnestly beg the people, for their own interest, to conduct themselves in a peaceable, orderly, and prudent manner."

Shortly afterwards, the squatters' claims were recognized. By 1801, the land John Hunt had settled became part of Claiborne County. When the new community held its first election, David Rodgers was elected sheriff, but was unable to post bond and Hunt was elected in his place. There were no facilities for the new government in Tazewell at the time, so the first term of court was held in the home of John Hunt. (This log cabin later became the first school in Tazewell.)

The sheriff was not only responsible for keeping the peace but was also responsible for administering justice. A book describing the early days of Tazewell included the following description of the sheriff's duties:

"A whipping post stood between the jail and courthouse. As near as I remember, it was made similar to two ox yokes, the one below fastened in a frame and turned upside down; the one above to fit down and form two holes large enough to confine the head and neck. Debtors were taken out two at a time and the duty of the sheriff was to whip them until they would promise to go to work and pay their debts."

Not exactly a job for the fainthearted.

John Hunt appears to have been living a fairly contented life. He had recently given land for a church and was a well-respected figure in the community. His daughter, Elizabeth, had married Samuel Black Acklin, the son of his old friend, Samuel Acklin. The newly married couple made their home with John and the rest of the family.

This was a busy time for Hunt. Besides serving as sheriff, he was also heavily involved in land speculation and running a stagecoach inn. Bishop Ashbury, in his travels through the south, spoke of staying, and preaching, at Hunt's Tavern.

Even though the Hunt family had prospered, John was already looking to the future. Hunt, along with the Larkins and many other families, had staked everything on Tazewell's future but the town simply refused to grow. The land was poor for farming and the community itself provided no incentive for commerce. The only thing the town had going for it was its close proximity to the Cumberland Gap, "gateway to the western lands."

By the time Hunt's term of sheriff was up on September 1, 1804, he had already made plans to leave Tazewell. In the previous six months he had been selling off land holdings that he owned in Tazewell and the adjoining areas.

Popular legend tells us that he went south in search of a big spring he had heard stories of. Again, the truth is much simpler. There were already rumors that territory belonging to Indians in what is now North Alabama would be opened for settlement. Anyone already living there would probably be able to exercise their squatters' rights by paying a small registration fee. Everyone else would have to purchase their land at a public auction, which by its very nature tended to drive land prices up.

John Hunt was determined to have squatters' rights.

Early in September 1804, John Hunt and Andrew Bean left their cabin in East Tennessee and struck out into the wilds on foot (not on horseback, as many historians have claimed).

They traveled in a southwestward direction, guided only by the sun and the stars. Almost a month later they arrived at the stream of water now known as Bean's Creek, at a spot near where Salem, Tennessee, now stands. At that place they made camp for several days in order to make observations and investigate the surrounding country. According to legend, it also became necessary to replenish the larder. Their unerring rifles soon procured several bear and fat deer, the choice parts of which were jerked and packed for future use.

Traveling further south the explorers came upon the newly completed cabin of Joseph Criner near the Mountain Fork of Flint River. Criner and his brother, Isaac, were the first white settlers in this area. According to later accounts given by Criner, Hunt and Bean spent the night and inquired about land further south. It was at this time that Hunt first heard of the big spring.

The next morning, Mrs. Criner made bread for their journey and the men left to seek out the big spring.

John Hunt and Andrew Bean were not the first white persons to reach the spring. Earlier, in 1802, John Ditto had built a crude shack there and camped for a short while before moving southward to the Tennessee River, where he opened a trading post. When Hunt arrived, he found the beginnings of a cabin that Samuel Davis, another early settler, had started. Unfortunately, Davis, in his haste to return to Georgia for his family, left the cabin unfinished and when he returned found Hunt had completed the cabin and was living in it.

The cabin was a rough one-room affair. People searching for it today will find only a parking lot across from the present-day Huntsville Utilities.

The land where John Hunt settled would be beyond comprehension to a resident of Huntsville today. The area above the bluffs, where the courthouse now stands, though reasonably flat, was a maze of thick vines and bushes. Below the spring, toward Meadow Gold Dairy, was an endless swamp inhabited by bears, geese, and rabbits. Where Huntsville

Hospital is now located was a thick hardwood wilderness teeming with deer.

After hastily completing the cabin (frontier law did not recognize a squatter's claims unless a home was built on it), Hunt and Bean turned their sights north. Bean had decided to settle near Salem, Tennessee, and Hunt returned to Tazewell for his family.

The early spring of 1805 found Hunt occupied in selling off the remainder of his land around Tazewell and making preparations to move his family to the "Big Spring." Other families, upon hearing of John's upcoming departure, also made plans to move.

Accompanying Hunt when he returned to the spring was his wife and three of his sons, William, George, and Samuel, as well as members of the Larkin and Black families.

It was early summer, 1805 when Hunt returned with his family. He spent most of that summer clearing and fencing a small field, which lay in what is now the best part of the city of Huntsville, running from Gates Street as far south as Franklin. The land was exceedingly fertile and produced bountifully in return for little labor. William Hunt would recall years later how he had killed a bear near the present location of the courthouse while clearing the field.

The brave old pioneer, scout, and hunter was now happily fixed; his farm gave him employment during the spring and summer. Hunting, fishing, and dressing meats and skins occupied his time in the fall and winter. Neighbors were few and highly valued in those primitive days. When the proper time arrived in the fall, all the hunters for miles around went out together to lay in their stores of meat for the year. Whenever a settler died, his family continued to share in the proceeds of the hunt when a division was made, a proportionate share of bear and deer meat was always taken to the families of widows. These rough men knew charity as well as courage. Legend has it that John Hunt was always foremost in providing for the poor and helpless. One Christopher Black, an Irish man, who assisted Hunt in removing his family from East Tennessee, was famous for delivering game to the fatherless and the widows.

Hunt's Station, as the spring was now called, was fast becoming the center of the community. More and more settlers were pouring into the valley. Much evidence suggests that Hunt, who had already enlarged his cabin, ran a public house at this time. A public house was where a traveler might get a meal or purchase a few basic supplies. This probably explains the persistent rumor today that Hunt operated a shop that sold castor oil.

In 1807, his daughter, Elizabeth, moved to Huntsville from Tazewell along with her children, husband, and five slaves. They had been delayed from joining Hunt until they could dispose of the inn.

Elizabeth and her family moved in with Hunt in anticipation of the land sales. Congress had already called for a land sale, with squatters being given preemptive rights to one section of land each. With the Hunts occupying the best land in the county, it seemed as if their fortunes were made.

Unfortunately, when the sales were held it was discovered that John Hunt had not registered his claims. The wealthy planter LeRoy Pope outbid the other purchasers and ended up with legal title to all of John Hunt's dreams. Hunt was forced to move from his beloved Big Spring.

With all the prime land in Huntsville already taken, Hunt purchased a quarter section of land far outside of town by paying eighty dollars as down payment. This parcel was located at approximately where the old airport on South Parkway is now. His daughter and son-in-law purchased the adjoining land.

Pope had forced the name of Twickenham upon the new community, but many people resented the fact that he had bought Hunt's land. One of the first actions the new city government took was to change the name to Huntsville, in honor of the intrepid pioneer.

The next few years of Hunt's life are well-documented. He joined the Masonic Lodge, served on juries, and was appointed coroner. In 1809 he sold his land to Abasalom Looney. By selling this land, he also lost the right to vote or serve on juries in the very city that he had founded.

According to the law of that period, a man could not do any of the above unless he was a landowner.

An old man by now, Hunt moved in with his daughter and son-in-law. In 1820, Hunt, probably prompted by his grandson who was studying law in Huntsville at the time, applied for a Revolutionary War pension, but was turned down because the unit he served with was not considered a part of the Continental Army.

Like old men everywhere, Hunt probably spent his last days recounting tales of when he was young and adventurous, hopefully surrounded by his grandchildren.

On February 27, 1822, John Hunt died at the age of 72. He was buried in the Acklin graveyard, now known as the Sively graveyard, a short distance from where he spent his final days.

Ironically, the grave of John Hunt, the man who founded Huntsville, lies unmarked, just a few feet from the city dump.

Chapter 5

Huntsville's First Hanging

An angry crowd gathered rapidly on the square as news spread that a murder had been committed and that the culprit was going to be tried in Huntsville!

For the young town, in 1812, this was startling news. The settlers, who were still building the town, took pride at living in a peaceful community. The few crimes that had been committed had been dealt with in timely fashion by "Captain Slick," a loosely organized group of vigilantes. Never had a murder taken place here.

As the facts of the murder emerged, the townspeople learned that a transient by the name of Eli Newman was charged with the crime. He had been employed as a deckhand on a flatboat taking goods to market in New Orleans.

After the goods were sold, Newman, along with the other deckhands, began the long walk home, as was the practice then. All the men had been paid and were anxious to get home to their families.

After several weeks of walking, the men camped one night near Huntsville, in the Chickasaw Indian Nation lands. Early the next morning as they prepared to break camp, Newman made an excuse to remain behind with a man by the name of Fetrick.

On June 6, Newman, according to court testimony: "Not having the fear of God before his eyes but being moved and seduced by the instigation of the Devil, took his razor and cut Fetrick's throat."

It isn't known whether Newman had deliberately intended to kill Fetrick or if the murder was the result of an altercation during the robbery. Regardless, when he caught up with the group several hours later, he was alone.

The men questioned Newman about Fetrick's whereabouts. Something about his demeanor caused suspicion among the others. He appeared nervous and evasive. Finally, the men insisted on backtracking to where Fetrick was last seen.

Within hours, they discovered the grim reality of Newman's treachery. Fetrick's lifeless body lay before them with his throat slit from ear to ear and pockets empty of his recent pay.

Although Newman professed his innocence, the men, after searching him and finding the dead man's money, quickly bound him and made him their prisoner. Newman was brought to Huntsville and turned over to the newly elected sheriff, Stephen Neal. Although there was no official jail, the prisoner was placed in a room with an armed guard.

The grand jury met on the second Monday in November. A murder indictment was returned and attorney John W. Walker, the son-in-law of LeRoy Pope, agreed to represent the prisoner.

The trial was held in a small log house situated on a large rock formation east of the Big Spring. This is the present-day location of the Regions Bank. On Friday, Nov. 13, the case was brought before Judge Obadiah Jones.

Although Newman was quickly found guilty, Judge Jones ordered a new trial because of a technicality.

Newman next appeared in court on Nov. 21, but the case was continued because not enough prospective jurors were in town on that cold day. Traditionally, jurors were selected from among businessmen and others who happened to be in the vicinity of the courthouse at the moment.

To prevent Newman's case from being delayed until the spring session of court, Judge Jones called a special session for

Dec. 1.

The trial continued all day and those involved consented to allow the jury to retire for the night to the house of William and Louis Winston in the custody of a sworn officer.

The next morning at 9 am, the trial continued with lawyers Walker and Winston presenting their arguments. Then, as the jury deliberated, a large crowd milled around the log house anxiously awaiting the verdict. A hush fell over the townspeople when James Ishma, foreman of the jury, appeared at the door to read the verdict:

"Guilty in manner and form as charged in the Bill of Indictment!"

At 10 o'clock the following morning, Newman stood before Jones for sentencing. The defense counsel rendered 13 technical reasons why the verdict should be overturned, but the judge denied the motions, proclaiming:

"You, Eli Newman, will be carried from hence to the place from whence you came, and on Saturday next the fifth day of this instant between the hours of ten in the forenoon and two in the afternoon you will be carried by the proper officer, to the place of public execution to be executed in or near the town of Huntsville, and there be hanged by the neck until your body be dead, and the Lord have Mercy on your soul."

On Dec. 5, 1812, at about noon, Newman entered history as the first man to be executed for murder in Madison County.

Chapter 6

The Battle of Huntsville

Terror gripped Huntsville as the horrible message spread throughout the community: "The Indians are coming! They're killing everyone!"

Men, women, and children, determined not to risk their fate at the hands of the bloodthirsty savages, began fleeing their homes. Within hours, the only people left to defend Huntsville from the impending doom were five courageous men who had barricaded themselves in the new courthouse. The year was 1813 and North Alabama was plagued by marauding bands of Creek Indians. The battle of Fort Mims had recently taken place, with Indians killing hundreds of settlers. Reports of hideous massacres, scalping, and other atrocities spread like wildfire with every passing stranger.

Huntsville's population was about 1,500 souls, of whom 250 were slaves. The town, in its few short years, had already become a prosperous and thriving community. On the grounds around the courthouse, which was the town center, people would gather under the big, sprawling oak trees to buy and sell cotton, swap tales, and quiz passing strangers about news from other towns.

The first word of the approaching Indians came from a thirsty traveler who had stopped to water his horse. The citizens gathered as he told of savage warriors he had seen on his journey. One local gent passed the stranger a jug of spirits. The news of the Indians seemed to become even more ferocious as the jug made its rounds from man to man. The stranger spoke of being chased to the very edge of town by the red men. You could have heard a pin drop on the old courthouse square that day as the townspeople clung to his every word. Gradually the crowd dispersed, with worried men pondering the best ways to protect their families. When a few men put their women and children in carriages for the journey north and out of harm's way, the panic began. Farmers left their tools lying in the fields, women left their food still hot on the stoves, everyone was trying to flee Huntsville as fast as they could.

Masters and slaves alike competed for any kind of transportation they could find. With the exodus north, plantations were abandoned, and families separated as the cry became "every man for himself".

In a few short hours, Huntsville had become a ghost town.

Meanwhile the famous Indian fighter, Andrew Jackson, who was camped 25 miles away at Fayetteville, Tennessee, had received word of the impending massacre. Rallying his troops, he ordered a nonstop march all the way to Huntsville, without rest or food. He reminded the soldiers of all the helpless families that would surely be lolled if the army did not reach Huntsville in time.

As the soldiers marched south to save Huntsville, the frightened populace continued its scramble north. Gloom settled over the town as it became abandoned, with no one left to defend it.

No one, that is, except for five brave men who barricaded themselves in the new brick courthouse, determined to defend to the death the town they had helped to carve out of the wilderness.

Captain Wyatt was no stranger to fighting Indians. He assumed command of the brave little group in the courthouse that day, knowing the odds were against him. But if he could delay the Indians, perhaps Andrew Jackson would arrive with his troops in time to save the day. Rumor had it that even Davy Crockett was headed toward Huntsville with his long rifle, determined to whip the red rascals once and for all!

It was a long, dark night as they paced to and fro in the courthouse, peering often out the windows. Capt. Wyatt, in an attempt to bolster his men's sagging morale, passed around a jug of whiskey, and then another ... and another.

Finally, with nerves at the breaking point, a shadow was seen darting behind the bushes in the courthouse yard. A shout rang out: "Indians, the Indians are here!" Men rushed to their posts and began firing.

The battle of Huntsville was on.

Gunshots rang out through the night as the stalwart defenders fired, reloaded and fired again, pausing only long enough to wipe the powder stains from their tired faces and to take another drink.

As the sun rose over Huntsville that next morning, it revealed a scene of utter devastation. All around the courthouse square, windows lay shattered, doors were shot off their hinges, and the acrid smell of gunpowder hung heavily in the air.

Gen. Andrew Jackson and Davy Crockett marched slowly into town at the head of the brave Tennessee volunteers. With guns primed and loaded, the soldiers slowly fanned out across the square. Veterans of a hundred Indian battles, they were amazed and at the same time terrified at the devastation the night's battle had wrought.

The great battle fought in Huntsville that night might have gone down in history books except for one small detail.

There were no Indians!

The brave courageous defenders of our fair city had been firing at shadows.

The stranger who had first spread the story of the Indians had long disappeared and the only hostile Indians within a hundred miles were those visions that emerged from the whiskey jugs.

Today, where Holmes Avenue intersects with Lincoln Street, one will see a historical marker that tells how Gen.

Jackson and Davy Crockett camped there after a long, hard march from Tennessee. The marker does not tell why they came here.

Now you know.

Chapter 7

Horse Race at the Green Bottom Inn

Most people think of Andrew Jackson as an Indian fighter, general and president. What they don't know is that he was also an avid fan of horse racing and a shrewd gambler.

Mr. John Connally, owner of the Green Bottom Inn, located where A&M University now stands, was also an avid horse racing fan and had built a race track in front of his establishment. Before long it had become a mecca for the gambling gentry.

Jackson became a regular visitor to Connally's inn during his frequent visits to Huntsville. Known throughout Tennessee and North Alabama for the fine race horses he raised, he was the center of attention whenever he showed up with a new racer.

He also won a lot of money.

One day the general arrived with a new horse. It didn't look nor act like a race horse, appearing more like an old plow horse.

The general hitched the animal to a rail and went inside where he proceeded to eat lunch.

One of the men at a nearby table finally gathered the courage to approach Jackson.

"General, you gonna race that horse?"

"Maybe! Maybe not," Jackson replied.

Local gamblers knew that Jackson was a shrewd judge of

horse flesh, so immediately they became interested in the horse.

"Wanna sell the horse?" they asked. "Might, might not," he replied. "Give you 50 dollars gold," one said.

"Horse ain't worth it," the general replied. "It's just an old nag."

"Give you a hundred!"

The general asked, "Gentlemen, do you realize the value of that horse? That's not just an ordinary racer! Why, I would be willing to wager you that there's not another horse here like him."

"Make it three hundred."

Reluctantly the general parted with the horse and the new owners made preparations to enter it in the next race.

Of course, the horse finished last. The group of disheartened (and broke) gamblers approached Gen. Jackson, who was sitting under a shade tree counting his winnings.

"General," they cried, "you said that horse wasn't any ordinary racer. What's so special about it?"

"Gentlemen, I really wished you had asked me earlier. Yep, that's a special horse. It's probably the slowest piece of horse flesh that I have ever seen."

Editor's Note: In a strange twist of history, one of John Connally's descendants, also named John, would play host to another president. A visit to Texas on November 22, 1963 by President John F Kennedy ended in the wounding of Texas Governor Connally and the assassination of the president.

On the president's agenda that day was a visit to Connally's farm where he raised thoroughbred horses.

Chapter 8

Brahan Spring Park Monument to a Swindler

He was an undisputed swindler who came to a disgraceful end, but, Huntsville heaped honors on him by naming one of its largest parks in his name.

We, of course, have numerous monuments to the city's pioneers. The city itself is named after John Hunt, its founder. The Von Braun Civic Center is named after Wernher Von Braun whose visionary foresight helped to make our country first in space exploration. We even have a community named for Lily Flagg, a prize-winning cow.

But one of the best known landmarks is Brahan Spring Park, used weekly by thousands of people who know nothing about the scoundrel for whom it was named.

We have an old-time city council to thank for naming the park after John Brahan. They also knew nothing about the man. If they had, they may have questioned their own wisdom. John Brahan was born in Fauquier County, Virginia, in 1774. His father, an Englishman who had settled in Virginia, was killed during the Revolutionary War while serving the American cause.

Brahan spent his early youth in the Old Virginia plantation environment. Though his family was impoverished when compared to their neighbors, he nevertheless made influential friends who would serve him in good form throughout his life.

Brahan's first brush with the "fine art" of swindling came

in 1808 when he convinced his friends to invest in a land company he was organizing. The company would buy land around Nashville, Tennessee, and, after a period of time, resell it for a large profit. He promised them riches, saying he'd do all the work if they would just put up the money.

After collecting what he thought was a sum sufficient for his purposes, Brahan went back to Nashville, leaving his friends in Virginia thinking about the fortunes that would shortly be coming their way.

When almost a year had gone by without any word from Brahan, his investors began to get nervous. "Please," they wrote, "let us know the state of our affairs." Still there was no word from Brahan or their money.

Finally, in a state of exasperation, they wrote Brahan to demand an accounting. "Our confidence in our joint venture has greatly waned since the last season. Please be so kind as to provide an immediate accounting of all sums invested."

Brahan wrote back explaining that he had bad news: "I am at a loss to explain the current market."

In other words, there was no money left.

Still, there was enough money for Brahan to construct a new home in Nashville and conduct an active social life. With his cultivated manners and fine clothes, he projected an aura of respectability in the new frontier community. Among the new friends he made were General Weakly and Andrew Jackson, who in turn introduced him to many other influential people.

With such people endorsing Brahan, it was fairly easy for him to gain an appointment to public office. One of the qualifications of holding an office of trust at that time was to put up a substantial bond to be forfeited in case of malfeasance. In May of 1809, Brahan was appointed Receiver of Public Monies for the Nashville land office. The bond was ten thousand dollars, which he did not have. Instead of declining the appointment, Brahan assured them that the bond was in the mail and then promptly forgot about it.

For some odd reason no one checked to see if the mail ever arrived.

Instead of settling down to earn a normal living, Brahan was still determined to make his fortune the easy way. His next victim was John Gachet, a friend of General Weakly, whom Brahan persuaded to put up a large sum of money to speculate in land. Again, Brahan was going to do all the work and all Gachet had to do was sit back and count the profits.

Of course, there was no profit, no land, and no money remaining. All Brahan could offer was another flimsy excuse about "market conditions."

Gachet was not as easy to put off as had been the Virginia investors. Not only was he persistent in his demands, he was also dangerous. Gachet had been involved in several "affairs of honor" and was widely known as a man not to be trifled with.

Unexpectedly, with all of Nashville waiting for the feathers to start flying, Brahan announced his engagement to Mary Weakly, daughter of General Weakly, who was also the close friend of John Gachet. Needless to say, General Weakly quickly smoothed over the whole unpleasant affair.

Again, Brahan should have been satisfied, but instead he began casting about for new ways to earn money. At about this time Brahan realized what a unique job he had. He was in charge of collecting and transmitting to the United States Treasury all proceeds from federal land sales. This put him in the strange position of collecting from himself for any lands he purchased at federal land sales. All he had to do was to list the account as paid and delay transmitting his reports into the treasury department until he could resell the land and balance his account.

It was like putting a fox in charge of the hen house. Within a year Brahan was on his way to amassing a small fortune. He had not yet learned the art of juggling books, so he stayed in constant trouble for his method of accounting.

On March 26, 1810, the Secretary of the Treasury wrote

Brahan:

"Your mode of conducting the business of your office being different from that of all other land offices, and causing much embarrassment in this department, it becomes necessary to point out the deviations to you."

Although authorities in Washington were beginning to question his accounting practices, Brahan was unfazed, citing the slowness of the mail as the primary reason for being slow in transmitting funds.

Madison County had become such an important part of the new territory that the decision was made to move the land office from Nashville to Huntsville. Of course, Brahan raised no objection as it put him closer to his "investments." Brahan selected a large section of land, later occupied by Merrimac Mills, and built a spacious home. By all outward appearances Brahan was a successful businessman. Appearances were deceiving, however, as Brahan's world was about to come crumbling down.

By 1818, land sales in North Alabama had come to a virtual standstill. As long as sales had been brisk, Brahan could buy land with government money. Then, when someone else bought land, he would take that money and replace the federal money he owed. Of course, the scheme depended on taking another purchaser's money to replace the first purchaser's money, and so on.

Brahan was determined to bluff it out somehow. When the treasury secretary wrote and demanded an accounting, Brahan put him off with the excuse that he was overworked and needed a clerk to help him balance the books. Brahan was well aware that the treasury had never authorized the hire of secretarial help before.

Unfortunately for Brahan, the treasury approved the hire of a clerk. The rest of the story can best be told by excerpts from the official records.

To John Brahan,

Having on the 8th day of December last, instructed the Commissioner of the General Land Office to inform the receivers and registers that a reasonable allowance would be made for clerk hire, I have felt some surprise at the delay which has occurred in the transmission of your accounts. You are now six months in arrears, and judging of the future, by the past, there is no reason to expect your accounts will be rendered more punctually during the ensuing, than they have been in the past year ... I perceive by your return for Sept., that more than $53,000 remained in your hands at the end of the month.

WM. Crawford, Sec. of Treasury

John Brahan to the Secretary of the Treasury:
Receiver's office, Huntsville, June 1819

SIR: I have the mortification to inform you that there is a considerable deficiency in my cash account, the cause I can only account for in part, the business being large & the time to sell & receive being only two weeks at each sale. I was always fearful that in the hurried state of things that I should sustain considerable loss. I am now convinced of the fact & beg leave to inform you that I am now closely employed in getting the books of the office up & as soon as that can be done, & I can procure & deposit the balance due to government, it will then be my wish to retire from an office of so much risk & responsibility as the one I hold. (It, in this circumstance, has given me more concern than any occurrence of my life; & the deficiency shall be made up as quick as possible, at any sacrifice. I think by the last of Sept.) I can make all square at all events & will do all in my power by that time. I have been in public service upwards of twenty years and this is the first time in my life that my accounts have ever exhibited any loss of public money.

I must therefore beg a little indulgence, to enable me to arrange the business, as it is my determination that the government shall not lose anything by me, even if it takes all I have to make good the loss—property of all sorts is very low at this time, & I am well aware that I must make a great sacrifice to raise the money, but I shall not hesitate to do it.

I have the honor to be, John Brahan

The Secretary of the Treasury to John Brahan: Treasury Department 12 August 1819
SIR: Your letter of the 28th of June last, but postmarked the 8th has been received.

The information which it contains has created no surprise. The withholding of your account and the retention of nearly $80,000 in your hands from month to month could leave no room of doubt of the misapplication of the Public money to that amount.

It is now important to secure with as little delay as possible to the government, the repayment of the sum which has been applied to your private use. For this purpose, I have requested a Gentleman of your acquaintance to call upon you to receive such security as shall be in your power to give. Considering the manner in which this demand has been created it is expected you will seize with avidity the earliest opportunity of repairing the injury which the government has suffered by your Acts.

I am, very Respectfully, Sir, Your obedt Serv', (Signed) Wm. H. Crawford

The Secretary of the Treasury To Obadiah Jones 12th August 1819
SIR: The failure of the Receiver of Public Monies at Huntsville to render his accounts with punctuality, and the state of such as were rendered, excited well-founded suspicions that he had applied a large amount of the Public Monies to his private use. Recently his accounts have been rendered as late as the month of April last, and show a balance retained in his hands of nearly $80,000.

A few days past, a letter was received from Mr. Brahan

bearing date the 28th of June last, but postmarked the 8th, in which he acknowledges a considerable deficiency in his cash account and ascribes it in part to the extensive sales which had been made and the short time allowed for the public sales. He has not stated the amount of the deficiency, but from the amount which he has retained in his hands for the last 6 months as appears by his accounts when rendered, I am persuaded it is not much short of $80,000.

It is perfectly idle in Mr. Brahan to attempt to conceal the cause of the deficiency. It is perfectly known here and still better understood by him. It is all important to the government that this sum should be immediately secured, if he has property sufficient to do it. I have therefore to request that you will immediately after the receipt of this letter proceed to Huntsville and require of Mr. Brahan to secure to the United States the amount of the deficit. If deeds of trust which authorize the Trustee to sell the property without any judicial procedure, are recognized by the laws of the territory, they will be preferable to mortgages which require time and involve expense. It is presumed that Mr. Brahan will not hesitate to execute any instrument or Deed which you shall deem necessary to secure the debt to the United States. Enclosed I send you a certified copy of his last return, which will enable you to ascertain the balance due by him. To this balance you will add the amount of monies received since, which can be ascertained by reference to the Books of the Register—from that sum deduct the sums which he has since paid, the difference will be the sum due according to his own statement. You will however avoid any expression in the writings which you may have executed that will preclude the government from making such further demands upon him as shall be found to be due upon the settlement of his accounts.

A reasonable compensation will be made for the services which you may render, which shall be remitted in a draft upon the Huntsville Bank as soon as your account shall be received.

I am, very Respectfully, Sir, Your obedt Serv',

(Signed) Wm. H. Crawford

General Land Office
Washington D.C.

In answer to your note of this day, that John Brahan's commission was sent from the treasury department, April 10, 1809, with the form of a bond for $10,000, which he was requested to execute, with one or more sureties: On the 12th of May 1809, he acknowledged the receipt of the commission and promised to send the bond. No bond can be found in this office.

Very Respectfully,
Josiah Meighs
Comptroller of the Treasury

It took the government almost twenty years to recover the money that Brahan had embezzled. Through the intervention of his friends he avoided being charged for any crime.

Chapter 9

Three Months to Live

She had always dreamed of her wedding day, imagining how her handsome husband would take her hand in his and pledge eternal love to her.

But, when that day came, and Mary Chambers took her wedding vows with William D. Bibb, they both knew she would be dead in three months.

Mary Smith Chambers was born in 1816, daughter of Dr. Henry Chambers, an early Alabama legislator who had been born in Virginia. Upon graduation from William and Mary College in 1808, he had studied medicine before coming to Alabama, a new territory at the time.

After serving as a surgeon on the staff of Gen. Andrew Jackson during the War of 1812, he made his home in Huntsville and was elected a member of the state constitutional convention in 1819.

The whole town took an interest in the fatherless young lady, Mary, constantly speculating as to who would make a perfect match for her. The local gossips, after exhausting their limited list of possible candidates, surmised that none were good enough for her. But that was before the dashing and handsome William Bibb appeared on the scene.

Bibb and his brother, David Porter Bibb, of Belle Mina, were both handsome, reckless, polished, and everything a young woman could want in a husband. Their father was Thomas Bibb, second governor of Alabama.

Whether by accident or intentional, both of the young people were invited to a party arranged by mutual friends. It was here that the brothers met the beautiful Mary and her cousin, Mary Parrott Betts.

As the Bibb brothers courted the two cousins, the older people watched with approval. Relatives on both sides agreed that they were perfect matches. These courtships seemed the logical preliminaries to unions that would connect these three prominent North Alabama names.

It was to no one's surprise that the brothers proposed marriage to the damsels in the fall of 1834. The proposals were accepted breathlessly. It was to be the most elaborate double wedding in the history of Alabama.

Orders were sent to Paris for elegant handmade wedding gowns. Both trousseaus were to be prepared of the finest materials and by the best designers possible.

Many parties feted the couples. Prominent citizens from here and adjoining counties celebrated the upcoming event extensively. The date, however, was yet to be set.

Christmas came and went with no word of the wedding day. January wore by. No one knew what was causing the delay, but the couples seemed as much in love as ever. The real reason for the delay was the fact that the wedding dresses had not arrived. Conversations circulated about the length of time required for goods to arrive from France by boat. The brides-to-be met each stagecoach as it rolled to a stop on the downtown square. They were disappointed time and again. Finally, in early February, a large package arrived that definitely looked like a wedding dress container. However, when it was opened the girls were heartbroken to discover that only one dress had been made. The seamstress had run out of material.

Days went by, then William Bibb and Mary Chambers declared their intention to marry at once, even though it meant there would be no double wedding. The other couple understood and arrangements were made for the ceremony to take place at the Chambers home. Excitement increased every day. There was a whirlwind of activity, with sewing, flower arranging, cleaning, cooking, and sending out invitations. Friends notified them that they were coming from many other states.

The couple was blissfully happy and the older folks envied them.

Then the unthinkable happened. A few nights before the wedding, Mary's old Negro mammy said to her and her cousin: "Let me make you some 'settling down' medicine so you won't be a bundle of nerves during all this wedding excitement. Gonna be a lot of handsome young men around here and you don't want your hearts a'fluttering."

The girls just laughed. They loved their old mammy, who had taken care of them since they were born.

The old woman came back in a few minutes with a small glass of clear liquid.

"What is it, Mammy? Will it make us more beautiful?" they laughed.

"Ain't nothin' but salts," she said. "Ain't gonna hurt you."

The girls couldn't decide who would take it first. "You're the one getting married, you take it first," Mary Betts urged.

So, Mary Chambers swallowed the liquid in one gulp, making a face for the mammy's benefit. But, as soon as she put the glass down, she knew something was terribly wrong. "My throat hurts! What's wrong with me? Help me, Mary!" she pleaded.

While her cousin soothed her, the mammy dashed into the other room, to return a moment later with her face covered in tears.

"Oh, what have I done to you?" she sobbed.

The "salts" had come from a bottle containing oxafic acid. A doctor was summoned and, after examining Mary, rendered his opinion: she could only hope to live for a short time, about three months at the longest.

Instantly, the Chambers home was buried in a deep depression. William Bibb was overcome with grief upon learning of the tragedy. For days he never left her bedside. During this time, he abruptly announced that he and Mary would be married immediately.

On Feb. 26 an entirely different wedding than that which had been planned took place. Friends and relatives, trying to act cheerful, watched as the Rev. John Allen, pastor of the First Presbyterian Church, united Mary Chambers and William Bibb in holy matrimony. The poignancy of the moment was such that words could not describe.

Mary Bibb lived three more months to the day. After her death, Bibb erected the finest monument money could buy. It was placed above her grave in Maple Hill Cemetery and was the first mausoleum ever built in the cemetery.

Across the face of this marker is inscribed the three major dates in Mary's life.

Mary S. Bibb
Wife of Wm. D. Bibb
Daughter of Doct. Henry Chambers Born
October, 1816
Married Feb. 24, 1835
Died May 26, 1835

Unfounded rumors have arisen through the years concerning the unusual mausoleum. According to one legend, the tall structure was built to house Mary, who had been buried upright, sitting in her rocking-chair. Like most legends, the truth is much simpler.

It was built by a grieving husband as a tribute to his wife, a testimony to two young people who were very much in love.

Chapter 10

First Bathtub in America

Among history's "firsts" is the unusual fact that Huntsville had the first bathtub. This splendid invention was the brainchild of Thomas Martin of Fairfax, Virginia.

He had learned, in 1808, of a new land opening up south of Tennessee. A territory that was said to be abundant with game and fertile land upon which crops of all varieties could flourish.

Martin, his wife, Sarah, and her parents left Virginia and soon settled near the big spring in the North Alabama territory that John Hunt had founded in 1804.

Huntsville, as it would soon be named, was a thriving community of 2,500 people.

Martin built a grand home for his family on the north-west side of Monte Sano and engaged in dairy farming. It was reported that he earned the considerable sum of $2,000 a year in this business. An enterprising young man, he decided to pipe water to his property.

Huntsville had become the first city in the United States to start a water works system and Martin copied the technique of hollowing out red cedar logs to carry the water.

Running the pipe from the Cold Spring to his milk house, he carved a limestone tub, placing it in the milk house, probably because it was against the law to bathe in the house. This was most likely due to the fact that open fires had to be used to heat the water for the bath.

The tub was five feet long, 19 inches wide and 12 inches

~ 47 ~

deep, with a hole carved in one end for drainage. It remained on Monte Sano for close to 50 years, then it was moved to a daughter's house on Holmes Avenue where it lay neglected until it was uncovered during excavation for the downtown post office.

For many years it sat unnoticed in front of the Post Office Cafe, where it finally became lost forever, leaving only the footnote that it was, as reported by a New York newspaper in 1916, "the first bathtub with running water in the United States!"

Chapter 11

Sally Carter Ghost of the Golden Ghetto

Drive down Whitesburg until you come to Drake Avenue. Look over at the corner of the intersection and you will see a high brick wall surrounding a group of homes. This development, with its stately antebellum home as a centerpiece, would be just another group of homes to the average passerby if it were not for the ghostly legend lurking within its walls.

Cedarhurst was built in 1825 by Stephen S. Ewing, who had become wealthy by speculating in land in the early days of Huntsville. The home became noted for its architectural beauty and the numerous social affairs held by Stephen and his wife, Mary.

In 1837, Sally Carter, the sister of Mary, visited Cedarhurst with the intention of spending the summer. Within days she became sick and a short while later died. She was buried in a cemetery located only a few steps from the home. According to legend, Mary was stricken with grief over her sister's death and sent to Nashville for an appropriate marker to place at the head of the grave. The inscription on the tombstone read:

"My flesh shall slumber in the ground
Till the last trumpet's joyful sound
Then burst the chains with sweet surprise
And in my savior's image rise."

Two years later, in 1839, the household slaves told of hearing an eerie sound late in the night. "The sound was almost musical," they said, "almost like a trumpet." The slaves were frightened and locked themselves in their cabins, anxiously waiting for daylight to come.

The next morning, the slaves told Ewing of the strange, frightening sounds they had heard during the night. Ewing, being a practical man, quickly dismissed the slaves and sent them about their chores. Later that morning, as he was walking by Sally's grave, he stopped and idly picked a few stray weeds that were growing around the tombstone. As he bent over to grasp the weeds, he froze, his attention riveted to a set of small, ladylike footprints in the heavy morning dew. There were only two footprints, not going anywhere and not coming from anywhere. Just two footprints in the middle of the grave.

Ewing sold the house in 1865 and moved to Mississippi. By then, there were few people left who could remember Sally Carter, but almost everyone could tell stories of her ghost. Tales were told of people walking past her grave on a dark moonlit night and hearing the sounds of chains rattling and trumpets sounding. But, of course, any educated person in town could tell you that it was ... just tales.

In 1919, J. D. Thornton bought the house. That same year, in the fall, Mr. Thornton's nephew was visiting when a terrible storm took place one night. The next morning, when the family came down to breakfast, they discovered the nephew sitting on the front porch, pale and trembling.

"Sally appeared to me last night," he said in a quivering voice. "She said her tombstone had fallen over and asked me to put it back up."

The other members of the family tried hard to control their laughter, and, in an effort to humor him, followed him to the graveyard.

Sally's tombstone had fallen down. The nephew, with a look of horror on his face, turned and ran back to the house.

The same morning, he packed his clothes and made

arrangements to return to Dothan, his home. He never visited Huntsville again.

The rest of the family, out of shock and fear, left the tombstone where it had fallen.

About this time other strange and unexplained things began to happen in the house. Ash trays would rise from a table and fly across the room. Overnight guests would hear the sound of footsteps in their room but upon investigating, the room would be found empty.

In the late 1970s, Cedarhurst was sold to a company that had plans to develop it as an exclusive complex. Brick walls began going up and security guards manned the gates. Lavish new homes were built and the old home was converted to a club house for the residents.

It seemed as if, finally, Sally was at rest in a home as magnificent as the one she had once known.

There was just one small problem. No development company wants to buy a piece of valuable property with a grave right in the middle of it. The grave had to go.

A plot in another cemetery was bought, disinterment permits were acquired, and men and machinery were hired. The first grave, that of Sally's sister, Mary, was uncovered and her remains moved with no trouble. What they discovered when Sally's grave was opened would leave everyone speechless, with no explanation.

The grave was opened and the vault was found to be intact, with no sign of damage. But when the vault was opened, Sally's body was not there. It had disappeared.

Workmen later said they dug an area of thirty to forty feet around the grave and it would have been impossible not to have found any signs of the body if it was there.

In 1985, the home was selected to be used as a Decorators Show House. Every year in Huntsville, decorators would select a home to showcase their talents, and Cedarhurst, with its prime location and rich history, seemed a logical choice. A local interior decorating firm was selected to decorate Sally's bedroom. A color scheme of teal blue and peach was used with bright fabrics for wall coverings. Crocheted bed coverings and period antiques helped to give the room a personal touch. It was a room that anyone would have been happy with. Well, almost anyone.

Several weeks after the Decorators Show opened, strange mysterious things began to happen. A vase of flowers would be overturned, a picture on the wall would be crooked. Small things, just enough to make the ladies laugh and tease one another about the ghost.

What happened next can best be described by an article that appeared in the Huntsville Times newspaper on May 19, 1985. "One night, the house was inspected before closing and all was found to be in order and ready for the next morning's visitors. The door was locked, and a security guard went on duty. No one entered Cedarhurst that night.

"The next morning, when the house was opened, Sally Carter's bedroom looked like it had been the scene of a teenager's tantrum. The antique diary was found pitched on the floor and artificial flowers strewn about. Most apparent of the disturbances was the disarray of the bed coverings."

No explanation has ever been found.

Talk of Sally's ghost has died down in the past few years. What was once her grave is now hidden from public view, and strangers are discouraged from entering the complex.

And so now, over a hundred and eighty years after her death, Sally Carter, her ghost hemmed in by tall brick walls, has entered Huntsville's folklore as, "The Ghost of the Golden Ghetto."

Chapter 12

Scandal on Randolph Avenue

When John C. and Emeline were married on Christmas Eve, 1829, no one would have predicted the unhappy and scandalous end their union would see. Emeline was many years younger than John, a prosperous and distinguished land owner, who had come to Huntsville with his parents in 1807. He was the ideal husband for the young Emeline, or so everyone thought.

Emeline was barely 18 when they married and was considered by many to be lighthearted and girlish. She possessed a trim figure and an extremely romantic and imaginative mind. In this last characteristic, she and her husband were totally different.

The couple were married in Courtland and moved to Huntsville after the wedding. They began their married life in the home of his mother, about a mile or so outside of Huntsville. Living with them were John's two sisters, older ladies who had never married. Both spinsters took an immediate liking to the bright and flirtatious young woman, and the three soon became good friends.

When his mother died in 1831, John and Emeline moved to the brick home at the corner of Greene and Randolph.

On August 9, 1836 the trouble began. There was a high board fence that surrounded the home, and on that day a handbill was dropped over it. It announced that a certain Henry Riley, "stage manager of many of the principal theaters in the Union," would present an entertainment consisting of recitals, imitations, and songs.

This handbill was found in the garden by Emeline's favorite Negro girl, Ann, and plans were made to attend. John however, was not a theater-goer and chose to stay home that night and read. So Emeline, with anticipation of a good time, set off for the event with her Ann.

Arriving at the theater, Emeline went directly to the choice seats always reserved for the ladies at the front. The first act was horribly boring to Emeline, and she fidgeted badly. But the second act was one she would remember forever. When Henry Riley first entered the stage, Emeline was struck. Here was her ideal of a man. As he began to give imitations of "celebrated performers," his glance fell often on Emeline who was sitting on the first row. Riley was intrigued by the young and flirtatious girl.

Although Riley had no chance to speak to Emeline that night, the whole city was soon aware of the looks exchanged between the two.

In a few days, a note from Emeline came to Henry, brought by the servant girl. He didn't respond, as he had asked a few questions of the tavern owner and had found out that Emeline was married to a powerful man in the community.

Another note was delivered in two days.

Henry, if you will come down to the theater this evening, I will go there and tell you where you may see me. Let no one know of this, not for your life. Mr. C. is in the country, I am all alone.
Your Emeline.

In no time this innocent flirtation exploded into a full-blown affair. Almost everyone in town was talking about it by now, except for John, who remained unaware.

Emeline now thought of Henry every waking moment. Even though she was acting cheerful at home with her husband, and as if nothing bothered her, she knew her heart belonged to Henry. Infatuated with her new love, Emeline wrote in her diary every day. *"My heart wanders like a drop from the ocean which cannot meet its kindred drop, like a voice which in all Nature finds no echo. Keep that ring I sent you in remembrance of me. One who loves you. Farewell. Farewell."*

A few days later, Henry met Emeline again in the garden behind her home. The garden adjoined the lot where the theater was located on and there was a fence between the two lots. They spent more time together than they had planned on, talking in whispers. When they separated, and Emeline ran toward the house, John stepped out the back door, anger clouding his face.

For several weeks John had ignored the whispers and gossip he had heard around him. But now, before he could stop, he found himself accusing Emeline of meeting someone in the dark. She remained silent. He demanded to know where she had been for so long but she still refused to answer. Once inside the house, John's rage exploded as he began shaking her violently, while shouting all kinds of accusations. Emeline remained strangely unemotional, not bothering to reply to John. Hours later, unable to sleep, Emeline was torn between loyalty to John and love for Henry. She thought of telling John everything, but she knew if she did John would kill Henry. On September 19, the actor was preparing to depart Huntsville when Emeline's servant girl brought him another note. It said that Emeline's husband had missed a favorite picture of her, the one that Emeline had given to Henry. She had to get it back, and in the note told him not to write her again.

She didn't hear from Henry for some time. He was now in Tuscumbia appearing in another production. Emeline, missing him terribly, sent word, *"Come to Huntsville to see me. I was once a bright jewel, but you have robbed me of its luster."* Whatever hope John had in saving their marriage now seemed to crumble. Since August, he had been anything but a happy man. When his mind was not on the severe problems he had in his business, he brooded often about the ugly and malicious rumors about his wife that had originated among the Negroes. Disturbing stories had been brought to him directly by his sisters, who by now had had a falling out with Emeline. A familiar face emerged around the middle of December, that of Henry Riley. Rumors traveled rapidly: why was he here, without his theatrical company, unannounced, and without any business? Then, around 2 o'clock on the afternoon of December 19, two men "minding their own business" saw Riley walking along Randolph, from the direction of the square.

As the actor passed Emeline's home, the two men saw the blinds of a window in the second story cautiously open and a piece of paper drop to Riley's feet. He hastily looked around him, picked up the paper, and quickly walked back toward the courthouse.

The two men could not keep information of this type to themselves, so they quickly went to the office of their friend, attorney James W. McClung, and told him what they had seen. McClung was a friend of John's, so he immediately rushed to the land office with the story. After hearing McClung's second-hand version, John C. sat back in his chair with a resigned look on his face. He said that, if there was enough evidence to prove that Emeline was unfaithful, he would proceed with a divorce.

The two men accosted Henry Riley a few minutes later in front of the Bell Tavern, and aided by a few curious bystanders, wrestled him to the ground. After a short struggle, they managed to pry the piece of paper out of the actor's hand.

"I am so much pleased to see you here once more, but it is impossible for me to speak to you. I am still the same and ever shall be. Return home, Henry, and forget me, if you please, but if it is ever in my power to become the bride of H., with honor I will, and as soon as I can, you shall know it. Keep my secret. Never betray me so long as you live. Write a letter this evening, and tonight, after tea, slip it through the window blinds of the arch. I will be there playing the piano. Adieu,

Henry, Yours."

John was still not satisfied with this latest proof, so he summoned his very best friend, Samuel Crusoe. He insisted that they should go to the tavern where Henry was staying and inquire as to whether or not Riley had any luggage with him. When the tavern keeper indicated that he did indeed have a trunk upstairs, John and Samuel insisted on searching the actor's room, over much protest from the tavern keeper. Up until this moment, John still did not believe that Emeline had been unfaithful to him. He remembered the early days of their marriage when every day was happy. He knew it could be like that again, if he would just be patient. But upon opening the trunk and gazing at its contents, John knew there was no more hope. He felt his heart sink within his chest and tried to fight back tears of rage.

The trunk contained very little, just a few clothes, a hat, and a large bundle wrapped in a theater program. When they opened the bundle, a small miniature of Emeline fell out. There was a picture of her in it, one that John had made the day after their wedding. Letters, all in Emeline's handwriting, made up most of the bundle. John did not have to read many of them to know the truth about Henry and Emeline.

That night, after a long and painful deliberation, John called his wife into the parlor of their home. Emeline could tell by the look on his face, that her secret romance had been discovered. Without any sort of preamble, John told her that she had to leave. Their marriage was over.

When Emeline began to weep, John announced that she would be sent back to her father's home on the very next stage out. He had already purchased a ticket for her. Late that night, in the midst of a blinding rainstorm, Emeline boarded the stage to leave Huntsville forever. There was no one to see her off. John sued for divorce the following March. The trial did not come up until October, and after reviewing all of the evidence for two days, Judge George W. Lane ruled in favor of the plaintiff.

Emeline's only comment about the decision was that she believed that John's associates had approached her under the guise of friendship and really desired to destroy his happiness and her reputation.

Saying thus, Emeline was forever driven away from the home on the corner which still stands as a monument to her ill-fated romance.

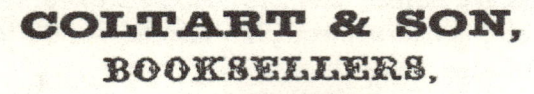

Chapter 13

The Indian Creek Canal

To bring the Tennessee River to downtown Huntsville was the dream of Dr. Thomas Fearn, and his dream was to become a reality through the construction of a canal linking Huntsville with Triana.

On December 21, 1820, the Indian Creek Navigation Company was chartered and Dr. Fearn, LeRoy Pope, Henry Cook, Sam Hazard, and Stephen Ewing were designated as commissioners and were empowered to issue stock in the company at $50 per share.

Under the charter, the corporation was given the rights to open, and improve for navigation, Indian Creek from the spring at Huntsville to the Tennessee River at the town of Triana, and to open the waterways for use as a canal. The corporation was also given the right of eminent domain for the purpose of acquiring the necessary lands and waterways. The company was empowered to collect tolls for the passage of all boats through the canal from Huntsville to Triana at the rate of two dollars for every ton of cargo the boat may carry. A notice appeared in the Alabama Republican on 30th March 1821, stating the "Indian Creek Navigation Company Stock is available for sale at the Planters and Merchants Bank in Huntsville."

At the end of August, it was announced that work on the canal was progressing rapidly and the canal would be open to shipping next season. But, in April of 1822, Dr. Fearn was receiving bids to complete the unfinished one-half of the canal.

Over the next few years, there was a lack of interest in the canal by the public and the feeling was that the canal would never be completed. Dr. Fearn and his brother, George, still had faith in the project, but it appears they were the only ones who believed the canal would become a reality.

An advertisement in the Southern Advocate, 27th January 1827, announced, "The Indian Creek Navigation Company is prepared to ship cotton from Huntsville to the Tennessee River. The canal is not completed, but presently will admit the passage of boats."

Work on Fearn's Canal, as it was now known, progressed slowly with alternating phases of "work" and "no work."

Finally, on April 5, 1831, two boats came up the canal to the wharf at the head of Big Spring Creek where they unloaded a cargo of merchandise. They loaded up with a cargo of cotton and passengers and successfully returned to the Tennessee River. Each boat was capable of carrying 100 bales of cotton and fifty passengers.

Unfortunately for the investors, the advent of the railroad spelled the end of the canal's future. The last time the canal was used was during the Civil War, when the federals shipped the stones that had been quarried for the uncompleted Catholic church to Ditto Landing, where they were used for fortifications.

Chapter 14

Blood Kin

The only record of Thomas Frazier is the 1830 census. He is listed as living with his wife, Mary, and their three children. No one knows where he came from or who his parents were. There are no records of how he earned his living, when he died, or even where he is buried.

Thomas Frazier left no mark on history by which he is remembered. He did not even leave a fine home for tourists to gawk at. He was just a plain, common, ordinary man.

The only legacy he left behind were his children and their future generations. Thomas Frazier had over sixty-two thousand descendants, most of whom still live in Jackson and Madison counties.

Chapter 15

The Forgotten Hero

For Peter Daniels it was just another day. An ex-slave who had purchased his freedom, Daniels had built up a good business in a little shop off the courthouse square where he worked as a barber. Although quiet-spoken, he was well respected by both the black and white communities.

He was probably cutting hair, or maybe sweeping up his shop, when he first noticed the excitement outside. Quickly finishing his chores, he made his way to the square to see what was happening.

A large crowd had gathered. Word had just been received of the massacre at the Alamo in a far-off place called Texas. A pall seemed to settle over the crowd as the news began to sink in. All the defenders had been slaughtered. Even Davy Crockett, who had visited Huntsville so many times in the past, was dead.

As is true with all major events of this nature, once the horrible news was realized, the citizens began to get angry. Immediately, talk began to circulate of forming a company to go to Texas and avenge the fallen dead.

One young man in the crowd, with a loud whoop, yelled, "All for Texas!"

The cheer was taken up by the other young men in the crowd and within minutes it seemed as if the whole population of Huntsville was about to march on Santa Anna. Fortunately, cooler heads prevailed.

Several old-timers, who had seen service in the War of

1812 and in the Indian wars with Andrew Jackson, convinced a local businessman by the name of Peyton White to organize a military company. White had experience in the military and he was also fairly prosperous, a major qualification for anyone who wanted to raise a company. In those days, the officers were expected to contribute to the expense of supplies, clothing, weapons, and various other things.

Peter Daniels, like everyone else that day, must have felt a surge of pride as the young men flocked to enlist. But what could he do? He was black and lived in a society that condemned men to perpetual servitude for the color of their skin. Slowly he made his way back to his shop. It was probably best to just put it out of his mind. Besides, there were a lot of other things to think about. It seemed as if everything in the world was happening right here in Huntsville. His thoughts raced:

"They are erecting a bank building on the square; people say the marble came all the way from Nashville. James Bierny is running for president on the abolition ticket; he used to live right here in Huntsville, and they got government troops over in Guntersville. People say they're gathering up all the Indians over there and sending them out west ... and besides, I've got my fife."

Daniels was known far and wide for his ability to play the fife, a flute-like instrument. Probably self-taught, he was an attraction whenever a crowd gathered in Huntsville. On muster days or when the local militia would practice marching in the town's dusty streets, Peter was often seen at their head urging them on with his fife. People claimed that he had a God-given talent with the fife, and though many people tried, no one could ever produce the stirring martial music the way Daniels could.

Over the next few weeks, the town was a flurry of activity as men prepared to embark for Texas. Women and children both were kept busy making the Lindsay hunting shirts that the men preferred to wear. William Wilson spent his time drilling the new recruits, while Peyton White huddled with the shopkeepers every day, trying to raise the necessary supplies. Daniels, like everyone else, must have been caught up in the patriotic fever that had engulfed the populace.

Today, it is impossible to know how Peter Daniels became part of the company. Possibly some of the troops saw him sitting outside his barber shop, playing the fife, and approached him. Or maybe he spent so much time playing the fife for the troops as they drilled that people just automatically accepted him.

We do know for a fact that he did not enlist as a regular soldier, as blacks were not allowed to carry guns or enlist in service. The most they could hope for was a job as a servant, or a teamster, or maybe, as in Daniels' case, a job that no one else could do.

Regardless of how or why, when Captain Peyton White and his small band of volunteers marched out of Huntsville early one morning in the spring of 1836, Peter Daniels was at the head of the company, blowing mightily on his fife.

From Huntsville, the troops marched to Ditto Landing where they boarded a boat that carried them to Muscle Shoals. There they were transported around the dangerous shoals by a horse drawn railway that had just been completed, saving the soldiers from a long, hot march.

After boarding another boat at the foot of the shoals, life for the volunteers must have settled down to an everyday routine of boredom. It was a long trip and as the flatboats slowly drifted down the Tennessee to where it met with the Ohio River and then over to the Mississippi, there wasn't much for the troops to do.

The men would occupy their time by cleaning their rifles, sharpening their Bowie knives, and of course, telling tall tales. Most likely, Daniels was not afforded the privilege of having much spare time. Even though he was the fife player, he was still black, and blacks were the people who did the chores.

Occasionally, they might meet with another flatboat carrying more volunteers to Texas. When this happened, it was a time of rejoicing and bragging, with each boatload trying to outdo the other with their boasts and achievements.

And finally, as always, after the men had exhausted every excuse for a conversation, someone would call for Daniels and his fife. It's easy to imagine now, over a hundred and seventy-five years later, how it must have sounded as the boats floated slowly in the current down the river with both banks covered by lush foliage. Men silently lying about the deck, lost in thoughts of home, or maybe, the approaching battles, while listening to the soulful music of Daniel's fife.

By the time the group reached New Orleans, word of Peter Daniels' musical ability had preceded him. Fife players were rare, and every self-respecting military company was expected to have one. One musician, Justin Jeffries of Mobile, was actually kidnapped by members of another unit. When the members of his company realized what happened, they armed themselves and went after the kidnappers with a vengeance, resulting in a near-riot.

Daniels was recognized as one of the best and he was besieged by generous offers from many companies. But Peter Daniels was not for sale to the highest bidder, and accordingly, when the small band of Madison County volunteers marched out of New Orleans, Peter Daniels, with his fife, was again at their head.

The war in Texas was entering a terrible period. Santa Anna, faced with ever-increasing swarms of American volunteers, hoisted the black flag. As with the Alamo, Goliad, and countless other places, there would be no surrender. If the volunteers failed in battle, they would be massacred to the last man. It is hard to imagine what must have been going through Daniels' mind as he marched across the barren plains of Texas with the volunteers. Everyday brought fresh reports of atrocities committed by the Mexican troops, and yet they kept marching bravely on.

The war consisted mostly of small skirmishes; small bands of men constantly harassing their opponents. Hit and run; hide for a while and then hit again. With few men, and fewer supplies, this was the only military tactic the Americans could employ.

It was during one of these skirmishes somewhere on the plains of Texas, the exact location has been forgotten for over a century, that Daniels was taken prisoner.

The Mexicans immediately recognized Daniels as the wonderful fife player they had heard so much about. The Mexican army was renowned for its military bands, so any prisoner with musical ability instantly became a topic of discussion at headquarters.

Santa Anna believed men fought better when inspired by music. Months earlier, at the Alamo, four regimental bands played constantly throughout the final battle, and even during the massacre that followed.

Daniels was taken before the Mexican officers, who after confirming his identity, offered him a position in their regimental band.

"No," replied Daniels. "I can't do that."

The Mexican soldiers explained to him that the only other alternative was death before the firing squad. Still, Peter Daniels refused.

The soldiers must have been impressed by Daniels' courage, for instead of ordering his immediate execution, they placed him under guard for the night. Likely, they were hoping that after having time to reflect on the matter, Daniels would change his mind.

A thousand thoughts must have played on him during that long, dark night. Thoughts of home and family and friends. Thoughts of the injustices that he had known. Thoughts of Huntsville that now seemed so far away.

And yet, he never wavered. His loyalty was not for sale... not even for his life.

As the sun began its slow climb over the bleak desert floor, the Mexican officers sent for him. Standing before them, likely with his fife in hand, Daniels was once again offered the choice. Join the Mexican band or refuse and die.

And like other men whose likenesses are carved in stone all across our nation had also chosen, Peter Daniels resolved to die as an American.

Peyton White and the rest of the volunteers returned to Huntsville at the end of the conflict. Daniels was the only casualty of the company.

For a while, whenever men would gather, they would talk about Daniels and his heroic choice. But then, as the years passed by, people began to forget and within the span of a hundred years he had become just a footnote in an old, dusty book locked away in the archives of the public library. Today, visitors in Huntsville are shown the fine antebellum homes of yesterday and they learn of the hardy pioneers who built them. They are told tales of the trial of Frank James and numerous other accounts of Huntsville's legendary figures, but not a word is ever mentioned about Peter Daniels.

No one remembers.

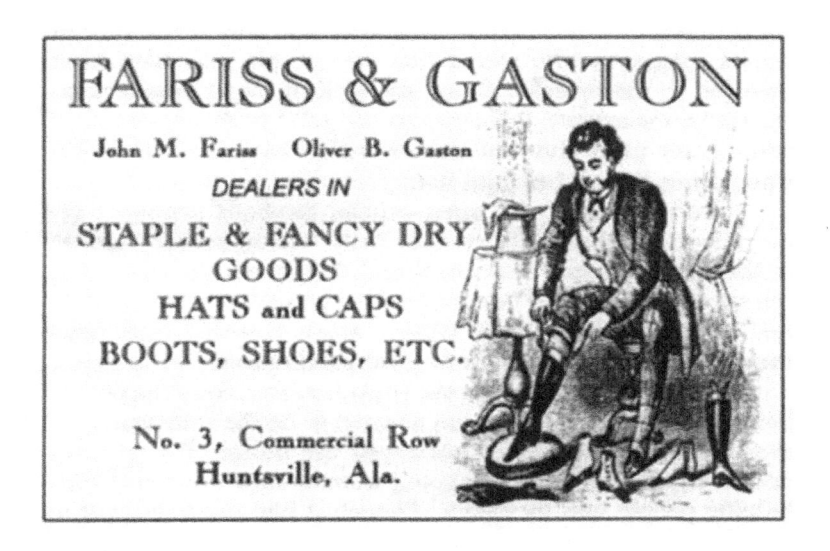

FARISS & GASTON

John M. Fariss   Oliver B. Gaston

DEALERS IN

STAPLE & FANCY DRY GOODS
HATS and CAPS
BOOTS, SHOES, ETC.

No. 3, Commercial Row
Huntsville, Ala.

Chapter 16

James Bierny
Presidential Candidate

Probably one of the most colorful and eccentric characters of all time to reside in Huntsville had to be James G. Bierny. Born in Danville, Kentucky, in 1792, Bierny was the son of a wealthy, slave-holding family. After attending the College of New Jersey (now Princeton), he moved to Huntsville in 1817, to seek his fortune.

Bierny at first tried his hand at cotton farming, but was a failure, as he had neither the experience nor inclination to learn the business. Fortunately, he owned numerous slaves and was able to earn a comfortable living by renting them to other plantation owners.

His curious ways first came to the notice of Huntsvillians when he began to condemn others for the practice of slavery. James Bierny had become interested in the Abolitionist movement and was an avid spokesman for its ideas. Anti-slavery meetings were held regularly at his home on East Holmes Street, opposite its intersection with North Lincoln Street. Again, in keeping with his contradictory ways, his servants provided refreshments and took care of all the chores while their master preached abolition.

When the first state legislature had convened, Bierny had been one of its members, and remembering this, the towns-people were at first tolerant of his unorthodox ways. Within a few years his fame as an agitator had spread, causing the

"American Colonization Society" to offer him the position of "agent for the states of Tennessee, Alabama, Mississippi, Louisiana, and Arkansas Territories."

James Bierny, upon receiving the offer, asked for time to think it over so he could "consult his conscience." In reality, he had asked for time so he could sell his slaves. Another factor influencing his decision was a series of articles he had published in local newspapers condemning slavery and dealing rudely with the South.

Where before, Bierny had been merely eccentric, with the publishing of his articles, he became known as a rabid abolitionist. Meetings were held in Huntsville where speaker after speaker condemned Bierny. As a result of these meetings, it was decided to "invite and persuade him" to leave town. A publication of the times states that "wisely he sought some other shore, where those who knew him less might praise him more."

In 1835, Bierny moved to Cincinnati where he published the "Philanthropist," the cause of numerous riots and threats. In 1837, he was again invited to move. Next, he moved to New York, where, in 1840, the Liberty Party selected him as their presidential candidate. He garnered 7,100 votes and in 1844, when he was again persuaded to run, he attracted 15,812 votes. Although he lost the presidential race, he had insured that slavery would be a major issue in any political race for many years to come.

James Bierny had two sons, both born in Huntsville. David Bell Bierny, the eldest son, graduated from Andover and became a lawyer in Philadelphia. He served the North as a general in the Civil War and was twice faced with charges of dereliction of duty. The charges were finally dropped.

William Bierny, the other son, was educated in the north and abroad. During the war, he became commander of a regiment of black troops. He is probably best known for the book he wrote about his father, titled "The Life and Times of James Bierny." William explains that his father left Huntsville because "moral conditions were so depraved, and shooting and drinking brawls so frequent, that one's life was not safe there."

Editor's note:
Strange as it may seem, early Huntsville newspapers often carried articles condemning slavery, although most of their business depended on support and advertising from the slave owners.

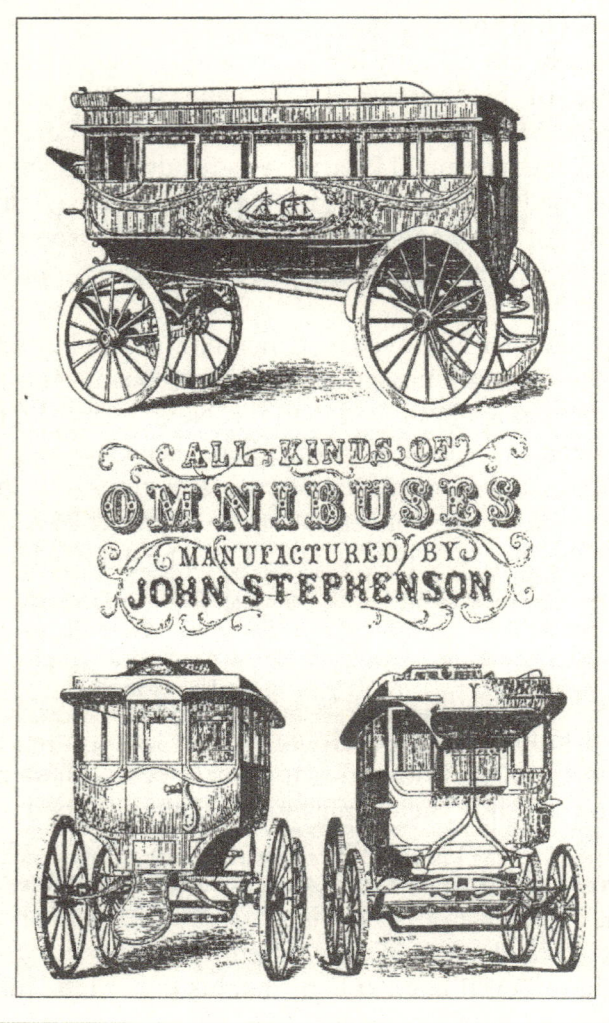

Chapter 17

The French Settlers

Huntsville woke up one morning in the late fall of 1818 to see one of the strangest processions in its short history pass through town. Hundreds of French citizens dressed in ceremonial uniforms with sabers and colored sashes, heavily jeweled ladies clothed in the latest fashions, all headed toward southern Alabama to try and recreate the glory of France in the Alabama wilderness.

It was an odd fate that brought these people to Alabama. When Napoleon was defeated at Waterloo, the elite of French society was forced into exile. The European countries refused their request of asylum, for fear of antagonizing the new French government. America was their last remaining hope. Supporters of the defeated general had already been welcomed in Philadelphia, but the city was not large enough to absorb the many hundreds of exiles now making their way across the ocean. After meetings called by the leaders, it was agreed that they should send out emissaries in search of a new home.

Many months later, the scouts reported back. They had found a land where all the immigrants could settle. It was a fertile land where vines and olives would flourish.

The group split into two parts. The first group followed the coastline down to Mobile and the second group went overland, passing through Huntsville on the way. Months later, after a hard and dangerous journey, the two groups met again at the Tombigbee River. Here the French aristocrats found only a few huts built of logs and clay. They named the settlement

Eaglesville in honor of Napoleon, but soon, envisioning a new world of friendliness among the peoples, they rechristened it Demopolis. The small towns around it began to take names such Arcola, Linden, and Moscow, all symbols of the past glory of the French empire under Napoleon.

Representatives obtained a land grant from the United States government signed by President Monroe. The grant was for four townships, each six miles square, at a price of two dollars an acre, made payable 14 years after the signing of the contract. The grant stated that this land was set aside for the cultivation of the vine and olive.

Then came the period of hope and enthusiastic labor. Veterans of many victorious campaigns began a new battle-against nature and the elements. Dressed in their rich uniforms, they cleared the land, ditched it, and plowed it under. Their wives, delicate ladies still clothed in Parisian gowns, milked the cows, carried water to the men in the fields, and cooked the meals over an open fire in the fireplace.

From old letters and stories of elderly people who knew the settlers emerges a picture of their existence in this harsh wilderness. The whole community began to take on the appearance of a French hamlet. Life was easy in some ways, there being plenty of wild game and vegetables from the gardens. Often, at the end of a hard day, the settlers would gather in a clearing with their musical instruments and sing the songs of their faraway homeland, while Indians and traders looked on with bewilderment. Aristocrats and their ladies, who had last danced at the imperial court in Versailles, now performed the same delicate steps by the light of a bonfire in a forest clearing.

General Desnouettes, richest of the exiles and the acknowledged leader, spent his entire fortune in clearing and cultivating the land. In the middle of his estate, and near his home, he built a log cabin. In this cabin he placed a bronze statue of Napoleon. Heaped at the statue's feet were swords and guns that he had captured in battle. On the walls were the captured banners and colors of the regiments that he had commanded. This cabin soon became a shrine to the settlers. Men would sit outside its door and smoke their pipes while talking of their former service under Napoleon. The ladies would bring the children to the cabin and tell stories of the homeland as the children gazed wide-eyed at the guns and swords.

Colonel Raoul, another exile who was not so fortunate in material wealth and who found agriculture to be entirely distasteful, soon lost his land and became a ferry man, transporting passengers across the waters of French Creek. His wife, the former Marchioness of Sinibaldi and once lady-in-waiting to Queen Caroline of Italy, cooked flapjacks for the hungry passengers.

No people would have been more unfit for the job of bringing the forest under cultivation. Not only were they inexperienced in farming, but the weather was against them. Each winter the frost would destroy what they had so painstakingly labored over all summer. The colony might have survived, however, had it not been for a stunning misfortune.

They had settled on the wrong land!

It was discovered that the land they held title to was located miles away, in the midst of swamp and canebrake.

Immediately, aggressive American squatters began filing land claims to the land that the French had cleared. Sadly, the French people moved deeper into the forest. The hope that had once fueled their ambitions was gone. Slowly the colony gave up its existence, until the only reminder of them were the French names they had given to surrounding landmarks. As the colony died, the French settlers became scattered across the southern part of the United States. A large number of them moved to New Orleans, while General Desnouettes settled in Belgium. He drowned off the coast of Ireland when the ship he was traveling on struck a reef. Colonel Raoul went to Mexico, where he became a soldier of fortune.

Chapter 18

The Man with No Name

John W. Hanner, a staff writer for the *Brooklyn Gazette*, while visiting Alabama in 1847, wrote a story about a slave in Huntsville who belonged to a Mr. McLemore. The slave had been born on the place where he lived but had never traveled more than a half-mile away from home.

Apparently, the slave was born retarded, but had become a favorite of his master. Although able to perform simple chores, the man was unable to care for himself. He slept in the main house, where someone could watch over him.

Mr. Hanner described the slave as a very large, but calm, person who was never known to tell a lie. His voice was low and his enunciation slurred. He never became angry or excited about any of the ordinary things of life. Like all other slaves at that time, he was unable to read or write.

What made the slave so unusual was the fact that he was a mathematical genius. The man did not know one figure or letter from another, but was able to add, subtract, multiply, and work complicated mathematical problems in his mind faster than most people could on paper.

Word of his unusual ability spread and before long he became a local curiosity. The Rev. John C. Burruss and Thomas Brandon, prominent men in the early days of Madison County, heard of the strange slave and decided to see for themselves.

Some of the questions used in testing the slave were as follows:

How much is 99 times 99?
Answer: 9,801.
How much is 74 times 86-1/2?
Answer: 6,401
How many 9's are there in 2000?
Answer: 222 with 2 over.
How much is 321 times 789?
Five-second pause. 253,269.
How much is 7 times 9,223?
Two-second pause. 64,561.
How much is 3,333 times 5,555?

This was the only question that seemed to stump the slave. He pulled at his clothing, wrung his hands, sucked his thumb and then ran out of the house into the yard where he began skipping and leaping into the air.

Satisfied that they had finally been able to best the slave genius, Burruss and Brandon were about to leave when the slave ran back into the room.

"18,514,815," he shouted to the bewildered guests.

A week later he was able to recall to the men what the last problem asked him on that day had been. He never had an explanation as to how he arrived at the answers, stating only, "I studies it up!"

When word of the slave's uncanny mathematical gift begin to spread, his master was besieged by requests from people wanting more information. One group of learned professors from Nashville spent three days with him in an effort to prove trickery. All attempts failed as the slave answered each question correctly.

Finally, in a last effort to discredit him, one of the professors asked how many stars were in the universe. The slave jumped up, ran out of the room and never returned. Almost an hour later the professor found him hiding behind a woodshed. "You don't know the answer!" exclaimed the jubilant professor.

"Yes sir, I knows the answer ... there jest ain't no word for a number that big."

No one knows whatever happened to the slave who was a mathematical genius. Years later, people could not even remember his name and he became just another footnote in old Huntsville's history.

THE WONDER OF THE BUGGY WORLD
LEATHER QUARTER TOP BUGGY

$31

SEARS ROEBUCK & CO
Cheapest Supply House On Earth

Chapter 19

Mystery Lady of Keel Mountain

For years, tales and legends have persisted about Keel Mountain, some with a basis in fact, others with none. Stories about Indian chiefs, hermits, and outlaws all make an appearance when groups of friends gather around a roaring fireplace on a cold wintry evening, but perhaps no story is as strange as the one we present here:
No one knows for certain where Eleanor came from; we don't even know her full name. According to legend, she made her first appearance around 1850. Farmers and travelers alike stopped to stare at the young woman trudging slowly up the road pulling a hand cart loaded with her few meager possessions. At every house she would stop and ask if, perhaps, they might have work for her, and possibly a place for her to sleep. People would later say that even though she always had a faint smile on her face, there seemed to be an aura of sadness hanging over her.
A short while later, those living in the community heard that she had taken up residence in an old abandoned hut at the foot of Keel Mountain. She made no attempt at farming and rarely, if ever, had contact with other people. She never visited the local store. People had no idea how she managed to survive.
Immediately, rumors began to spread about the peculiar woman living in the broken-down hovel at the foot of Keel

Mountain. Woodcutters and hunters told stories about passing by her place and seeing deer, raccoons, and other wild animals following the woman around as she went about her chores. The animals seemed to have no fear whatsoever of this strange but gentle lady. She was seen feeding deer by hand. The closer you got to her place, the louder the birds got. When at her place, they all appeared to coexist in a peaceful kind of harmony. It was rumored that the animals protected her from harm and would let her know when strangers drew near. Other people claimed that it was Eleanor who protected the animals.

The rumors might have eventually died down, had not two young men decided to go torch-hunting one night. There used to be a clearing on the top of Keel Mountain where deer would congregate and feed at night, and it was there the men decided to try their luck.

Quietly picking their way through the woods, they stopped at the edge of the field. Their hunch had been right; a whole herd of deer were feeding in the clearing, with one huge, solid-white buck standing guard. Suddenly, for no explainable reason, the buck's head jerked up and every muscle in his body went tense. The rest of the herd immediately took flight, while the white buck stood perfectly still.

In the last second before the white buck was about to flee, the young men raised their rifles and fired. Dropping their rifles and racing to the spot where they had last seen the deer, they came to an abrupt stop. The buck had vanished; no tracks, no blood-trail, nothing. It had completely vanished. The only evidence of anything ever being there was a blood-soaked shawl lying in the spot where the deer had disappeared.

The young men were at first puzzled, and then frightened as the idea began to sink in that, perhaps, they had shot a person. But no, that was impossible. They both agreed they had seen the white deer fall.

Returning home, the men told their families what had happened. Quickly, the neighbors organized a search party just in case there was a person lying on the mountain, wounded. As the search party fanned out across the mountain, it quickly became apparent that something was different. There were no birds in the trees, no deer running in front of the search parties, not even a fleeing rabbit. It was almost as if all the animals had deserted Keel Mountain.

After searching for most of the next day and finding nothing, the men finally gave up. Coming down from the mountain, they decided to stop at Eleanor's house and get a drink of water. It would also give them a chance to satisfy their curiosity about the strange woman about whom they had heard so many rumors.

As they approached the house, they shouted out a hello. No answer. They shouted again. Still no answer. The house looked like it was deserted. The door was hanging off of its hinges, and most of the roof had long since disappeared. The men were about to leave, when all of a sudden, a huge white buck walked out of the woods.

It was later said that the deer just stood there, looking at the hunters.

Several of the men raised their rifles and shot at the buck. The animal just stood there calmly, watching them. Other men began blasting at the buck, which stood motionless while the deadly barrage was taking place, until finally it slowly turned around and walked back into the woods.

Some of the men in the group were the best rifle shots in the county, yet they could not hit a deer standing only fifty feet away. Others in the party who were standing off to one side later said that when the men began shooting at the deer, they could see bark flying off the trees directly behind. It was almost, and they said this very hesitantly, "like the bullets were passing right through the deer."

In the late fall of 1923, John Ingrams was returning home from a hard day at work. As he approached the foot of Keel Mountain, in the midst of a freak snowstorm, he was suddenly forced to slam on his brakes. Standing in the middle of the road, directly in front of his car, was a woman. Leaving his car,

John approached the spot where he had seen the woman a few moments before. The woman had disappeared. No sign of her could be found anywhere. The only sign in the fresh snow was a set of enormous deer tracks. Being curious about the strange tracks and the disappearance of the woman, John followed the tracks a short piece up the road to where a bridge crossed the stream. The bridge was gone, it had collapsed. Amazed and confused at the good fortune that had saved his life, John was about to return to his car when his attention was drawn to the other side of the stream. Standing there calmly, not moving a muscle, was the largest buck he had ever seen... and it was pure white.

No one has ever been able to explain the strange facts surrounding the woman, and while almost everyone living near Keel Mountain has seen a white deer at some time or the other, no one has ever seen or heard of one being killed. Maybe it was something that could not have been harmed by mortal man.

$13.95

BUYS THIS BIG 475-POUND, HIGH SHELF, COMBINATION WOOD AND COAL, SQUARE OVEN, RESERVOIR RANGE.

———— AT ————

$13.95

YOU ARE GETTING THIS STOVE AT LESS THAN 3 CENTS PER POUND, AND YET IT IS ONE OF THE STRONGEST, HANDSOMEST AND THE BEST LARGE, RESERVOIR RANGE MADE. IT IS THE EQUAL OF RANGES THAT SELL GENERALLY AT $30.00 TO $40.00.

From the illustration engraved from a photograph, you can form some idea of the appearance of this our big IDEAL ACME KING high shelf Range, but you must see it to appreciate what it really is.

Chapter 20

A Man Named Sam

His name was Sam. No middle name. No last name. Just plain Sam. For any traveler passing by the cotton fields on the outskirts of Huntsville, there was nothing to distinguish him from countless other slaves.

Simply another faceless slave, bent over in the hot sun picking cotton. A human chattel worth about five hundred dollars on the open market.

But if the traveler had paused in his saddle long enough to take a good look at this particular slave, he would have seen the face of a man destined to become one of the most controversial people in our country's history.

Although historians cannot agree on Sam's exact year of birth, most agree that it was probably around 1795. He was born in Southampton County, Virginia, on a plantation near Edom, owned by a planter named Peter Blow.

Peter Blow actually owned two plantations, one near town, and the other, a large spread of 860 acres, about twenty miles away, near a community called Sweet Gum.

As was common in the days of slavery, Sam was raised on the same plantation where his master lived. This was not an act of kindness; it was pure economics. Young slaves grew up to become adult slaves, and adult slaves were worth a lot of money. Infant mortality among slave children was high, so Blow, like most other planters of that day, kept the infants near the "big house" so he could constantly monitor their health. At the age of eight or nine, Sam was sent to Blow's other plantation. This farm was a typical cotton plantation, which meant that everyone had to work in the fields. Although children of that age were too young for much physical labor, they were nonetheless valuable at many chores.

Southampton County had been the site of several small slave uprisings, and Sam undoubtedly heard stories of them as he labored in the fields. Many of Sam's fellow workers were from Africa and it was their stories of a long-lost freedom that inspired many of the young blacks. Ironically, on a nearby plantation just seven miles from where Sam labored, another slave also grew up listening to the same stories. This slave, named Nat Turner, would also end up in the history books.

Peter Blow's father had been moderately successful as a cotton grower and plantation owner. Unfortunately, by the time Peter inherited the land, the already-poor soil had been depleted by years of continuous cotton growing. In 1814, 1815, and 1816, young Peter had to borrow money to keep the plantations going. Not only was the soil practically useless by now, the price of Virginia cotton had plummeted to an all-time low.

To compound his problems, Peter had acquired a habit of excessive drinking. Normally a well-spoken, quiet man, he became abusive when drinking. Unable to see his own faults as a poor businessman, he blamed his financial reversals on those around him, including his slaves.

By early 1818, Blow's creditors were demanding payment. He reasoned that the best thing to do was to go somewhere and start over again. He had been hearing reports of new land down in a territory called Alabama. This land was supposed to be reasonably cheap and fertile for growing cotton.

With a decision made, Blow began to sell off his Virginia holdings. Along with the land, he sold many of his slaves. Most of the money went to pay off creditors. He had no feelings for Sam the slave and therefore made arrangements to sell him also.

When Sam's mother, Hannah, heard of the impending sale she implored Blow not to go through with it. Hannah was Blow's house servant and had been given to him by his father. Blow reversed his resolution to sell Sam, most likely because he realized he would need field hands when he got to Alabama.

Books of Huntsville's early history are full of descriptions of new settlers migrating to Madison County. In one instance, probably typical of the Blows, a writer tells of a family moving from Virginia with "the husband walking in front of an ox-pulled cart heavily laden with all sorts of household goods. Following the cart came the slaves, herding all types of fowl, milk cows, goats and other farmyard beasts."

On Oct. 5, 1819, Peter Blow purchased a quarter section of land from the United States Land Office for his new plantation in Alabama. Immediately, to be ready for the next planting season, he started Sam and the other slaves to clearing the land and erecting crude shelters against the oncoming winter. Ironically, this quarter-section of land is now the home of Oakwood College, one of the most prestigious black colleges in the United States. When Oakwood College was founded, some of the students were housed in old log cabins that were originally slave quarters. Tradition has it that these cabins were some of the earliest buildings built on the grounds. If so, it is quite likely that some of the college students were housed in buildings that Sam helped build.

Though now in a new land, Peter Blow's fortunes and disposition had not improved. He had not calculated how much time and money it would take to start a new plantation. His disposition was probably not helped any by Sam.

The slightly built slave had become "careless in dress, had a swaggering walk and a tendency to gamble," none of which endeared a black slave to a white master. Whether it was the alcohol that Blow was consuming in prodigious amounts or Sam's troublesome behavior that caused Blow to begin to whip him, no one knows. Taylor Blow, Peter's son, in an interview with the St. Louis Dispatch, stated that one of his earliest memories was of being forced to watch while his father whipped Sam.

During this time, Sam met and began courting a young woman who was a slave on a nearby plantation. They were soon married. Whether they were legally married or merely "jumped over the broomstick" is not known. All records and memories of this marriage are lost in the mist of time. Nothing indicates what her name was or whether their union produced children.

Most slave families were close and there is no reason to believe that Sam's was any different. When one of his younger brothers died, Sam, for some unexplained reason, perhaps affection, began using his name. Now, instead of Sam, he insisted on being called Dred.

By 1821, Peter Blow finally realized he was not cut out for the life of a cotton grower. A few miles west of Huntsville, in Florence, fortunes were being made. The new town had attracted investors such as Andrew Jackson, James Madison, John Brahan, and LeRoy Pope. The more Blow heard about the new settlement, the more he became determined to move there.

Short of cash, as usual, Blow borrowed $2,000 from John Jones of Huntsville until he could sell his property as security, he put up his land and slaves. Fortunately for Blow, a buyer by the name of James Camp soon came along and purchased the land for $5,000, enabling him to repay the loan.

While Blow was preparing to move, Sam, now known as Dred, was caught in a moral dilemma that had faced his people since the beginning of slavery: Obey the law of the land, move with his master, and leave his wife, or? There was no other choice. Some historians have claimed that Dred tried to run away during his sojourn in Huntsville, but no proof was ever offered.

In the end, Dred moved to Florence with his master, Peter Blow, and his wife remained in Huntsville. They would never see one another again.

At first, prosperity smiled on Blow. He gave up the idea of being a cotton planter and opened a hotel bearing his name in Florence. The Peter Blow Inn was evidently a leased building, since there is no record of purchase.

In his 1876 memoirs, Judge William Basil Wood identified the inn as one of Florence's early hotels and wrote that Dred served in this establishment as the hosteler, or keeper of the horses, for the guests.

Taylor Blow, Peter's son, held a deep affection for the slave now known as Dred. Though much of this affection probably stemmed from the natural relationship that occurs when two people grow up together, one must wonder how much of it was caused by a mutual disliking of the elder Blows drinking and abusive nature.

For the first time, it appeared that Peter Blow was going to be a success. His inn had become a popular gathering place for travelers and by 1827 he had grown prosperous enough to buy two town lots in downtown Florence. The first was purchased Feb. 28, 1827, from the trustees of the Cypress Land Co. Less than a month later, he bought the adjoining lot from Patrick Andrews. Today, a parking garage and a church occupy the lots.

Florence, like other boom towns, began to temporarily decline after its first spurt of prosperity. By 1829 Blow had decided to again seek his fortunes elsewhere. This time his sights were set on St. Louis, Mo., the great gateway to the west.

At 53, he no longer had the grandiose visions he had as a young man. Now he was satisfied to become the proprietor of a men's boarding house. He owned five slaves, including Dred, and employed them in his new business.

Within two years Blow had run up large debts and was forced to close the hotel. Though the town was full of single men looking for a place to sleep, he just was not a business person. Suddenly, on June 23, 1832, Peter Blow took sick and died.

When his creditors heard of his death, they all demanded

payment from the estate. The slave named Dred, being probably the most valuable property that Blow had owned, was seized and sold to satisfy the creditors' claims.

He was purchased for five hundred dollars by Dr. John Emerson, who was about to enter the military. Over the next decade, Dred traveled with Emerson, as his body servant, to numerous outposts throughout the west. At one such post, soldiers after observing Dred's small build (he was only 4 feet 11 inches) began to jokingly compare him with General Winfield Scott, a veritable giant of a man who stood well over six feet. The nickname stuck and Sam, the slave who had changed his name to Dred while living in Huntsville, became known in our history books as Dred Scott.

In 1846, Dred Scott filed a petition in the Missouri court at St. Louis. In his suit, Dred maintained that as he had lived in states and territories where slavery was illegal, he was therefore no longer a slave. His case would drag on in court for almost 10 years, capturing the imagination of every man, woman and child in the country.

The decision handed down by the Supreme Court, called the Dred Scott Decision, ruled against Dred and served to inflame the already hostile tension between the North and the South.

Most historians agree that the Dred Scott Decision helped to put the country on the collision course that led to the Civil War.

Dred Scott died on May 4, 1858, in St. Louis. On the preceding day, in a town 120 miles away, Abraham Lincoln and Stephen Douglas resumed their arguments of the Dred Scott Decision in the fourth of their historic debates. Lincoln's arguments in this debate were a major factor in his winning the presidency of the United States.

Chapter 21

The Black Widow

"Tall, dark-haired, and beautiful. She had a penchant for attracting husbands ... and then burying them," is how one local wag described the mysterious Elizabeth Flannigan, one of the most notorious figures ever to live in Madison County.

The mysterious happenings that took place in her home near Hazel Green may have been accidental or may have been violently purposeful. The first sight to greet any visitor who happened to visit the home was a massive oak hat rack, placed in the most prominent part of the foyer, upon which she hung six hats—one for each dead husband. For some curious reason known only to her, she made a point of displaying the hats, perhaps as a morbid reminder, or maybe as a warning to her next unfortunate lover.

The antebellum home was built on the site of an Indian mound about a mile east of Hazel Green. The original log cabin was erected in 1817 in the middle of a 500-acre plantation by Alexander Jeffries, an early Madison County settler. He was an older man who had met and immediately became infatuated with the young widow.

After a courtship lasting only several weeks, they married in 1837. If Mr. Jeffries had any thoughts of a long marriage, they were dashed two months later when a servant found his body lying lifeless in the barnyard. His cause of death was listed as heart failure. The fact that Jeffries was presumably in good health at the time was never explained.

Fortunately, the young, grieving widow had by this time

acquired experience at burying husbands and so within hours of Jeffries' demise his body was consigned to the graveyard.

As a young woman, Elizabeth had met and married twice in short succession. Her first husband was a Mr. Gibbons, a wealthy man who was many years her senior. They were married only a few months when a mysterious malady struck the new bridegroom. Neighbors later claimed that Gibbons took sick one morning, died at lunch, and was buried before dinner. The cause of death was never explained.

Shortly afterwards, she set her sights on another neighbor, Mr. Flannigan, who becoming instantly taken with the young widow's charms, insisted they be married immediately. Flannigan was also a wealthy plantation owner and when he too died three months later, Elizabeth became one of the wealthiest people in the community.

Apparently, Elizabeth did not believe in long mourning spells, as her latest husband was buried before she took the time to inform the neighbors of his sudden departure.

The widow was now forced to look elsewhere for her next spouse, as the supply of eligible bachelors in the neighborhood had been depleted considerably. Within a few months, Elizabeth, while visiting friends in Limestone County, announced her impending marriage to Robert A. High, who was a state legislator. He was also very wealthy.

He must have spent a lot of time away from home, as it took almost two years for him to succumb to the same malady that had claimed his predecessors. He too was buried immediately, leaving behind a hat on the foyer hat rack and a considerable fortune.

Having tried plantation life and politics, Elizabeth decided next to marry a merchant. Absalom Brown was a wealthy businessman from New Market. After spending most of his fortune on his new wife, he died as well. This came as a shock to everyone, as Mr. Brown was a very healthy and virile man. The unknown malady that he was stricken with caused his body to swell so much that it was necessary to bury him immediately after his death. None of the neighbors ever saw the body.

Once again, not believing in long spells of mourning, Miss Elizabeth Flannigan Gibbons Jeffries High Brown roused herself out of her depression long enough to many Willis Routt, her sixth husband. He died, amazingly, just like the others, in a short time.

At about this same time, Elizabeth, or Mrs. Routt, became involved in a controversy with a neighbor, Abner Tate, over loose livestock and other matters. Tate was completely blind to her beauty, which infuriated her, and had been observing the home and its occupants for many years. He openly charged her with murder. He backed up his suspicions with the hat rack in the parlor that was in open sight, on which hung six old hats—the blatant proof of Tate's accusations.

Maybe Abner Tate should have been forewarned of crossing the notorious widow, for shortly afterwards, he was wounded by a shotgun blast. Though proof was lacking, gossip had it that Mrs. Routt had hired one of Tate's slaves to do him in. The slave, not having the courage to do the dirty deed himself, in turn hired another man, who allegedly pulled the trigger. Mr. Tate, shortly afterwards, sold all of his slaves.

By this time, Tate was furious with his neighbor and determined to see justice done. When he went to the authorities he was informed that "nothing could be done unless you can find some evidence. Maybe all of her husbands did die natural deaths. Maybe the slave did shoot you by accident. Maybe it's just all coincidence. There's nothing we can do."

Beside himself with rage, Tate was determined that his neighbor would not get away with her dastardly deeds. He began writing a book in which he described the mysterious happenings at the antebellum home. He wrote about how the succession of husbands made her prosperous and wealthy, and how she would treat them all with disdain, once she had captured them. He noted how the intervals between weddings and deaths became shorter and shorter, as she acquired "more experience and practice."

When the book was published, it created a scandalous sensation in Madison County. Half of the county believed she was guilty while the other half swore to her innocence.

Needless to say, the merry widow was not a pleasant lady to be around when she heard news of the book. She immediately drove her buggy into Huntsville, where she consulted an attorney and brought charges against Abner Tate for defamation of character.

When the case finally came to trial late that fall, the courtroom was packed. The courtroom became a battleground, with plaintiff and defendant hurling insult after insult at each other. Accusations followed from each of the attorneys, while the judge rapped repeatedly for order.

The crowd of onlookers became so large that it overflowed onto the courthouse grounds. It was said a tavern in town was taking bets as to how the trial would end.

The judge, after listening to as much as he could stand, continued the case, hoping both parties would calm down enough to be rational.

After a short while, Mrs. Routt dropped the charges. Even today, the debate goes on in Madison County.

Why did she drop the charges? Was it because she was tired of constantly being the topic of gossip, or was she worried about some new information that Tate's attorney had recently uncovered?

Shortly thereafter, Mrs. Routt and her son moved to Mississippi. She never again returned to Madison County. No one knows why she moved, but on the day of her departure, witnesses swear that they saw her in a carpenter's shop, getting a seventh peg added to her hat rack.

Chapter 22

The Last Gathering

The Grants first moved to Jackson County, Alabama, around 1834, settling on 200 acres of land granted to Thomas Grant for his service in the War of 1812.

By the time the Civil War began, Thomas Grant had nine grandsons. Five of them enlisted in the Confederate army, while the other four became Union soldiers. All of them served in North Alabama, within a few miles of where they grew up. In 1864, while cutting wood, Thomas Grant suffered a fatal heart attack.

Word was sent to all the children and grandchildren of the upcoming burial. The next day saw the whole family gathered at the cemetery to pay their last respects. Five young men dressed in Confederate gray stood on one side of the casket and the four Union men stood on the other side. When the time came to lower the casket, all nine young men helped, and when it was done, they looked at one another across the grave. Slowly and almost awkwardly, they reached across the still open grave and shook hands with one another.

Almost seventy-five years later, Mrs. E. Grant still remembered the tears on her uncles' faces that day. She said it was almost as if they were saying their last good-byes before they got back on their horses to return to the war.

Out of the nine grandsons, four were killed in battle, one was captured and died in a Federal prison, and two others were wounded. The family never got together again.

Chapter 23

War Comes to North Alabama

Headquarters Third Division,
Huntsville, Ala., April 11, 1862
Capt. J.B. Fry:
Sir: After a forced march of incredible difficulty, leaving Fayetteville yesterday at 12 pm, my advanced guard, consisting of Turchin's brigade, Kennett's cavalry, and Simonson's battery, entered Huntsville this morning at 6 o'clock.

The city was taken completely by surprise, no one having considered the march practicable in the time. We have captured about 200 prisoners, 15 locomotives, a large amount of passenger, box, and platform cars, the telegraphic apparatus and offices, and two Southern mails. We have at length succeeded in cutting the great artery of railway intercommunication between the Southern States.

Respectfully,
O.M. Mitchel, General

Headquarters Third Division,
Huntsville, Ala., April 11, 1862
General Buell:
The work so happily commenced on yesterday has been completed today upon a train of cars captured from the enemy at Huntsville. A heavy force of the Ninth Brigade (Ohio and Wisconsin troops), under command of (Joshua W.) Sill, was ordered to drive the enemy from Stevenson in the east, while

an equal force from the Eighth Brigade, upon captured cars, was directed to seize Decatur upon the west. Both expeditions proved eminently successful.

To prevent the enemy from penetrating toward Nashville, I ordered the destruction of a small bridge between Stevenson and Bridgeport, which we can replace, if necessary, in a single day. The expedition from the Eighth Brigade, under the immediate command of Colonel Turchin, proved eminently successful. To arrest his advance, the enemy fired a bridge on the farther side of the Tennessee River, but our troops reached it in time to extinguish the flames. A small force of the enemy fled from the town, leaving their tents standing and their camp equipage behind them.

Thus, in a single day we have taken and now hold a hundred miles of the great railway line of the rebel Confederacy. We have nothing more to do in this region, having fully accomplished all that was ordered. We have saved the great bridge across the Tennessee (at Decatur), and are ready to strike the enemy, if so directed, upon his right flank and rear at Corinth.

Respectfully,
O.M. Mitchel, General

Headquarters Third Division,
Huntsville, Ala., May 4, 1862
Hon. E.M. Stanton:

I have this day written you fully, embracing three topics of great importance-the absolute necessity of protecting slaves who furnish us valuable information, the fact that I am left without command of my line of communications, and the importance of holding Alabama north of the Tennessee. I have promised protection to the slaves who have given me valuable assistance and information. My river front is 120 miles long, and if the Government disapproves what I have done, I must receive heavy reinforcements or abandon my position. With the aid of the Negroes in watching the river I feel myself

sufficiently strong to defy the enemy.
O.M. Mitchel, General

General Mitchel,
Huntsville, Ala.
Sir: Your telegrams of the 3rd and 4th have been received. No general in the field has deserved better of his country than yourself, and the Department rejoices to award credit to one who merits it so well. The Department is advised of nothing that you have done but what is approved. The assistance of slaves is an element of military strength which, under proper regulations, you are fully justified in employing for your security and the success of your operations. It has been freely employed by the enemy, and to abstain from its judicious use when it can be employed with military advantage would be a failure to employ means to suppress the rebellion and restore the authority of the Government. Protection to those who furnish information or other assistance is a high duty.
Edwin M. Stanton, Secretary of War

Headquarters Third Division
Huntsville, Ala., May 5, 1862
Hon. E.M. Stanton, Sec. of War:
The occupation of Huntsville and this railway line by my troops seems to have produced among rebels the bitterest feeling. Armed citizens fire into the trains, cut the telegraph wires, attack the guards of bridges, and cut off and destroy my couriers, while guerrilla bands of cavalry attack whenever there is the slightest chance of success. I have arrested some prominent citizens along the line of the railway and in this city. I hold some prisoners (citizens) against whom the negroes will prove charges of unauthorized war. Am I to convict on the testimony of the blacks? Have I your authority to send notorious rebels to a Northern prison? May I offer the protection of the Government to the negroes who give valuable information?

O.M. Mitchel, General

Hon. E.M. Stanton, Sec. of War:
No answer has been received to my request for authority to send two or three notorious rebels to a Northern prison. Judge (George W.) Lane and Senator (Jeremiah) Clemens believe it necessary. Would it avail anything for General Clemens to appear in Washington as the representative of the citizens of Northern Alabama, his object being to learn unofficially in what way the existing controversy might be ended? He will come if you approve it. Since the driving out of the regular troops, guerrilla warfare has been commenced, and advocated by the very men I wish to send to a Northern prison. The failure to occupy Tuscumbia, I fear, is to become a frightful source of trouble. (John Hunt) Morgan is said to have crossed below Florence, and it is now said other cavalry, and even (Sterling) Price's infantry, are now crossing. I have not heard from General Buell or General Halleck in two weeks. No re-enforcements have reached me. If guerrilla warfare is to be waged, I must have a large force of cavalry. Am I to expect soon any addition to my command?
O.M. Mitchel, General

Headquarters Third Division
Camp Taylor, May 19, 1862
Hon. E.M. Stanton, Sec. of War:
My line of posts extend more than 400 miles. My own personal attention cannot be given to all the troops under my command.

The most terrible outrages-robberies, rapes, arson, and plundering-are being committed by lawless brigands and vagabonds connected with the army, and I desire authority to punish all those found guilty of perpetrating these crimes with death by hanging.

Wherever I am present in person all is quiet and orderly, but in some instances, in regiments remote from headquarters,

I hear the most deplorable accounts of excesses committed by soldiers.

I beg authority to control these plunderers by visiting upon their crimes the punishment of death.

O.M. Mitchel, General

Huntsville Carriage Works

J.W. Skinner, Prop.

**Carriages
Buggies
Landaus
Phaetons
Victorias
Road Carts
Harness
Whips
Robes**

Repairing A Specialty

Repository and Works, Corner Clinton and Green Streets

Chapter 24

Frank Gurley
Fugitive in Gray

Something was up. You could feel it in the humid, late summer air. Union General Don Carlos Buell's Yankee soldiers could feel it. The Rebel horsemen under General Nathan Bedford Forrest could feel it. There was an ominous sense of impending tragedy afoot. Something was up.

The month was August. The year was 1862. That dreadful saga that was the American Civil War was a little over one year old. In the east, the Union army under General George McClellan had been stopped cold in its drive toward the Confederate capital at Richmond, Virginia. In the west, the Union army under General U.S. Grant had steamrolled its way through western Tennessee by taking Forts Henry and Donelson. It had lost some of its steam after being terribly blooded at Shiloh, but had gone on to take Corinth and Iuka, Mississippi from the equally blooded Confederates. Now Grant's army was stalled. It was spread out over western Tennessee and northern Mississippi in several garrisons thanks to Grant's cautious superior, General Halleck. That left the middle.

Yankee operations in Middle Tennessee were under the command of General Don Carlos Buell, who like Grant, also reported to General Halleck. Buell had left his headquarters in Nashville and personally led part of his "Army of the Ohio" to help Grant out at Shiloh. After that battle, he ordered one of his army commanders, Ormsby Mitchel, to strike south from Middle Tennessee into North Alabama.

The target for Federal operations in North Alabama was originally the Memphis and Charleston Railroad. This line was one of the vital supply arteries for the South, connecting east and west with north and south within the Confederacy. It was also vital to an invading Yankee army if it was going to eat. So General Mitchel plunged southward.

In early April of 1862, Mitchel's army marched from Fayetteville, Tennessee and stormed into Huntsville, Alabama. He captured the railway station, the roundhouse, locomotives, rolling stock, Confederate soldiers on leave, a fledgling foundry, and anything else in town he wanted. Once Huntsville was secure, he sent elements west to take Decatur and east as far as Bridgeport.

Now the focus of operations shifted. Mitchel believed that given enough men he could take Chattanooga, Tennessee. Whoever controlled Chattanooga would control East Tennessee, but even more important, the door to Atlanta would be open. Buell thought it was a good idea. Buell's superior, Halleck thought it was a good idea. The War Department thought it was a good idea and started clamoring for action. Buell marched the rest of his army from Mississippi through Tuscumbia, Florence, and eventually headquartered in Huntsville, Alabama. Before it was over, Buell had assembled some 55,000 men and had more in Iuka, Mississippi if he needed them.

All he had to do was keep the rail lines open, the bridges repaired, stockpile supplies at Stevenson, Alabama, and it was on to Chattanooga. Then disaster struck.

Buell's captured prize, the Memphis and Charleston Railroad, was fast becoming a mill stone around his neck. To keep his army going, he needed some 300 tons of food and forage daily. Assuming he had the necessary engines and rolling stock, this would be a tall order for the railroad even in peacetime.

But this was war, and disaster for Don Carlos Buell had two names: John Hunt Morgan and Nathan Bedford Forrest.

The Rebel raider Morgan had been causing general havoc up in Kentucky, but now he dipped down into west Tennessee destroying tunnels, burning bridges, and tearing up track; effectively blocking Buell's supply line to Louisville, Kentucky. But, the lines to Nashville, Tennessee were still open.

Enter Forrest.

While Morgan might be causing general havoc, it would be Forrest that would play sheer hell with the Yankees in Middle Tennessee and North Alabama. Not content with just destroying sections of the railroad, Forrest would capture garrisoned towns full of Yankees. He would supply his men with Yankee guns and cannon and feed them Yankee food. What he couldn't use he would burn. He would attack repair parties, trains, and even the sawmills pressed into service by the Federals.

Now Buell was bogged down. His demoralized army was spread all over Middle Tennessee and North Alabama guarding the railroad. There would be no march on Chattanooga that year.

Forrest was no stranger to the area that Buell was trying to operate in. He was born in Chapel Hill, a small town in Middle Tennessee. He was also familiar with North Alabama. Earlier in the year, in February, he had spent a three-week furlough in Huntsville, Alabama.

Several companies of his best men had been recruited from Huntsville and Madison County. Men like Captain D.C. Kelley, a Methodist preacher who could preach the gospel and fight Yankees with equal fervor. There was also another lad that Forrest had his eye on, young Frank Gurley. Gurley hailed from the small town, not far from Huntsville that bore the name of his ancestors who had settled in the area. Forrest had mentioned Gurley in some of his earlier reports, commenting on his courage and intelligence in battle.

It had been a busy year for these men, but now something was up. You could feel it in the late summer heat.

Everywhere Confederate armies began to stir. Like hungry animals on the prowl, they moved out looking for Federals to feed on. In the East, Bobby Lee's Army of Northern Virginia would find and crush Pope's Union army at the Second Battle of Bull Run, then head north into Maryland. In the west, Rebel Generals Van Dom and Price would harass Grant and attempt to retake Corinth, Mississippi. That left the middle.

While Morgan and Forrest tied down Buell's Union army in North Alabama and Middle Tennessee, Confederate General Braxton Bragg consolidated his Army of Tennessee and crept northward. Crossing the Tennessee River at Chattanooga, he embarked on what would be his invasion of Kentucky.

These momentous events would of course affect the lives of thousands of individuals, North and South. For the young Frank B. Gurley, Bragg's invasion of Kentucky would trigger a series of circumstances that would bring untold misery into his life.

As Bragg's Rebel army cautiously crept northward through east Tennessee, Buell was inundated with alarming reports from his scouts. Fearful that Bragg might be moving on Nashville, Buell began moving his army out of North Alabama, consolidating it and keeping it between Nashville and the Confederate army. Buell was to move his headquarters from Huntsville to Decherd, Tennessee, where he could keep a closer watch on the unfolding events.

As the Union army moved north, one of Buell's brigade commanders, General Robert Latimer McCook, was also on the move. McCook was one of the 17 fighting McCooks from Ohio. His father, his uncle, nine other brothers, and numerous cousins were to serve the Union cause, either in the army or the navy. McCook didn't know it yet, but he had an unfortunate date with destiny. In this case destiny's name was Frank B. Gurley.

Gurley had been detailed by Forrest to recruit from North Alabama additional men for what was eventually to become the 4th Alabama Cavalry. Operating under the collective noses of the enemy, Gurley had succeeded in raising a company of stalwarts. Meeting up with another company of fresh recruits near New Market, Alabama, Gurley and his men headed out to find Forrest. As fate would have it, he also found General McCook.

While following Buell's earlier advance along the Memphis and Charleston Railroad, General Robert McCook had taken ill and was confined to an ambulance. McCook in his ambulance and with a small cavalry escort, was scouting in the New Market area on his way to Decherd. When his party stumbled into Gurley's party, all hell broke loose.

Upon seeing Yankee soldiers, Gurley ordered his men to charge. To the outnumbered Yankees it must have been a fearsome sight as this rough crew of horsemen rode them down. Gurley's recruits hadn't had time to be properly outfitted and were dressed in a motley assortment of homespun civilian clothes and armed with shotguns, pistols, and whatever else they brought from home. In truth, they looked more like common outlaws than Confederate soldiers.

The Union horsemen broke and ran, being hotly pursued by the Rebels. As Gurley rode after the escort he passed the ambulance. Glancing over, he saw a figure in Yankee blue whipping the horses to a higher speed. Gurley fired at the figure as he passed it. Robert McCook fell mortally wounded in the abdomen.

When Gurley returned from the chase, he discovered who he had shot. The Confederates took the mortally wounded officer to a nearby farmhouse so that he might be more comfortable. Gurley spent some time talking to the man before he died the next day. Apparently, McCook believed Gurley and his men to be legitimate soldiers for he never said anything to the contrary before he died. Unfortunately for Gurley, the North didn't see it that way.

The word that got back to the Federal officials was that McCook's men were attacked by a band of ruthless guerrillas. Furthermore, Robert Latimer McCook had been cruelly murdered while he lay in the captured ambulance bed. Now a different kind of hell broke loose as outraged Union soldiers scoured the countryside looking for Gurley and his men. The farmhouse that had given General McCook succor while he lay dying was burned to the ground. A Rebel lieutenant on furlough was found and shot. Old men and boys for miles around were arrested. The Yankees had blood in their eyes. While it was true that Forrest had given Gurley a commission to raise troops, technically it was illegal since under Confederate law only Jeff Davis could grant that authority.

In reality, Gurley was acting as a Confederate soldier doing his duty as he saw it in a country at war.

Gurley was commissioned as captain, Company C, 4th (Russell's) Alabama Cavalry later that year and went on to ride with and fight many more battles for General Forrest.

After the fighting at Chickamauga, illness and exhaustion forced him to go home on leave. At this time Madison County was again under Federal occupation and on the Yankee books Gurley was still an outlaw-at-large.

In October of 1863, Gurley was arrested at his home. Jailed in Huntsville, then Nashville, he was found guilty of murder on January 11, 1864, and sentenced to hang by the neck until dead. When Confederate authorities got wind of this they threatened to hang Yankee prisoners in retaliation. This probably had a bearing on the fact that his execution date was continually postponed. In January of 1865, apparently by mistake, he was exchanged. After the close of the war, Gurley returned to his Madison County home to try to pick up the pieces and start a new life. But it was not yet to be.

A nationwide manhunt was launched late in 1865 to find the "murderer" of Robert McCook. Now, Frank Gurley found himself once again to be a fugitive from Yankee justice. Once again, he was arrested at his home and once again he was scheduled for a date with the hangman's noose. Strangely, two days later the proceedings were postponed by none other than Andrew Johnson. Living in jail, not knowing if each day was to be his last, Gurley was finally released in April of 1866.

His ordeal finally over, Gurley at last was able to get on with his life. Every year he would host reunions for his old regiment at his Madison County home. He became a respected farmer and pillar of the community, always ready to assist his friends and neighbors endure the ordeal of Union Reconstruction.

Frank Gurley was probably the only man in Madison County history to have his exploits recognized by two American presidents. President Jefferson Davis honored him for his faithful actions in the service of the Confederacy. Andrew Johnson, president of the United States, pardoned him for the very same actions.

LARCOMBE'S

PHOTOGRAPHIC & AMBROTYPE GALLERY,
Franklin Hall, Franklin St, near Public Square,
HUNTSVILLE, ALABAMA.

Chapter 25

Court Martial of the Mad Cossack

The crowd hissed and booed as Colonel Ivan Turchin, surrounded by an armed guard, was escorted into the Huntsville courthouse.

A Russian emigre, he had offered his services to the Union and became the symbol of all things considered despicable by the people of North Alabama.

Brigadier Gen. James Garfield, presiding officer of the court martial, made several attempts to start the proceedings, but his demands for silence were repeatedly drowned out by the ugly scene from outside the courthouse. Finally, angrily, he ordered the guards to clear the entire block surrounding the building.

The crowd, prodded by bayonet tips, grumbled but slowly dispersed, making sure their utterances reflected their condemnation of the beast who was standing trial.

Peace finally restored, the crowded courtroom's attention centered on the presiding officer. It was Garfield's first time to preside at a court martial and he found the assignment distasteful.

Curtly ordering the clerk to read the charges, he seemed in a great hurry to complete the entire affair.

"How do you plead?" He asked the short, heavy-built man in the defendant's chair.

Col. Turchin, a haughty figure in his full spit-and-polish

parade attire, jerked himself erect in a military manner reminiscent of his Prussian background. Delaying his response long enough to assure that he was the center of attention, he barked in a loud and commanding voice:

"Nyet guilty!"

He had been named Ivan Vasilvetich Turcheninov at birth, in Russia, and had pursued a military career before emigrating to America in 1856 with his wife, Nadine, a dark-haired beauty.

The outbreak of the Civil War found America's Union army woefully short of trained officers. Through the efforts of his friend, George McClellan, Turchin was commissioned a colonel in the Nineteenth Regiment Illinois Volunteers.

From the beginning of his American military career, Turchin had trouble obeying orders. Openly contemptuous of his commanders, he constantly reminded all within earshot that "the way to win wars is by fighting, not pulling garrison duty guarding potato patches!"

In addition, while wives of military men were forbidden to follow their men on military maneuvers, Turchin's wife accompanied him on his various campaigns. This caused considerable consternation among his junior officers and animosity among the other wives. He even had a uniform altered to fit Nadine, who often rode alongside her husband at the head of the column of troops.

On April 11, 1862, General Ormsby Mitchel captured Huntsville in a surprise raid. After securing the town as a base of operations, he sent various units into the surrounding areas to occupy and guard them from Confederate forces.

Col. Turchin was sent west toward Tuscumbia and Sheffield to block the movements of Confederate units. One of these Rebel units was under the command of young Col. Ben Hardin Helm, a longtime thorn in the Union's side.

A brilliant officer of the Confederate army, Helm was, ironically, President Lincoln's favorite brother-in-law.

Turchin quickly realized it would be impossible to

conquer the Shoals area without maintaining a permanent garrison there. He would occupy a community one day, but as soon as he left, the citizens would, once again, defiantly raise the Stars and Bars.

After weeks of fruitless maneuvering and being taunted by Confederate sympathizers at every turn, Turchin's patience wore thin. He knew these people were aiding the Rebel cause while at the same time asking for Union protection, but army regulations forbade him from taking any action against the citizens.

By May 2, 1862, when the 19th Illinois marched into Athens, Turchin was ready for revenge. What happened next became one of the bleakest episodes in Alabama's history.

After assembling his troops in the middle of downtown Athens, Turchin sat on his horse and stared at the soldiers for what seemed an eternity. Finally, he spoke in his heavily accented voice:

"Men, I close mein eyes vor von hour." Dismounting, he turned his back on the troops and walked across the street to the hotel.

At first the troops remained in formation, confused at what they had just heard. Finally, a grizzled old sergeant who had served with Turchin on earlier campaigns, let out a loud whoop and hurled a rock through a store window.

"Come on, boys," he yelled, "the town belongs to us!" Instantly the soldiers, a normally well-disciplined unit, became a wild, lawless mob. Surging through the streets surrounding the square, they demolished doors and pillaged stores and homes in their frenzied delight. Residents who tried to resist the intrusions were cruelly beaten and, in many cases, the women raped.

One squad, which apparently included a demolitions expert, took vaults from the stores and blasted them apart in the middle of the street.

Within minutes the streets were littered with Confederate money, bonds and stock certificates. The only valuables the

Yankee soldiers were interested in were Union greenbacks.

Had the scene not been so horrible, the townspeople might have laughed at some of the incidents unfolding before their eyes.

Three of the Yankee soldiers, in a drunken craze, plundered a woman's wardrobe and paraded up and down the main street wearing petticoats. Other soldiers, heeding the proverb that "an army travels on its stomach," chased chickens and turkeys through the streets.

Meanwhile, Col. Turchin availed himself of the best room in the hotel, puffed a cigar and calmly read from a book on European history. His solitude was interrupted by a knock on the door.

It was the colonel's adjutant. "Sir," he said, "the hour is up."

"Are the men done?" asked Turchin.

"Well, sir, they are scattered all over town." Taking a long draw off the cigar, Turchin reflected on what course to take next. If he did not stop his men now, what other atrocities might be committed?

His next comment shocked no one who knew him: "Let the men continue."

At the outset of the looting, several townspeople had mounted fast horses and rode to Huntsville to seek protection from Gen. Mitchel.

At first Mitchel refused to believe the reports, but as word of more atrocities were received hourly, he became alarmed. Quickly he dictated a telegram to Turchin, demanding to know the cause for the accusations reaching Huntsville.

"Isolated incidents," replied Turchin. "I have everything under control."

Although Turchin may have tried to stop the looting in the days that followed, the situation had gotten out of control. The crimes continued. Over the next several weeks, Gen. Mitchel repeatedly admonished Turchin to bring his troops under control. It was to no avail, however.

Finally, an exasperated Mitchel sent Turchin the following dispatch:

"I would prefer to hear that you had fought a battle and been defeated in a fair fight than to learn that your soldiers have degenerated into robbers and plunderers."

A few days later, court-martial charges were filed against the man who had become known as the "Mad Cossack."

The court-martial began on July 7 in the Athens courthouse. Twenty separate charges of rape and pillage were filed against Turchin. As presiding officer, Gen. Garfield was so shocked that he wrote his wife:

"I cannot sufficiently give utterances to my horror of the ravage and outrages which have been committed. There has not been found in American history so black a page as that which will be the record of this campaign."

The townspeople of Athens made no secret of their hatred of the accused. Within two weeks, Garfield was forced to move the trial to Huntsville, hopefully to a more impartial atmosphere.

A recurring bout with jaundice had so weakened Garfield that he had to be carried into the Huntsville courthouse on a stretcher. In less than a month he had lost 43 pounds. His ill health, combined with having to live in the midst of Confederate sympathizers, caused his attitude toward Turchin to slowly change.

Although never a friend of the South, Garfield's bitterness toward the Rebels seemed to increase every day of the trial. A few days earlier, he had written: "Until the Rebels be made to feel that rebellion is a crime which the Government will punish, there is no hope of destroying it."

Now, as he listened to Turchin's testimony, he felt he had found a kindred soul.

"Since I have been in the army," testified Turchin, "I have tried to teach these Rebels that treason to the United States was a terrible crime. My superior officers do not agree with my plans. They want the rebellion treated tenderly and gently.

They may cashier (discharge) me, but I shall appeal to the American people and implore them to wage this war in such a manner as will make humanity better for it."

The trial lasted thirty-one days. Toward the end, Garfield was very sympathetic with Turchin, saying, "It would be good to have a few towns in Kentucky, Indiana, and Ohio suffer the same treatment."

Regardless of personal feelings for the defendant, the court was forced to find Turchin guilty because of the overwhelming evidence. The man now known as the Mad Cossack was found guilty of nineteen of the twenty charges and was ordered dismissed from service.

Despite the findings of the court, Garfield recommended that Turchin be granted clemency.

Weeks later, the dismissal came to President Lincoln's attention.

Lincoln was keenly aware of the publicity his "Southern in-laws," Ben Helm in particular, were generating in the Washington papers. Already, one New York paper was editorializing that Turchin had been dismissed because of his pursuit of Lincoln's brother-in-law.

Col. Turchin's wife, the elegant Nadine, who was now in Washington, made sure the President read these editorials. A short while later, Turchin's dismissal was overruled by Lincoln, who also raised him to the rank of brigadier general.

However, the rank and file of the Union army never respected him, and Turchin finally resigned in disgust.

Ironically, his nickname, the "Mad Cossack", became prophetic. He died in 1901 as a raving maniac in an insane asylum in Illinois.

As for Lincoln's brother-in-law, Ben Helm, he died heroically on the field of battle while leading his Kentuckians at Chicamauga. Lincoln reportedly wept when he heard the news. Helm's widow and children, Confederate to the core, were taken to Washington and became residents of Lincoln's White House.

Such furor arose over Mrs. Helm's constant outbursts against the Yankees, however, that Lincoln was forced to send her across the line to her old Kentucky home, along with her children, who had unnerved the White House staff by raising a Confederate flag on the presidential lawn.

Helm's son had also raised eyebrows by running through the White House yelling, "Hoorah for Jeff Davis!" and arguing with Lincoln's son over who the real president was.

Despite his sentiments that other towns deserved the same treatment as Athens, Alabama, Gen. Garfield, upon returning to civilian life, entered politics and was elected President of the United States.

He didn't get many votes in Huntsville.

Chapter 26

A Love Story

April 11, 1862: On the morning of April 11, General Mitchel's division took possession of Huntsville. There was no opposition, only a few sick and wounded Confederates in town. They entered at daybreak, first taking possession of the railroad. The Southern was just coming in, having on board 150 Confederate soldiers, some wounded, going home on leave. The train endeavored to make its escape but was fired on by two cannons. All aboard were taken prisoner. The well soldiers were confined to the depot house and the wounded remained in the railroad cars.

This is how Jane Chadwick, writing in her diary, described the events of that day, thus marking the beginning of one of the strangest legends in Huntsville's colorful history.

Emily McClung was at the depot that morning when the cannons opened fire on the train. Her fiancé had been wounded at the battle of Vicksburg and was coming home to recuperate when the train was captured that morning. She watched with terror as the blue-coated invaders herded John and the other prisoners to the depot at the points of bayonets. John and Emily had been childhood sweethearts for as long as anyone could remember. People used to tease their families that if John ever got lost, all they had to do was to find Emily; John was sure to be close by. When the war began John enlisted into the Confederate army, postponing their plans for marriage. When Emily received word that John had been wounded and was coming home, she immediately started making plans for their wedding.

Years later, people would talk about how sad it was to watch Emily standing off at a distance, staring at the depot with tears in her eyes while John would stand in the window helplessly looking back at his love.

The other prisoners, upon learning of John and Emily's plight, began conspiring to help John escape. Word was passed to Emily that she should be waiting across the road from the depot at the stroke of midnight.

Late that night, John put on a Yankee officer's uniform, and while the other prisoners created a loud commotion, he walked boldly out the front door. Walking slowly at first in order not to draw attention to himself, he made his way across the road.

But upon seeing Emily waiting for him, John, unable to wait any longer, began running toward her, with his arms spread. A Union guard seeing what he thought was a fleeing prisoner ordered John to halt. When John continued to run, the guard opened fire. After firing the first round, the guard noticed another figure across the road. The gun roared again, leaving both Emily and John lying in the road dead.

The Union soldiers placed their bodies in an empty railroad car until they could make arrangements to bury them. The next morning, a burial detail went to remove the bodies, but they were gone. A guard had been posted all night and it would have been impossible for anyone to approach the railroad car without being seen.

An alert was sounded, but the bodies were never found.

1884 - People waiting to buy tickets at the depot told of seeing a young couple walking and holding hands late one night. The man was dressed in an old-fashioned Federal uniform. When the couple were approached, they disappeared.

1890 - A man by the name of Dilworth buys the property and builds a lumber supply store. While building the store he experiences problems with his horses. Regardless of how well they are fenced in, the horses refuse to spend the night on the property. Every morning, upon arriving at work he would find the fences torn down with the horses standing across the road trembling as if in terror.

1909—Police are called to the lumber yard. Neighbors had called and complained of a loud party, with people dressed in Confederate uniforms. One man was supposed to have been dressed in blue, escorting a beautiful young lady. The police could not find any signs of a party.

1933—Mr. Dilworth is called to the lumber yard early one morning. It had been snowing the night before and the night watchman had found fresh footprints in the snow. Mr. Dilworth and the guard followed the prints to where they disappeared into the side of his warehouse. After a complete search, they were still at a loss to explain the strange trail that led to nowhere.

No one has ever been able to offer an explanation for the curious events surrounding this legend. Maybe there is no answer.

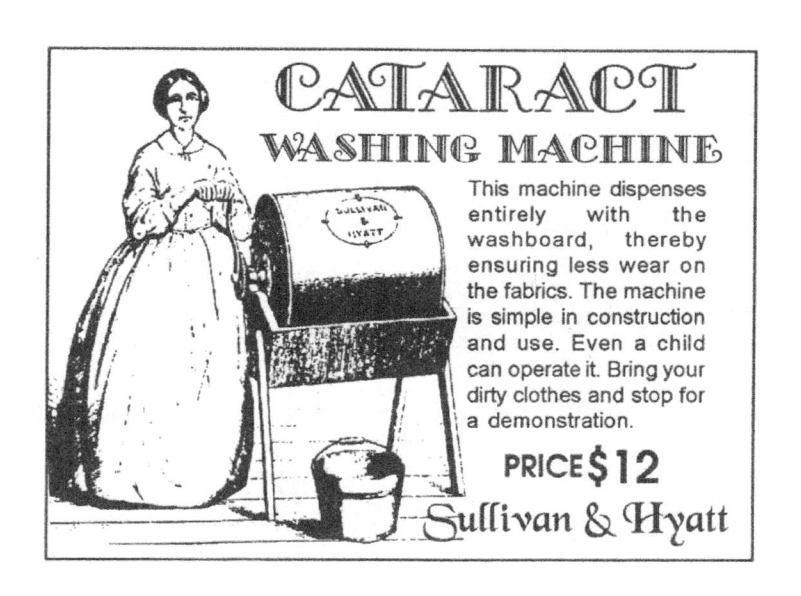

CATARACT WASHING MACHINE

This machine dispenses entirely with the washboard, thereby ensuring less wear on the fabrics. The machine is simple in construction and use. Even a child can operate it. Bring your dirty clothes and stop for a demonstration.

PRICE $12

Sullivan & Hyatt

Chapter 27

A War Letter

Dear Ma,

I hope that this letter finds you in good health. We are in camp now in a place called Huntsville. The people here aren't too friendly and there is not much to do. There is a big spring here and that is where people go to see other people.

They say that Morgan is going to try and take the city back but we are ready for him. We got a lot of defenses and no one would try to overcome them. We march all the time. Last week we went to New Market and I saw the elephant. Seven of our boys got killed and a bunch more got shot up.

This war cannot last much longer because people are going to get tired of killing. People can't kill but so much and they will get tired of it and then there will not be any more wars.

Give Nessie my regards and tell her that she can use my room until I get home. Roy is coming back home on leave soon. He got a bullet but not bad. I hope this war will be over by Christmas and I can come home. Please send me a comb and some real sugar if you can, we don't ever get none of that here.

Don't forget me Ma,

Your son Ben

Chapter 28

A Captured Flag

Most people in Huntsville are familiar with the statue of the Confederate soldier standing next to the courthouse. And almost any school boy can tell you stories about our heroes of the Confederacy, such as LeRoy Pope Walker and John Hunt Morgan.

But the most ironic untold story of a Civil War hero can be found inside the Madison County courthouse. If you wander around the bottom floor you will see a display on one wall honoring natives of Madison County who fought in our wars. Among the many names listed you will see Richard Taylor, who won the Congressional Medal of Honor for fighting against his own people.

Taylor, a native of Madison County, was serving in the Union army when he was awarded the medal for capturing a Confederate flag.

Richard Taylor was born just south of New Market around 1833, the oldest of ten children. His father, James, was a shoemaker and from all indications not very prosperous. There are no records of the family buying or selling any property in Madison County.

In the 1850s, Taylor moved to Davies County, near Washington, Indiana. His family remained in Madison County. Family tradition indicates he worked as a stationary engineer in a flour mill. When the Civil War began, Richard immediately enlisted as a Union soldier. His enlistment was for three years and his occupation was listed as an engineer.

On January 1, 1864 while stationed at Indianola, Texas, he reenlisted with the rank of private.

Meanwhile, back in Madison County, evidence suggests his brothers enlisted in the Confederate army. Most historians would agree that the family was not very close!

In June 1864, Taylor's regiment received orders to Washington, D.C., to help defend the Capital. Confederate General Early had moved his army to within five miles of the Capital before being repulsed. On October 19th, General Early, in a surprise move, again moved his troops northward to Cedar Creek, Virginia. In the bitter fighting that took place, Richard Taylor managed to capture a Confederate flag, and for his bravery, was awarded the Congressional Medal of Honor. The citation is the shortest one ever presented: "Capture of flag."

Opposing Taylor and his regiment were four Confederate infantry units from Alabama.

At the end of the hostilities, Taylor was mustered out of the Union army in Darien, Georgia, on August 28, 1865. Rather than return to his family in Madison County, he chose to make his home in Indiana, where he died in 1890. After the war he never saw his brothers and sisters again.

Years later, his granddaughter would recall, "He would not talk about his family in Alabama."

Over a hundred years passed before Madison County would recognize Richard Taylor as a Civil War hero.

Chapter 29

Black Confederates

He was a Confederate hero. Born in Huntsville, Alabama, Henry Bolden served in many theaters of the war and saw action in the battle of Nashville. When the Union troops began to overrun his position in bloody hand to hand fighting, Bolden, who did not have a gun, picked up a stick and began swinging it furiously. When the battle was over, five dead Yankee soldiers lay sprawled about his feet.

Later, when asked how he did it, his only reply was, "I knocked them in the head."

Henry Bolden was a black man.

Although few people realize it, there were a number of black Confederate veterans in Madison County. These men, all of whom were valued and respected citizens, earned a unique place in Huntsville history.

Essex Lewis, one of the best known and highly respected, went to war with his master, Colonel Nick Lewis, and saw action in Virginia, Tennessee, Alabama, and Georgia. After the war, he returned to Huntsville, where he worked as a farmer and as a janitor at the post office. Lewis was a loyal member of the Egbert Jones Camp of Confederate veterans here in Huntsville.

In 1910 he was chosen to represent the Huntsville camp at a Confederate reunion in Richmond, Virginia. When Lewis died at the age of 106, his funeral was attended by an honor guard consisting of ex-Confederate soldiers.

Another Huntsville black who saw service in the Civil

War was Matt Gray. "Uncle Matt," as he was known, always wore an old gray uniform with the bronze "medal of the Confederacy" pinned to his lapel. He also was a member of the Confederate Veterans organization here in Huntsville and had the distinction of a "special" chair being reserved for him at the monthly meetings. According to newspaper accounts of the day, the only meetings he ever missed were when he was sick. At his death, the Huntsville newspaper ended his obituary with, "Now Uncle Matt has gone himself to aid with the Rebel yell."

Historians researching this period of our history might be interested to know that Huntsville was not an unusual case. During a Confederate reunion held in Tampa, Florida, in the early 1920s, twenty-five black veterans attended. Dan Winset, another black veteran, lived at the Confederate Old Soldiers home in Little Rock, Arkansas, while New Orleans had a militia made up entirely of black soldiers who served the South.

But perhaps the final word was spoken by Essex Lewis in 1898 when soldiers were stationed here during the Spanish-American war. While walking downtown one day a group of soldiers rode hurriedly by, splashing mud on his trousers. Essex glared at the soldiers and bent down to wipe the mud off, muttering to himself between clenched teeth, "Damn Yankees!"

Merrimack Manufacturing Co.
53 STATE STREET, BOSTON, MASS.
PLANTS: — HUNTSVILLE, ALA., AND LOWELL, MASS.

Corduroys, Velvets, Wool and Rayon Fabrics
SELLING OFFICE —1450 BROADWAY ▶ NEW YORK CITY

Print Cloths, Bag Goods
SELLING OFFICE—40 WORTH STREET . ▶ NEW YORK CITY

Chapter 30

The Last Surrender

In the spring of 1865, the South was a defeated nation. General Lee had surrendered at Appomattox. Confederate soldiers everywhere were returning home. The only organized resistance were the group of small bands hiding in the hills, who refused to be conquered. One such group was the 25th Battalion, Alabama Cavalry, which was commanded by Col. Lem Mead.

At war's end, the Alabama 25th numbered no more than a few hundred members. Too small and too weak to fight in battle, they were forced to conduct hit and run raids on the enemy's supply lines. This not only harassed the Yankees, it also supplied a source of badly needed food and weapons. It also incurred the wrath of General Granger, commanding officer of the Federal troops stationed in Huntsville.

General Granger sent word to the Rebel troops that Lee had surrendered and that they should lay down arms also. The war was over. Col. Mead, after consulting with his men, refused to surrender.

Once again, Granger sent word that "Officers could keep their side arms, and officers and enlisted men would be allowed to keep their personal horses, but they must surrender." If not, they would be treated as "outlaws and horse thieves." Col. Mead still refused.

After weeks of constant harassment by the Federal troops, the Alabama 25th was finally cornered near New Market on May 6, 1865. A pitched battle was fought, and twenty-five

Confederates were captured, three of whom were executed on the spot. The last remaining Confederate forces were badly split up and the command fell to the leadership of Major M. E. Johnston. With Federal troops everywhere, Johnston had no choice but to retreat once again to the hills. The Federal troops had threatened to burn the home of anyone caught helping the Rebels. They were cut off from food and supplies and now they faced the prospect of being hung if captured.

Sadly, Major Johnston agreed to surrender. He was informed that Col. Given, a Federal officer, would accept the surrender at a place on Monte Sano Mountain known as Cold Spring.

On May 11, the weary soldiers, 150 strong, marched into the clearing and formally ended their rebellion against the Union.

The Yankees, undoubtedly happy to see that the fighting was over, had provided two brass bands and a ten-gallon demijohn of brandy. As the paroles were being given out, it began to rain. The roads soon became too muddy for the wagons to haul the captured weapons down the mountain. The soldiers who had just finished surrendering were once again ordered to pick up their arms. They then marched to the depot, where for the last time, they gave up their arms.

One of the most intriguing legends of that day concerns the weapons that were surrendered. While stacking arms at the depot, it was noted that "probably a sorrier set of guns could not have been gathered in all of Dixie." Major Johnston later admitted to hiding his company's weapons before surrendering. He also said that "no better arms existed in the whole U.S. than those hidden."

No record has ever been found of these guns being discovered. In all probability they are still hidden in a cave somewhere on Monte Sano mountain.

Chapter 31

Bloody Bill Quantrell

The Civil War was over. Men who had once watched their comrades-in-arms die on a thousand bloody battlefields were now faced with the task of rebuilding their homes and plowing the fields that had lain fallow for almost five years.

For most men, their service to the Confederacy was a point of pride. Even the lowest private would spend hours rehashing past battles and remembering, and political careers would be built by men with the prefix of Captain or General added to their names.

A few men, however, wanted to forget. They knew that even the mention of their names would make the Yankees start scurrying to place nooses around their necks. The Tennessee Valley, with its strong anti-union sentiment, was a perfect place for such a man to take on a new identity and hide.

One of these men was William Clark McCoy, a Methodist minister who was ordained here in Huntsville. During the War, many people believed he had become synonymous with bloody massacres and terror. While few people recognized the name McCoy, everyone had heard what was widely believed to be his real name, William Clark Quantrell.

Our story begins in 1857 on the Kansas border. An undeclared border war had been raging for several years between Unionists and Southerners. Bands of outlaws, Union sympathizers calling themselves Redlegs and operating under the guise of patriotism, murdered and pillaged the countryside. In this conflict there was no middle ground, you were either for them or against them. A choice either way made you eligible for a bullet in the back and your home burned to the ground.

It was into this conflict that William Quantrell rode in the summer of 1857. Quantrell was a native of New Jersey whose older brother had moved to Kansas several years earlier. Shortly after Quantrell arrived, the two brothers decided on a trip to California. The first part of the trip was uneventful until they reached Cottonwood, Kansas, and made camp for the night.

Late that evening, after supper was finished, a group of Redlegs approached the camp. At first the brothers were not alarmed, strangers were always welcome in their camp. Suddenly, without warning, the leader of the group pulled his gun and began firing at the hapless brothers. Quantrell was severely wounded, his brother dead, and all their worldly possessions stolen.

According to legend, Quantrell lay there for three days, near death, guarding his dead brother's body. Finally, an old Shawnee Indian stumbled across the camp, helped bury the older brother and carried Quantrell back to his home where he nursed him back to health.

It took Quantrell almost a year to completely recover his health and the whole time he had but one thing on his mind; vengeance for his dead brother. During this time he listened and learned. He learned that the group of Redlegs that had ambushed him were part of an outfit operating under the leadership of a notorious guerrilla chieftain by the name of Jim Lane.

Quantrell grew a beard, changed his name, and began making friends with the guerrillas. Now known as Charles Hart, he was quickly accepted as a member of the band of cutthroats. He enrolled in a company that contained all but two of the men who had murdered his brother. Enlisting as a private, he was soon promoted to an orderly, and as his leadership skills became evident, was advanced in rank to the position of sergeant.

Before long, Redlegs began to disappear. First one or two would be found hung, or maybe with a bullet in the back of the head. Then it got to the point where scarcely a week would go by without another dead body being found. Men began to whisper about the unknown Judas in their midst. Even the bravest men were terrified.

One night about a year after he joined the band, Quantrell was sitting around the campfire listening to the men speculate on the identity of the assassin. One man brought up the story about the time he and a group of other men ambushed two brothers on Cottonwood River.

"That's a funny thing," he said, "all those men are dead. I'm the only one left alive."

"Not for long," Quantrell said as he casually pulled the trigger on his pistol, sending the Redleg to burn in Hell.

William Quantrell was a wanted man now, with a price on his head, dead or alive. Word of his exploits galvanized Kansas and Missouri and it wasn't long before he began attracting recruits for his own private army. Jesse and Frank James, their homes burned by the Redlegs, joined as did Kit Dalton, Cole Younger, and many other young men thirsting for vengeance.

Although it has never been verified, rumor has always persisted that Quantrell was commissioned a Colonel in the Confederate army. This, however, is highly unlikely due to his tactics. Quantrell's army, fighting under the black flag, did not take prisoners.

His most infamous deed was the August 21, 1863, raid on Lawrence, Kansas, where he and 273 of his men captured the city and put one hundred and fifty of its citizens to death. On May 10, 1865, Quantrell and his men took cover from an afternoon thunderstorm in a barn belonging to a Mr. Wakefield. Coming from the opposite direction was a column of 120 Union soldiers commanded by Captain Edward Terrell. The Union soldiers, seeing the fresh footprints leading to the barn, decided to investigate.

Immediately, shots rang out. During the furious gun battle, most of Quantrell's men were able to make an escape, leaving only five men behind, two wounded and three dead. Captain Terrell, upon questioning the two wounded men, was shocked to hear one of the men confess his identity as that of William Clark Quantrell.

The man purporting to be Quantrell was badly wounded. He had suffered gunshots to the shoulder in addition to a broken back. It was obvious the man was mortally wounded.

"Please," said the man, "leave me here in peace to die." After checking the man's wounds, the union captain agreed to the wounded man's request. Calling for his men to mount up, the officer led his men back to town, satisfied that he had caused the end of Quantrell. Unfortunately, his commanding officer was not as happy.

Angry at the fact that his men had left Quantrell to die in peace, the Commander sent another squad of soldiers to recover the fallen chieftain.

By most established reports, Quantrell died about two weeks later of his wounds while being held a prisoner in Louisville, Kentucky. Before dying he was supposed to have been converted to the Catholic faith and made a full confession. His remains were buried in a local graveyard with no marker. The burial marked the beginning of a mystery that continues to this day. No one who had ever known Quantrell stepped forward to identify the body. The only proof the soldiers had was the wounded man's own statement. Even the confession, and the account that he had converted to the Catholic faith, began to lose credence once it was pointed out that William Clark Quantrell was a Methodist.

Even the local newspapers hesitated to identify the person as being Quantrell. *The Louisville Times*, May 14, 1865, reported:

"Captain Twirl and his company arrived here yesterday from Taylorsville. They brought with them the guerilla who bears the name 'Quantrell.' It is not the Quantrell of Kansas notoriety, for we have been assured that he was at last account a colonel in the rebel army under Price. This prisoner was shot through the body in a fight in a barn near Taylorsville on Wednesday last. Several others were killed at the barn, but what their names are we have not been able to ascertain. The prisoner brought here is confined to the prison hospital and is in a dying condition."

Adding further to the confusion is a newspaper article dated June 7, 1865, that throws the whole question of a confession into doubt.

"It will be remembered that a guerilla calling himself William Clark, captain in the Fourth Missouri Rebel Cavalry, but generally supposed to be the infamous monster Quantrell, was wounded and captured on the 10th of May and placed in the military hospital of this city. He died of his wounds yesterday afternoon, about four o'clock."

If Quantrell had confessed, why did the paper still identify him by the name William Clark and state that "he was generally supposed to be Quantrell?"

And so, for lack of a better answer, the military authorities buried an unidentified body and wrote finish to the bloody chapter of William Clark Quantrell.

Or so they thought. When Quantrell's mother had the body exhumed to move it to a family plot, the corpse was discovered to have red hair. Quantrell's hair was black.

Almost two years later our story takes another bizarre twist. A young man by the name of William Clark McCoy appeared as a Methodist circuit rider in the Tennessee Valley. According to the story given at the time, McCoy was an ex-soldier who had served briefly with Quantrell and then later joined Stonewall Jackson's army as a courier. At the end of the war he learned there was a reward offered for members of Quantrell's band, so instead of returning home, he made his way south to Alabama where he became a minister.

A search of all the records would later reveal no William Clark McCoy serving with Quantrell or Jackson. Even more confusing was the fact that years later his wife, before her death, admitted there was a $50,000 reward offered for the capture of her husband. Quantrell was the only member of his group who had a price on his head at the end of the war. Rumors surrounded McCoy as to his real identity from almost the first day he moved to the valley. Photographs of Quantrell had been circulated throughout the country and there were thousands of ex-soldiers returning home from the war who had fought with Quantrell or had seen him. Surprisingly, no one at the time thought it was strange that the man once known as "Bloody Quantrell" was now seeking salvation through religion.

After accepting the Methodist faith, McCoy became an active worker in the church. One of the anecdotes about McCoy handed down through generations had to do with his helping raise money for a church. The church was having a picnic along with games and contests. One of the contests was a shooting competition with the winner receiving a freshly baked apple pie. Unfortunately, even with the low entrance fee of 25 cents, the contest did not generate much interest.

Some of the local men, having heard the rumor of Quantrell being in their midst, and noticing the brace of pistols he wore underneath his coat, appealed to McCoy to try his luck. Maybe if the crowd saw him entering the contest it would encourage other men to do the same.

At first McCoy refused, but after many appeals to his charitable nature he finally agreed.

The crowd grew silent as he approached the firing line. Twelve bottles sitting in a row at a distance of thirty paces was the target. Slowly he pulled one pistol and, after carefully taking aim, hit the first bottle dead center. The second shot came a few seconds later and another bottle disappeared. As the gun began to feel comfortable in McCoy's hand again, the crowd watched with amazement as his body went into a crouch, firing at the bottles so rapidly that it was impossible to tell one shot from the next. Moving so fast that his hand seemed to be a blur, he dropped the empty pistol and drew the other one. This time, instead of shooting with one hand, he threw the blazing gun from hand to hand as bottle after bottle exploded into thousands of pieces of glass.

People later said that after McCoy had finished firing, he stood there for a long minute, staring at the spot where the targets had stood, and as he slowly turned around to leave, reached down and unbuckled his gun belt. Though he taught all of his children to become expert marksmen, and gave occasional shooting demonstrations, he never strapped on a gun belt again.

During this time, McCoy had been ordained as an elder in the Methodist church here in Huntsville. According to legend, when McCoy signed the notice appointing him a minister, he signed with the name William Clark Quantrell. The Bishop then penciled in the name "WC. McCoy" and kept the papers in his personal collection.

Word of his eloquence began to reach the church superiors and in almost an unbelievably short period of time he began to advance in his newly chosen career. Besides serving in the pulpit of churches in Guntersville, Birmingham, and Decatur, he was appointed the editor of the Christian Advocate in 1886 and served as financial agent for Southern University.

Even with the good work that McCoy was doing, rumors persisted as to his being Quantrell. Neighbors and friends tried to get an answer from him, but McCoy, a man of God, refused to give any information about his past. As his children began to grow older, they also heard the rumors. In a youthful attempt to learn the truth, his children questioned him about where he grew up. He refused to talk about it. They asked him about his family and again he would not talk. Finally, exasperated, they asked him if he really was Quantrell. McCoy, by this time one of the most respected ministers in Alabama, refused to either confirm or deny the stories.

McCoy's son, Dr. J.H. McCoy, who at the time he related this story was a Bishop in the Methodist church, told about an incident that seemed to confirm, to him, his father's real identity.

The sons had heard the rumors about their father being Quantrell and they had also learned that Quantrell had a tattoo of an Indian maiden on his left forearm. Their father, however, always refused to take his shirt off. Even in the hottest part of the summer he would not roll up his sleeves. One hot August day McCoy and his sons were working in a field next to a cool, flowing creek. Late that afternoon the boys suggested a dip in the water to cool off. "Go ahead," McCoy said, "I'll be along directly."

After the boys had finished their refreshing dip, they dressed and went in search of their father, who in the meantime had disappeared. Walking down the creek they found their father with his shirt off, bathing in the creek. Seeing the tattoo of an Indian maiden on their father's left forearm, the boys began to ask questions.

McCoy, highly agitated, quickly put on his shirt and told the boys, "Now listen to me, you haven't seen a thing, not a thing, you understand?"

One evening, while still a pastor at Haney's Chapel, near Guntersville, McCoy read in the newspaper that Frank James was being held prisoner in the Huntsville jail. Summoning his brother-in-law to accompany him, he told his wife, "I must go to Huntsville and see Frank James."

After arriving in Huntsville, they quickly received permission to talk with the prisoner. The Huntsville city jailer at that time and McCoy's brother-in-law both verified what happened next.

As the door to the cell opened, Frank James was sitting on an army cot idly glancing through a book. Looking up and seeing that he had visitors, he started to speak, and then fell silent with a look of astonishment on his face. "Bill," James cried out. "Everyone said you were dead!"

McCoy asked the other men to step outside so they might talk in private. Again, true to his character, he refused to ever reveal what they talked about. Later, when his wife questioned him, McCoy simply chuckled and replied that James had said, "If you can become a preacher, anyone can."

The years wore on and more people stepped forward claiming that Reverend McCoy was really Quantrell. He finally admitted to knowing and having been friends with Jesse and Frank James, the Younger brothers, and numerous other members of the outlaw band, but he still refused to give an answer to the question that was on everyone's mind.

William Clark McCoy died in 1891 in Decatur, Ala. His children, knowing that their father kept a collection of old papers, wanted to settle the matter of who he really was. They were too late. Their mother, upon his death, had burned the papers. While she readily admitted that McCoy was not his real name and that there had been a $50,000 reward for his capture, she refused to reveal his real name. "I promised your father to never talk about it" was all she had to say.

McCoy's children and grandchildren, some of whom went on to become noted professors, judges, and pastors, traveled thousands of miles, spent untold hours poring over old records, and interviewing countless people in order to establish a genealogical record of their family. In all of their research, the only thing they could establish was that no such person as William Clark McCoy existed before 1866. The only records were those that he chose to give. Even these records present a puzzle. In the course of twenty years, he listed four different places of birth and four different birthdays. Was the quiet spoken Methodist preacher really the bloodthirsty William Clark Quantrell? Although his family believes it to be so, possibly no one will ever be able to prove it conclusively.

The one thing that we can be certain of is that his name was not William Clark McCoy.

Chapter 32

Was McCoy Really Quantrell?

Both were the same height, same weight, same color hair, and both had eyes described as "steely blue." Both had a tattoo of an Indian maiden on their left forearm.

Both were expert pistol shots.

Both had the same first names, William Clark. Quantrell had been known to use an alias.

Both had the first joint missing from the little finger of their right hand.

Both were known to be excellent public speakers.

McCoy became a Methodist preacher and Quantrell had taught at an eastern Methodist college.

Both had excellent writing skills. McCoy was editor of the Christian Advocate and Quantrell had taught English at an eastern college.

McCoy's wife, though supposedly eligible, never applied for any sort of a pension for her husband's wartime service in the Confederacy.

Both exhibited traits as natural leaders.

The only mention McCoy ever made of his family was that one of them had been killed by the Yankees. Quantrell's brother had been bushwhacked by the Yankees.

Methodist church records identify McCoy as a former guerilla during the War Between the States.

Chapter 33

A Successful Man

A few years after the Civil War, Thomas Townsend, by any definition, was a successful man. He owned a palatial home on Adams Street, had a large plantation near Hazel Green, was a successful attorney and had been elected as a Huntsville city alderman.

None of this would have been unusual except for the fact that Townsend was an ex-slave in an era when racism controlled every facet of the community's social, business, and political life.

And he was also related to many of the most prominent white families in Huntsville.

Townsend's father, Samuel Townsend, was one of the wealthiest and largest planters in North Alabama. He owned a total of eight plantations, seven of which were in Madison County and the 8th in Jackson County. The main plantation where he lived consisted of over 1,700 acres near Hazel Green and was worked by hundreds of slaves.

Samuel Townsend was a hard, shrewd businessman who was known to spend hours poring over ledgers trying to squeeze an extra dollar's profit out of a cotton crop. He reportedly did not drink, smoke, or indulge in any other of the numerous vices common to the wealthy elite of that era.

The only weakness he had was Hannah—a tall, dusty, and slender slave who worked as his housekeeper and shared his bed at night.

Hannah was reputed to be the daughter of a Huntsville

attorney whose illicit affair was discovered when his wife's serving girl became pregnant. The wife, after questioning the servant, discovered her husband was the father.

Fearing a scandal, the wife ordered her husband to send the slave to New Orleans to be sold. Instead, the attorney sold his pregnant mistress to Samuel Townsend where he continued to visit her. After Hannah was born she lived in the "big house" with her mother who became Townsend's housekeeper.

Townsend evidently was intrigued by the young girl. He insured that she was taught proper manners, dressed properly and was even taught to read and write.

At a very young age (some accounts say that she was only 13 years old) Hannah was taken by Townsend as his mistress.

Hannah took a keen interest in everything that transpired on the plantation. Townsend was often gone weeks at a time on business and he began delegating much of the supervision of the plantation to his mistress. Strangely, given the climate of the times, Townsend made no particular effort to hide his relationship. Even when she began to bear him children, nine in all, they all lived in the "big house" as a normal family.

When Thomas, the eldest son, was born, Townsend doted on him the same way any loving father would. Thomas often accompanied his father on trips into Huntsville where he was undoubtedly the subject of much speculation and gossip.

Many people were infuriated that Townsend had hired a tutor to educate his son. This was a violation of Alabama law forbidding slaves from having an education. Huntsville was a small town and although almost everyone realized who Thomas' grandfather and father were, in the eyes of the law he was still a slave.

When Samuel Townsend died in 1855, his will stated that his entire estate was to be liquidated with the proceeds going to his children and mistress. He also made provisions for Hannah and the children to be taken North and freed. Under a law passed in 1834, slaves who were freed by their master could not remain in the state of Alabama.

Thomas and his siblings were sent to Wilberforce, Ohio where they were enrolled in a private boarding school.

Repeated efforts were made to have the will declared invalid but they all failed. Townsend had anticipated the efforts and, before his death, had hired some of the best attorneys in the state to draw up an iron-clad will.

Finally, a much simpler strategy was created to deprive the family of their inheritance.

The administrators of the estate simply took their time in liquidating it. Part of the land was sold to friends on credit. Other parts were leased, with the rent going back to the estate where the administrators and attorneys lined their pockets.

Between 1855 and 1860 the family had received less than $7,000 out of an estate that was valued at almost $250,000.

Meanwhile, Thomas, the eldest son, had completed his education in Ohio and was devoting almost all of his time attempting to claim his inheritance.

The Civil War brought a temporary end to the settlement, when it was declared illegal to transfer money or property to anyone at war with the Confederacy.

In 1866 Thomas finally gained control of the estate but was immediately confronted with new problems. Much of the property had been sold on credit but, in a country ravaged by the Civil War, there was little money for anyone to pay bills with. Thomas decided to return to Huntsville to try and put the family's affairs in order.

Although Thomas probably thought his visit would be short, he almost immediately became involved in community affairs. He became a teacher for one of the first Black schools organized in Huntsville and was instrumental in starting several programs designed to aid the ex-slaves in their new-found freedom.

In 1868 the estate was finally settled. Thomas received less than $4,000 after the money was divided and attorney's fees paid.

Undaunted, Thomas rented the Wade plantation, part of

the original Townsend estate, and began farming. Many of the blacks working on the farm were undoubtedly the same people he grew up with as slaves.

As the plantation began once again to prosper, Thomas became even more active in community affairs.

Respected by both the black and white communities, Thomas Townsend became a bridge across the racial barriers. When the government began issuing pensions for the black soldiers, Thomas became a claims attorney and worked with several white attorneys, helping to secure pensions for many of the black veterans.

In 1880 Thomas Townsend was elected as a city alderman, the first black to ever hold the position. He carried both the black and white sections of Huntsville.

As hard as it may be to believe, he was appointed to a committee overseeing the public schools even though blacks were forbidden to attend. He later served on the advisory board for the fire department and worked as a writer for the *Huntsville Gazette*.

When he died in 1916 he was eulogized by all the Huntsville newspapers.

As a tribute to a man who was born into slavery and became one of Huntsville's most respected citizens, the city voted unanimously to name a street after him. Townsend Street is located between Madison and Franklin Streets near Huntsville Hospital.

THOMPSON'S
[FORMERLY BLAKE'S,]
BONNET BLEACHERY
AND MANUFACTORY,
WASHINGTON STREET

Every variety of Straw and Fancy Bonnets altered to fashionable shapes, cleansed and pressed in the very best manner. Also, Gentlemen's Summer Hats. Straw Bonnets Colored. Milliners furnished with Bonnet Blocks of the latest patterns.
Goods forwarded by Express, &c., will receive immediate attention.

Chapter 34

The Rebel Yankee

Of all the Civil War veterans who called Huntsville home, Major S.E Sweinhart must have been the most unusual. An ex-Yankee soldier who moved to Huntsville after the war, he earned the respect of his former enemies and was accorded an honor unique in Huntsville's history.

Major Sweinhart was a member of an Ohio volunteer regiment and had participated in some of the bloodiest fighting of the war. While stationed in Alabama, he was captivated by the warm climate and the natural beauty of the Tennessee Valley.

When the war was finally over, and the soldiers had stacked arms for the last time, Major Sweinhart moved to Huntsville, determined to make it his home.

Feelings were running high at the end of the war, so it is not surprising that he was greeted with scowls and bitterness. "Damn Yankee," the Huntsville natives would say as they passed him on the streets.

"Damn Rebels," the Major would mutter under his breath, while looking straight ahead.

But time has a way of healing all wounds and as the Major grew into old age, he began taking his place on the old courthouse bench, reliving and refighting the battles of his youth. An old Yankee officer and a group of old Confederate veterans, with nothing in common except the blood spilled on battlefields years before.

Slowly the town began to accept the old soldier and the

~ 135 ~

scowls he used to encounter on the streets turned to smiles. Sweinhart became involved in the community and became active in veterans' affairs. Of course, the only other veterans in Huntsville were ex-Confederates.

In 1927, Major Sweinhart was awarded the highest accolade ever given to a Yankee by Confederate veterans. The story can best be told by a newspaper article of the day:

He was invited this week to attend a dinner given by the Daughters of the Confederacy to members of the Egbert Jones Camp of Confederate Veterans at the home of Robert A. Moore, acting adjutant for the Third Brigade, Alabama Division.

He was welcomed with hand clasps and smiles. After dinner, the old veterans invited him to attend their business meeting. When discussions lagged a little, Major Sweinhart, who had remained in a corner deep in thought, rose and stood at attention.

"Men," he said, with a shake in his voice, "I've lived down here so long I feel like I belong here." His voice quivered again as he added, "And by golly, I want to belong to you."

The Confederate veterans gave a hearty cheer, and one of them proposed Major Sweinhart for membership. The proposal was accepted immediately, and the major was accepted as a member of the camp by unanimous vote.

He now belongs to the Egbert Jones Camp of Confederate veterans and is believed to be the only Union soldier in the country who has experienced such a transformation.

When Major Sweinhart died, an honor guard consisting of ex-Confederate soldiers stood guard during the funeral ceremony. His body is buried in Maple Hill Cemetery, next to the other veterans he had grown to love.

Chapter 35

"Devil" Monroe

The citizens of Huntsville anxiously peered from behind drawn shades and locked doors as the strange procession slowly made its way downtown. Heavily bearded and dressed in rough homespun clothes, with a shotgun lying loosely across his saddle, "Devil" Monroe Evans led the caravan.

Next to him rode his son John, dressed in unkempt clothes and also carrying a shotgun. They were followed by two wagons surrounded and guarded by a motley, slovenly band of men, all heavily armed and eyeing the townspeople suspiciously.

In the middle of the strange caravan, riding in the two wagons, were the Devil's wives ... all seven of them.

"Devil" Monroe Evans was bringing his family to town to do their shopping.

The townspeople had good reason to fear the man known as the "devil of the mountains." William Monroe Evans, during a span of almost thirty years, terrorized the Tennessee Valley, killing, hanging, and burning anyone or anything that dared to stand in his path. Not even the Yankees, under General Ormsby Mitchel's command, would be guilty of such savagery and cruelty.

Evans was born on the Madison—Marshall county line around 1842 to a family whom history has forgotten. From the few accounts available it seems that his family eked out a living on a few acres of land where they worked halfheartedly, growing a garden and raising a few pigs. The farm, if it could be called that, was located in the mountains now overlooking Lake Guntersville.

Evans learned at an early age that the mountains, almost completely inaccessible and hidden from prying eyes, were a perfect place to hide any livestock that happened to become separated from its rightful owners.

Finding the life of a brigand more to his liking than working on a hard scrabble farm, he quickly embraced his newly chosen career. Gathering about him a few other miscreants and establishing a base camp in the hills, he quickly established himself as the leader.

The years preceding the Civil War were good ones for the band of budding desperados. Money had no real meaning to them as there were few places to spend it in the hills. They were content to rustle an occasional beef, and driving it back into the mountains, slaughter it when they were hungry. The remainder of their time was spent lolling about the crude shacks and lean-tos they called home and drinking the cheap homemade whiskey that they concocted.

If ever the need for hard money arose, all they had to do was to sneak into the outlying areas of Huntsville, New Hope, or Guntersville and burglarize someone's home.

Unfortunately, the "lowlanders," as they were called, soon put two and two together and decided that they were financing the outlaws' life-styles through their involuntary contributions of beef. At first, the citizens were content to post guards, but try as they might, they could never catch the outlaws in the act.

Evans seemed to find this highly amusing. Repeatedly, after confiscating some beef from its hapless owner, he would appear in town the next day as if daring someone to speak out against him.

Showing up in New Hope one day, after a particularly successful foray the night before, Evans began to taunt the farmer whose cattle he had stolen. The farmer was evidently afraid of Evans, and as the outlaw realized this the more brazen his abuse became. Finally, the farmer, unable to take anymore, mounted his horse and left town.

The whole incident might have ended there if Evans had left town too, but instead he chose to stay, along with his comrades, and spend the day drinking in a saloon.

Late that afternoon, with the sun still shining brightly, the brigands wobbled out of the saloon and staggered to where their horses were waiting, when all of a sudden their drunken revelry was interrupted by a loud shout.

"Evans, I want my cattle back!"

It was the farmer and, in his hands, pointed straight at Evans, was a shotgun.

Evans made a sudden move, and when he did the farmer blasted away. Although the shot missed Evans, it tore a gaping hole in the shoulder of one of his men.

As Evans stood there unharmed, a cruel and vicious sneer spread across his face when he realized the farmer's gun was now empty. Slowly raising his revolver toward the defenseless farmer, Evans was heard to mutter, "self-defense." Then he cold bloodily killed his first man.

Where before, Evans had been a troublesome thief, now he was a killer. Many people later said that with his first taste of blood he had become the devil incarnate. With his hideouts in the surrounding mountains, it was not long before he became known as the "devil of the mountains."

At first Evans seemed to relish his new-found notoriety. The people in the surrounding communities, never overly fond of him, now shunned him completely. Men who at least had tolerated him before now hung their heads and made excuses to leave whenever he entered a building.

This only served to enrage Evans and drive him to further extremes. With no friends except his motley gang of brigands, Evans became embittered, some people claimed, at the whole human race. A person could look at Evans in a quizzical manner and find his barn burned the same night. A bartender who refused to serve him might end up with a load of buckshot in his back.

The law was helpless. With no witnesses or evidence there was little the sheriff could do. Anyone who spoke up against Evans was destined to feel his vengeance.

When the Civil War broke out, there lived in the northern part of Marshall County a man by the name of John Dickey; a man who was known for his hatred towards his neighbors. After federal troops took control of the area north of the Tennessee River, Dickey offered his services to the union commander. Dickey's hatred for his own people was wrongly interpreted as patriotism to the Union, and so the Yankees commissioned him a captain of scouts with the power to organize a company to operate in North Alabama.

This new company was composed mostly of men who had deserted the Confederate army or had been dodging conscription. Many of these men were also wanted by the law. Lured by the opportunity to pillage and plunder at will, Evans joined the company and found to his pleasant surprise that he was in his element. John Dickey and Devil Monroe Evans cut a swath of vengeance across the valley that would terrify even their own band.

Men were dragged from their homes and murdered, some of them in the presence of their families. Volney Elliot was shot in the back, Alfred Clark was hung near New Hope, Davis Russell was shot and his body cruelly mutilated. Fletcher Lewis was found hung a few miles outside of Huntsville.

For most of them, their only crime was in crossing paths with Devil Monroe Evans and John Dickey.

The Confederate army was powerless to stop these atrocities and the Federal government refused to. Evans, Dickey and men like them, the federals reasoned, were helping the Northern cause by keeping the Rebel sympathizers in check.

By war's end, Evans and Dickey were the most hated men in the Tennessee Valley. Although legally, operating under the auspices of the Federal army, they had committed no crimes, the ex-Confederate soldiers returning home saw things differently.

John Dickey, deciding discretion was the better part of valor, pulled up stakes and moved to Texas. Evans, with his small band of cutthroats, retreated into the hills above New Hope in anticipation of impending retribution.

An uneasy truce seemed to prevail for a while. The people in the valley stayed out of the mountains and Evans rarely if ever went to town. When he did, he was always carrying his shotgun.

Again, the whole affair might have ended there if Evans had not become smitten by a comely young lass on the outskirts of town. Soon he became a regular visitor to the young lady's farm in an attempt to woo her hand. The girl's father had no use for Evans. He repeatedly told his daughter that he would never stand for Evans marrying her as long as there was any life in his body.

To Evans, that was talk he could understand.

Riding up to the girl's home late one afternoon, he killed the father and carried the girl off into the mountains.

The good folks of New Hope were outraged. A mob began to gather and there was talk of bringing Evans to justice. The sheriff brought them back to their senses. "No one witnessed the shooting except for the daughter," he said, "and if Evans is married to her now that means she can't testify."

In public, the men agreed with the sheriff but in private they had other ideas.

One of the little-known facts about New Hope concerned the Masonic Hall in town. Besides being used for other functions, it was also the meeting place for the local Ku Klux Klan. And it wasn't long before Evans and his wicked ways came to the attention of the local, night-shirted gentry.

According to popular legend, the Klan placed a two-hundred-dollar bounty on Evans' head and within days, he was playing dodge the bullet whenever he wandered down from the hills.

This was more than Evans' pride could bear. Calling his

men together he laid plans to dynamite the Masonic Hall and the Methodist church, both strongholds of his enemies. Fortunately for the townspeople of New Hope, word of the scheme leaked out and before Evans could act, warrants were obtained for his arrest.

After several long and hard days in the saddle, the posse cornered Evans and his men near the present-day city of Arab. The pack resisted arrest and in the ensuing gunfight six gang members were shot to death. Evans escaped, although severely wounded. He hid in the mountains until his injuries had healed sufficiently enough to allow him to travel. Deciding that both Madison and Marshall counties were dangerous to his health, he moved his wife and what was left of his gang to the mountains of Morgan County.

Cast out of the hills that he called home and with no friends, Evans began to look for other means of solace. It didn't take him long to find what he was looking for.

Cloaked in the veil of religion and casting himself as a modem-day Gabriel out to rid the world of wickedness, Evans proclaimed himself a converted man—a prophet of God.

Of course, cattle and hogs kept disappearing and he still carried the same shotgun wherever he ventured.

Traditional religion must have weighed too heavily upon his shoulders. Instead of spending his time in church spouting hell-fire and brimstone, he began to have visions.

"God," he said, "has told me to punish the nonbelievers."

This punishment usually took the form of larceny, to the delight of his slovenly gang. Next, he had visions of many wives.

"God," he said, "has instructed me to take more wives so that our truth might be spread."

Devil Evans believed in practicing his newly discovered religion and it wasn't long before there were seven wives living in his shanty, with a multitude of miniature devils playing in the yard.

It would be satisfying if we could, at this point, record that

Devil Evans became a changed man, but alas, if anything, he became even more cruel. Despite his many wives, (or maybe because of them) he began spending more time with his gang of brigands.

And now, with a Bible in one hand and a shotgun in the other, he considered any livestock that wandered his way donations for the Lord's work.

Evans would call on some hapless farmer, and with his shotgun lying across the saddle in front of him, inform the man that he would surely die and go to hell unless he saw it in his heart to make a sizable contribution.

Whenever someone would protest he would find his home or barn burned to the ground. If he continued to protest, he became a leading candidate for a midnight ambush. Every grand jury that was impaneled between 1875 and 1891 tried to indict Evans for his many crimes, but through perjured testimony and intimidation of crucial witnesses he managed to overcome their every effort.

Many people began to think that the Devil was truly invincible.

In the summer of 1891, Evans and his son John were again out collecting contributions for their work. Unfortunately, a man by the name of Pierce Mooney returned home in time to catch the duo burglarizing his home. Mooney pulled his gun and began shooting and father and son headed for the woods. The next morning as Mooney was feeding his livestock, he was ambushed in the back by someone firing a shotgun. Although in critical condition, Mooney was able to crawl back to the house, and there, his wife sent for the doctor. This was not exactly what Evans had planned for. A live witness could cause trouble. Evans knew Mooney was in critical condition, so he waited in hiding for the doctor on the way to the patient's house. No doctor, he figured, no witness. The physician, after being warned not to attend the wounded man, made as if he was going back to town. Instead, he cut through the woods and returned to the house by another route.

Next, Evans and his son tried to run Mooney's wife off. Hiding in the woods, they fired their weapons at the house and in loud voices warned her that if she did not leave, she too would be shot.

Meanwhile, word had reached town of the dastardly attack and the Devil's attempt to silence the witness. That same afternoon Evans' son rode into town to pick up some supplies and was promptly arrested and carried to Baileyton for trial. When Evans received word of his son's arrest, he mounted his horse, and carrying his shotgun, rode into town. As he slowly made his way down the street he could not have helped but notice the small groups of men gathered on every corner, eyeing him with hatred in their eyes.

Evans was arrested by the authorities before he even had time to dismount his horse. He, too, was placed in an empty store building under guard until the authorities could decide what to do with them.

The father and son duo were not unduly worried. No witness, no crime.

The same stark realization began to dawn on the townspeople. Evans would go free and their families would continue to be terrorized.

Late that night, August 15, 1891, a mob of almost two hundred people approached the store and demanded custody of Monroe Evans and his son. The guards offered up no resistance. The condemned men were tied up and marched outside to the nearest tree limb.

Devil Evans departed this world with a curse on his lips and the gleam of a fanatic in his eye. His son, John, began crying and begging for mercy as the noose was placed around his neck.

According to one account, seconds after the hanging took place a violent thunderstorm swept over the valley, with horrendous claps of thunder and solid sheets of rain pulverizing everything in its path.

"The Devil," they said, "was taking his due."

The next week the following item appeared in the *Alabama Tribune* newspaper:

"Rube Burrow was shot down by Carter and his name was lauded to the skies as a hero. Ford, in a most cowardly manner, shot and killed Jesse James, but the state of Missouri paid him large sums of money. Both of these men had some redeeming qualities. They were true to their families and true to their friends. But this man had none.

"He was not true to his country or his family. But the men who relieved North Alabama of the presence of this man are called by some misinformed persons brutes and murderers.

"Evans' poor wife is in a better condition. The man who wrecked her life and educated her son for the gallows is gone. She will no longer be insulted by the presence of her husband's harem. His gang is scattered to the four winds and peace and order have taken their place. The last stronghold of the Devil in the Tennessee Valley has been destroyed and the people say Amen."

Chapter 36

Frank and Jesse James Ride Again

The paymaster looked at the four horsemen with anger and bewilderment. What sort of men, he wondered, would have the audacity to rob a United States Army paymaster?

As the bandits wheeled their horses around and started to leave, one of the strangers, with a wide grin on his face, hesitated. "Mister," he said. "You can tell your grandchildren that you've had the pleasure of meeting Frank and Jesse James!"

For years rumors had circulated in North Alabama about the James brothers. One of the gang members, a man by the name of Ezzel, actually lived a few miles outside of Florence, and it was he who had first brought the robbery plan to the James brothers' attention. After observing the paymaster for several weeks at various saloons around the Florence area and listening to his talk of carrying "a big payroll" every week to the men working on the dam, Ezzel sent word to Jesse and Frank.

Frank and Jesse James had "retired" from the life of banditry and were living just outside of Nashville. Evidently, the life of a pig farmer just did not appeal very much to Jesse, because when he received word of the Muscle Shoals payroll just waiting for an honest bandit to rob it, he called his band back together again.

On March 11, 1881, a cold and wet afternoon, Alexander

THE WAY IT WAS

G. Smith, the payroll master, was barely two miles outside of Florence, when four horsemen appeared out of the woods. After tying Smith's hands behind his back, the robbers relieved him of the army payroll, his gold watch, and $221 of his own money. Smith had been saving the money to buy a farm, and when he told this to the bandits, they returned part of his money, after first asking if he was a "damn Yankee."

No such luck for the payroll itself, within minutes the bandits had made away with over $5,200 - $500 in gold, $4,500 in fifties, and miscellaneous smaller bills.

The bandit leader carefully divided the money equally among his partners and himself, and then, after untying the unlucky paymaster, headed north with his gang toward Tennessee.

Posse's were formed and rewards were offered, but no trace was found of the outlaw gang. They had, apparently, just disappeared into the cold, drizzly night.

In all likelihood, Jesse and Frank might have lived their lives out in and around Nashville, with no one suspecting who they were, if one of their cohorts had stayed sober.

Most folks who knew "Wild Bill" Ryan agreed that he couldn't hold his liquor, so it didn't come as any surprise when he pitched a "rip-roaring drunk" and shot up a local saloon in Nashville. What did come as a surprise were the two six-shooters, a sack of gold coins, and a fist full of greenbacks found on his person when the sheriff arrested him. In all, the money added up to $1,300, exactly one-fourth of the money taken in the Florence payroll robbery.

The sheriff wasn't too slow in realizing there must be a connection somewhere, and within days the suspicions were verified.

The James brothers knew that it was only a matter of time before the law started breathing down their necks, so deciding that discretion was the better part of valor, the brothers left Nashville.

Within weeks, the James brothers had settled in St.

Joseph, Missouri, and had begun their outlaw careers anew. Every week, it seemed, the newspapers were carrying new accounts of the latest robbery committed by the infamous brothers. The gang struck in Winston, Missouri, killing two men, and next in Gallatin. Robberies were committed in Booneville, Blue Cut, Haneyville, Sawyer's Ford and Heflin. There seemed to be no end. Rewards failed, bounties failed, even the famous Pinkerton Detective Agency could produce no results.

In the end, governor Crittenden of Missouri was forced to resort to the one weapon that has struck terror in the hearts of outlaws since the beginning of time. He hired a stool pigeon. Bob Ford had been a loyal member of the gang for a long time, but when the governor sent word that he wanted to have a "secret" meeting with him, he didn't hesitate. Meeting in a Kansas City hotel at midnight on January 13, 1882, the governor promised to pardon Ford for his "past indiscretions" and to pay $10,000 each for the bodies of Jesse and Frank James. On April 3, Bob Ford shot Jesse James in cold blood while Jesse had his back turned, adjusting a picture on the wall of his home. The pearl-handled, silver-mounted pistol that Ford used was the same one that Jesse had given him earlier, as a token of lasting friendship.

What would Frank do? Newspapers everywhere speculated on the fate of Bob Ford. How long would it be before the surviving James brother sought revenge? Days, weeks, and months went by, but nothing happened.

On October 5, Frank James calmly strode into the Missouri state capitol, wearing both of his six-shooters on his hip. People began running and hiding as James pushed open the door to the governor's office and walked in. The infamous outlaw stood there, staring with hatred at the man who had caused the death of his brother. Slowly, he reached for his pistols, and laid them butt first on the governor's desk.

Frank James, the most sought-after man in America, had surrendered, in exchange for the promise of a fair trial.

As the state prosecutors began preparing their case against the former outlaw, certain problems arose. Witnesses, citing health reasons, declined to testify. Evidently, they thought that facing Frank in a courtroom might be injurious to their continued good health. When the prosecutors were finally able to bring Frank to trial on one charge of murder, the jury returned the verdict in a matter of moments with "not guilty."

Unfortunately for Frank, the authorities down in Alabama had not forgotten about him. Jesse was dead, Wild Bill Ryan was serving twenty-five years, and Frank was the only one left to face the music. He was promptly rearrested and shipped to Huntsville to stand trial for the payroll robbery.

During the months he spent in the Huntsville jail, he became an instant celebrity. While he was lodged in the jail, his wife and child had more spacious accommodations at the old Huntsville Hotel. His cell quickly became the top tourist attraction in North Alabama. Many of his visitors left with the feeling that "he didn't look and act like an outlaw, and besides, it was just Yankee money!"

Newspaper men from all across the country gathered in Huntsville to cover the trial. One of the first things Frank did was to invite the press for an interview. "You boys ought to thank me," said James. "Jesse and I have given you something good to write about for almost twenty years." He asked the press not to be too critical of him, as he had recently lost his dear brother to a "back-shooting assassin" and now the same people were trying to do him in.

It was a gloomy, rainy day when the trial began. Crowds had started gathering early that morning and when Frank, surrounded by armed deputies, walked in, wild cheering broke out. The judge had to rap repeatedly for order.

The trial began with the witnesses for the government. These witnesses had delivered testimony that had sent Wild Bill Ryan to jail for the same robbery. But in a surprise move, four of them suffered from severe memory loss when they confronted a real, live Frank James sitting there in the courtroom, casually cleaning his fingernails with a pocket knife.

The fifth government witness, Dick Liddel, insisted that Frank had committed the robbery. Unfortunately for Liddel, the defense was quick to point out that he had been in cahoots with Bob Ford, the back-shooting assassin of brother Jesse. Dick Liddel soon lost whatever popularity he had enjoyed in Huntsville.

When Frank James' legal counsel, Gen. LeRoy Pope Walker, ex-Secretary of War for the Confederate States, began his summation in front of an "impartial jury" of 12 loyal ex-Confederate veterans, it seemed as if the only thing missing was the waving of the "old flag."

The jury seemed rapt with attention as Gen. Walker testified about being proud to defend James, a loyal Confederate. The General heaped scorn upon the government's case, saying that Liddel was just a common horse thief

Complicating matters even more for the prosecution was the testimony of a Nashville policeman who claimed that Frank could not have committed the crime. The officer swore that Frank was in Nashville, testifying in court, the very day of the robbery.

After hearing all the evidence, the jury retired to deliberate on the verdict. Thirty minutes later they returned with a verdict of "not guilty." Later that night Frank James was seen meeting and drinking with members of the jury at the Huntsville Hotel. He seemed to be in fine spirits and was heard to entertain his listeners with many exploits of his past.

Frank James was never convicted of any of the crimes that he committed. He became a model citizen, holding various jobs such as a race starter, shoe salesman, and his longest, doorman for a burlesque house in St. Louis. When Frank James died, he was a pauper.

He never visited Huntsville again and, no, he did not rob the bank downtown and, no, he did not jump his horse off the cliff at the Big Spring.

THE DEMOCRAT:

The oldest Newspaper in Huntsville, Alabama. Established by PHILIP WOODSON, October 8th. 1823. Published weekly (Wednesdays,) by

J. WITHERS CLAY, Editor and Proprietor.

TERMS OF SUBSCRIPTION.

One copy per annum, strictly in advance..$2 50
"   "   if paid within six months,....................................... 3 00
"   "   if paid after six months,.. 4 00
Ten copies, "   in one package, ($2,25 each,) in advance,............22 50
Twenty copies per annum, in one package, ($2,00 each,) in advance,...40 00
☞ Persons sending five or more new subscribers, and $12,50, will receive one copy of the Democrat GRATIS.

JOB OFFICE.

The proprietor of THE DEMOCRAT has an extensive and superior JOB OFFICE, with one power and two hand presses, and a great variety of Types, Cards, Paper, and can have executed cheaply, expeditiously, and in the best style,

Cards,

(Business, Visiting, Party & Wedding.)

LETTER HEADS & ENVELOPES,

RAILROAD RECEIPTS, SCHEDULES, &C.

Bill-Heads, Pamphlets, Druggists' Labels, Bank Checks,

WAY-BILLS, CIRCULARS, PROGRAMMES,

And almost any other Printing, Plain, Ruled or Fancy, in Black or Fancy Colors. Deeds, and Chancery, Circuit and Probate Court and Justices and Constables' Blanks, kept on hand.

Chapter 37

Days of the Ku Klux Klan

On January 3, 1869, a school teacher by the name of Jonathan Everest was taken from his home and hanged by the Ku Klux Klan. Before putting the rope around his neck, they allowed him to write a letter to his wife who lived in Illinois.
Part of his letter read:
"I know I will never see you again, as they are about to kill me. Please take care of our son and tell him when he is grown how much I loved him. Please do not grieve too much... you are a young woman and I hope you will marry again so to have someone to take care of you in your old age. They say it is time. I have to go."
Jonathan Everest's only crime was being a Northerner who had the misfortune to be assigned a teaching post in Alabama.
The Ku Klux Klan was originally founded in Pulaski, Tennessee, in 1865 and the idea of it quickly spread to other parts of the South. Disorganized bands of men calling themselves Ku Kluxers began operating in Madison County as early as 1866, independent of each other with no central control.
Huntsville and Madison County were in the grip of carpetbag rule. Men were being denied the right to hold political office because of their wartime service to the Confederacy and the men and women of Huntsville were starving. In 1865, over 5,000 rations were distributed in one month in an effort to alleviate the hunger. With the advent of

the Klan, Southerners saw a way to fight back through fear and intimidation. In the spring of 1867, a group of leading citizens from Huntsville traveled to Nashville where they met with a representative of General Nathan Bedford Forrest and received a charter to open a Den (local branch). General Forrest was the Imperial Wizard (president) of the national organization of the Ku Klux Klan.

Evidence suggests the first meeting of the newly chartered Den was held at the Otey Mansion in Meridianville, where a man with the initials F. G. (Frank Gurley?) was elected Grand Cyclop. An individual by the name of Coltart or Coltard was elected Grand Magi (vice-president) and the post of Grand Turk (adjutant) went to a Mr. Jenkins.

The Den moved quickly to take control of all the unorganized bands operating under the auspices of the Klan. Within months new Dens were formed throughout Madison County, while the Huntsville branch assumed control of all North Alabama Klan activities.

The citizens of Huntsville were quick to embrace the Klan and its law and order platform. Veterans who had returned home after the war to find their whole way of life destroyed were again part of an organization fighting for the Southern cause. Widows and housewives showed their support by sewing Klan robes and acting as informants. By 1868, the Ku Klux Klan in Madison County had grown to over three thousand members.

A common misconception today is to think of the Klan as a few diehard radical racists struggling to maintain the remnants of a society based on slavery. This is not true. Unfortunately, it had wide support among all segments of society. It would be a safe assumption to say that almost every Southern born public official in Huntsville at that time was a Ku Kluxer or a sympathizer. The Klan had become one of the major powers in Madison County.

In early 1868, Union military troops were sent to New Market to arrest a man accused of being a Klan member. Every few miles, between Huntsville and New Market, the soldiers would spot small bands of robed men on the horizon, sitting absolutely still on their horses ... watching. Entering the small town, the soldiers found the streets deserted. Not a soul was to be seen anywhere—except for 150 robed and hooded Ku Kluxers.

Klansmen were lined up on both sides of the road and at the shrill command of a whistle, reined their horses into formation completely blocking the street.

The soldiers paused, and deciding discretion was the better part of valor, turned their horses back toward Huntsville, without the prisoner.

On November 8, 1868, a meeting was held in Huntsville on the courthouse square by the freed slaves and "scalawags." Speeches were made protesting the reign of Klan terror, with carpetbag politicians promising to put an end to it, if they were elected.

Midway through the meeting, the speeches were interrupted by the loud piercing shrill of a whistle. Obeying the command of the whistle, Ku Kluxers mounted on their horses, began encircling the square. Later, a congressional investigation would estimate there were at least 500 robed Klansmen taking part.

The crowd grew silent, intimidated by the robed threat. A shot rang out. No one knows who fired it. Instantly, the courthouse square became bedlam as carpetbaggers and freed slaves all began firing. The square became a battleground with bullets ricocheting off buildings and bloody, bruised bodies lying everywhere. When the firing ceased, Judge Thurlow of Athens lay dead.

Historians would later claim that the Ku Klux Klan fired no shots.

Ex-Confederates were not allowed to vote and were terrified the newly freed slaves would take control of county and state politics. The Klan's primary function (as they saw it) was to insure this did not happen.

The Klan terror began to escalate, with no one being safe from the midnight riders. A husband accused of not working was taken out and whipped. Black men would be hanged for not being "respectful." A tenant farmer would be threatened with a whipping if he tried to leave and work for someone else. But the best way to incur the Klan's wrath was to vote Republican. The Klan was also impartial—it would whip or hang anyone, regardless of their race.

By the early 1870s the once-proud Ku Klux Klan had become an object of revulsion to most people in Madison County. The organization that was once controlled by the aristocrats of Huntsville had become a catchall for riffraff and "white trash."

Klan terror had become so bad in Madison County and surrounding areas that the United States Government sent a congressional committee to Huntsville to investigate the outrages and try to put a stop to them. The testimony they heard was so damning that even the Klansmen were disgusted.

Huntsville's leading citizens were called to testify about their knowledge of the Klan. Supposedly, they knew nothing. The most damning testimony came from the victims. Among the crimes the Klan were accused of were:

Caleb Beasley — whipped
Thomas Regney — whipped
Clem Dougerty — hung
Lisa Meadows — raped
John Clark — whipped
Henry Clung — hung
Williams — shot
Elliot Fearon — shot

John Wagner, a Northerner who had been collecting information on Klan activities, testified to reports of Klan atrocities of which he had personal knowledge:

"Elijah Townsend, men in disguise took his gun, and William Thompson at the same time was whipped by these men in disguise. Matt Hammond reported that last spring,

1870, he received a letter sent to him by the Ku Klux ordering him to leave his home and stating that he should not live within twenty miles or he would be hung. John Jones was confronted at the same time and was whipped. He reports that his wife was sick in bed, on her death bed, and these men, to scare her and make her tell where Jones was, shot their pistols off over the bed."

In all, the commission heard reports of almost one hundred crimes committed by the Klan in Madison County. The townspeople, once loyal supporters of the Klan, were shocked when confronted with the evidence.

On November 23, 1873, a meeting of the leading Huntsville Klan officers was held at the McGee Hotel in Huntsville, where it was officially dissolved.

Sporadic attempts would be made over the years to form another Klan, but never again would they enjoy the support of Huntsville's citizens.

READING GLASSES
$3.00
FOR LATEST STYLE SHELL FRAMES. ANY STYLE OR SIZE DESIRED.

See Moore and see better

Post Office Row   Huntsville

Chapter 38

Howard Weeden

We are all too familiar with fictionalized accounts of Southern women. But for a hundred years appreciators of Maria Howard Weeden, known to the world as Howard Weeden, have kept her life, her works, and memory of a true Southern lady alive. A plaque on the Federal-style house, located on Gates and Green Streets in Huntsville, attests that it is "the home of poet-artist Howard Weeden."

Born on July 6, 1847, in the very house that stands today, Howard—as she chose to be called, adopting the family name of Scottish ancestors as her given name—was tutored as a lady.

Her father, Dr. William Weeden, died before she was born and left the family with the beautiful town home, a complement of servants, plantations properties, and other real estate from which the family's income and life style was derived. Early in her life she demonstrated a talent for drawing and received lessons from a local portrait artist—Mr. William Frye. During the Civil War, when Huntsville was occupied by Federal troops, the Weeden House, known as "Aspen Place," was taken over by the commander of the occupying army. Mrs. Weeden and her daughters Kate and Howard were forced to move into the adjacent servants' quarters. As family members were in the Confederate army, the relationship between the family and the Federal officers, who had taken over the house, became intolerable. The family, feeling as prisoners and hostages in their own home, fled Huntsville with their servants accompanying them and went to Tuskegee in South Alabama.

There, Howard met Dr. George WF. Price and his daughter, Elizabeth Price, who became a lifelong friend, supporter, and biographer of her life. At the Tuskegee Methodist College for Women, Howard studied painting and developed her exquisite talent in watercolor.

After the War, the Weeden family returned to their family home in Huntsville. What was valuable in the home had either been stolen or destroyed.

With the family fortune gone, Howard turned to painting to help provide needed income for the family. Howard conducted art classes for young ladies and produced hand-painted greeting cards and placards. This work further contributed to the development of her particular and unique, largely self-taught style. She also wrote poetry and her works were published under the name of "Flake White" in the Christian Observer, a Presbyterian paper.

In the late 1800s Southern writers became recognized—especially with their stories of old plantation life. Howard Weeden read these stories and not only emulated the art of the day, she surpassed it. She was adept at drawing flowers, animals, decorative designs, and portraits.

While attending the Columbian Exposition at Chicago in 1893, she saw the unflattering sketches of Negroes by the leading illustrators of the day. Seeing this challenged and inspired her. She began to paint portraits of blacks accurately, and with dignity. It was a style unusual for any era. Due to fragile health and modest finances, she was unable to travel and so used local people around Huntsville as her subjects. With delicate care, using a brush with only three hairs, she recorded for posterity, both visually and poetically, the character and dignity of the vanishing race of ex-slaves.

She chronicled her subjects in watercolor with the accuracy of a portrait photographer and the sensitivity, simplicity, and feeling of a painter. But Howard Weeden went one step further—she wrote words to her pictures.

Her "Mammies" were not caricatures, but real as the

beloved persons themselves, as a few lines taken from "When Mammy Dies" attest:

"We're always young till Mammy dies, but when her hand no longer lies, as once it did upon our head, we feel that youth with her has fled."

Uniquely blending pictures and poems, she illustrated the gaiety, the sadness, the real lives of people with more than dramatic technical skill—it was genius. In her poem "The Worst of War" she relates in sixteen lines more than the horror of war—she captures the utter sadness, loss, and personal tragedy felt as the ex-slave recalls taking the riderless horse of his slain young master and officer back home:

"I led his horse back home where dey sat expectin' him, an' I saw Mistis' and Master's hearts when dey broke, an' dat was de worst of war."

The verses, she said, wrote themselves out of the Negroes' own words.

As the reputation of this refined, gentle woman grew, orders came in from all over the world for her works. In 1898, her little published book became the premier Christmas gift. She had to do all she could to meet the demands with what her pervasive ill health and nearsightedness would allow.

Praises came from near and far. Joel Chandler Harris, referring to the highly popular and published Southern writers of the day, called her the "best of us all...."

Extolling the virtues and realities of black people, she demonstrated her own uncommon, gracious brilliance. Pertaining to the ex-slaves she painted and wrote about, *The New York Times Book Review* of December 30, 1899 stated, "She revealed the whole race."

On April 12, 1905, she died at her home. But Howard Weeden passed on a treasure of extraordinary published works, which include: "Shadows on the Wall" and "Bandanna Ballads" published by Doubleday and McClure in 1899; "Songs of the Old South," and her last book, "Old Voices" in 1904.

Chapter 39

The Sleeping Preacher

Constantine Blackmon Sanders was born on July 2, 1831 near Hazel Green, about sixteen miles north of Huntsville. He was the youngest of ten children, eight girls and two boys. When Sanders was six years old his father died, leaving the family almost destitute. Out of necessity all the children were forced to labor in the fields.

People who knew Sanders when he was young described him as a tall, well-built lad, with a sheaf of unruly red hair, and always with a serious, though pleasant, disposition. From an early age he was attracted to religion. Friends later told how he would preach sermons to barnyard animals and when a chicken died, would hold a funeral. While other boys his age were more interested in swimming in the nearby creek, Sanders would coerce his playmates into conducting mock baptisms.

At the age of twenty, Sanders attended a revival meeting at a small country church. The sermon was about people who were possessed by the devil. Most likely, Sanders had never pondered the subject before as he went home and stayed awake all night reading from his Bible, searching for answers. The next day he joined the Cumberland Presbyterian Church at Concord. The young man, with his zealous religious fervor, was a welcome addition to the congregation. Almost immediately people predicted great things for Sanders.

Sanders had never received the benefit of formal education, so in 1854, after deciding to become a minister, he enrolled in a private school in Elkton, Tennessee. Shortly after his enrollment, the aspiring young minister became ill of a flux (diarrhea or dysentery), followed by a severe attack of typhoid fever.

The illness lasted for several weeks, with Sanders being delirious much of the time. It was during this period when he is supposed to have received his first visit from X+Y=Z, a mysterious spirit that seemed to enter his body at will and cause him to exhibit psychic powers.

One day while recuperating at the home of Mr. and Mrs. M. A. Harlow, Sanders appeared to go into a deep trance. Although he seemed unaware of his surroundings, he was still able to talk.

Mrs. Harlow later reported the strange events that day. "He remarked to me, 'There will be a burying here tomorrow evening, but it will not be any of your family.' About one hour after this, a gentleman rode up and requested the privilege of burying a corpse in our private cemetery the next day, which was granted. This death occurred some three miles distant, and we had not even heard, and I am confident Mr. Sanders had not, of the sickness, nor the death of the individual."

If the event seemed bizarre to the Harlow family it was nothing compared to the terrifying description given of Sanders while in the trance.

"His head split open from just above his eyes in the center of his forehead to the top, and from the top down near each ear. His head grew until the features of his face seemed to be reversed. His hands drew into an immovable position against his chest and throat. His feet and legs twisted into a position almost opposite their normal position. His eyes bled and the blood ran down his cheeks."

Mrs. Harlow stated that the separation of the skull was large enough to lay her little finger in near the top.

When news of the bizarre happenings began to circulate throughout the religious community it created a sensation. Religious-psychic phenomenon was not unknown in the middle 1800s. Many new religions in America had been founded on visions their leaders supposedly received. In almost every case the visions had appeared as a result of an illness or injury.

The Cumberland Presbyterian Church, of which Sanders was a member, were divided in their opinion. While the church itself condemned spiritualists and psychic phenomenon, many of the members were devout believers.

After being ordained in 1862, Sanders pastored several churches including Maysville, Meridianville, and Mooresville. He also served the communities as a dentist, a trade that was evidently self-taught. Possibly hoping to make up for his lack of formal education, he became an avid reader, eagerly devouring every book that came into his possession.

If there was a dark side to Sanders life, it was the fact that the spirit of $X+Y=Z$ continued to haunt him. Often while reading a book, or in conversation with an acquaintance, or even while riding in a buggy, Sanders' face would begin to contort as he fell into a semiconscious state. He would have no memory of what had occurred upon awaking.

Since he gave the appearance of sleep, he became widely known as "The Sleeping Preacher."

Legions of witnesses described the strange phenomenon. A house guest told how Sanders would write long discourses. At first the writings were mainly on religious subjects but later began to include diagnoses of illness for patients he had never seen as well as prescriptions for their illness.

He also translated Latin texts without error, although he claimed to have never studied the language. Numerous friends told how Sanders would locate lost articles for them while under the influence of the secondary personality.

Sanders suffered from excruciating headaches for most of his life. Often times he would take to bed for days trying to find relief from the pain. Although he led a normal life in most respects, numerous friends later testified to the fact that he only slept for two to three hours a night.

In February 1866, Sanders was confined to his bed with a

dislocated hip. J.W. Pruit reported that during a visit that Sanders began to laugh. When Pruit asked him why he was laughing, Sanders said he was laughing at DeWitt who was "having a hard scuffle to keep from falling off the fence, for the top rail was turning with him and he was trying to keep from falling over it."

According to Pruit, about ten or fifteen minutes later, Mr. DeWitt arrived carrying a bowl of custard and a bag of peas his wife had sent to Sanders. DeWitt related his difficulty in negotiating the rail fence with his hands full. He stated that the fence shook and twisted and he nearly fell off. To Pruit, it sounded curiously like what Sanders had laughed about fifteen minutes before.

Reverend G.W. Mitchell and Dr. Blair of Athens reported that on either October 31 or November 1, 1866, Sanders was sitting in front of a window when he began to say, "poor fellow" and "what a pity." Sanders began to exhibit signs of sadness and distress and said, "He's gone! Gone! Gone!" When questioned about his actions, Sanders told the men that Lieutenant McClure had just died from an internal hemorrhage near Clarksville, Tennessee.

Early the next morning, Lieutenant McClure's wife in Athens received a telegram informing her of her husband's death some one hundred and fifty miles away near Clarksville, Tennessee of an internal hemorrhage.

In October 1866, Sanders encountered Mrs. Mary A. Brown in Meridianville. Mrs. Brown expressed concern for her relatives in Salisbury, North Carolina whom she had not heard from in a long time. Mr. Sanders informed Mrs. Brown that he had gone to see them the night before and they were well as usual. Sanders also told Mrs. Brown that there had been a fire in Salisbury the night before. He told her the fire had started in a tin shop and burned to the corner of the Wheeler block. He assured the woman that all her relatives were safe. Mrs. Brown wrote a letter to her sister living in the Salisbury area and inquired about the fire. In time she received a reply which confirmed all Mr. Sanders had said including the time it occurred, the tin shop where it started, and the extent of the damage.

In the summer of 1867, Sanders told Miss Sallie Humphey that Miss Mattie Banks in Decatur had just been struck by lightning and described her injuries. Miss Humphey told her sisters what Sanders had said and the three decided to check the next newspaper to see if any account was given of the incident. When the paper arrived, it contained the story of Miss Banks' accident confirming what Mr. Sanders had said down to the time and specific injuries he had mentioned. More than sixty people, including physicians, ministers, civic leaders, judges, and people from all walks of life, of high moral character, gave written testimony to his psychic powers. Over the years Sanders and those who saw him perform these feats believed they were witnessing something that could not be explained. As might be expected, not everyone in the community believed Reverend Sanders had the ability to perform the psychic feats for which he had become known. While many believed the power was the work of God, others credited it to the devil, and still others thought that the accounts of his prowess were a complete hoax.

The debate became so heated in the church as well as in the community that many of the church leaders began a movement to have Sanders dismissed from the ministry. Only fear of causing an irreversible split in the church caused the leaders to halt their actions.

Two of the church leaders, Dr. Ross and H.R. Smith, expressed open contempt for the backwoods preacher whom they considered to be a charlatan. They would later have cause to reconsider.

One evening in 1874, Reverend Sanders, who lived in Meridianville, desired to go to Huntsville, twelve miles away, to hear a sermon by Dr. Ross, but was unable to attend. That night, under the influence of the $X+Y=Z$ personality, Sanders called for a pen, ink and paper. In his "sleep" he wrote for more than an hour. The following morning, he was told by his wife about the writing. Upon reading his writings, he found an outline of the sermon delivered by Dr. Ross the previous evening in Huntsville.

Sanders took the train to Huntsville that morning and went directly to the home of Reverend H.R. Smith. Mr. Smith expressed his regrets that Mr. Sanders had not been able to hear the previous night's sermon.

Sanders informed him that he had heard the sermon and enjoyed it all very much. He then preceded to give a detailed description of the sermon including text, major subjects, and leading thoughts from beginning to end. Mr. Smith stated that it was impossible for Mr. Sanders to have been informed of the sermon in such detail since it had been preached the night before while Sanders slept and he had come directly from his home in Meridianville to Smith's home in Huntsville early the next morning.

Both Ross and Smith became strong believers of Reverend Sanders and the mysterious X+Y=Z.

On many occasions over the years, he begged the secondary personality, to no avail, to leave him. X+Y=Z, it appeared, took an almost perverse delight in tormenting the country preacher.

In 1875, a newspaper reporter from Nashville, Tenn., heard about the controversial Reverend Sanders and wrote several stories about him and the secondary personality, X+Y=Z. Although knowledge of Sander's psychic abilities was well known in the Tennessee Valley, he seemed distressed by the thought of gaining widespread attention.

On February 2nd, 1876, X+Y=Z, calling Sanders "My Casket" as he always did in written communications to him, consented to leave him for an indefinite time. In this communication, X+Y=Z also promised (or perhaps threatened) to return at a later date. There is no written documentation as to whether the secondary personality actually kept his promise to return although rumors abound.

According to one report, Sanders was visited by X+Y=Z one last time in 1889. The mystical spirit is said to have revealed horrible details of future events and allowed Sanders a glimpse of the spirit world from where it came.

Constantine Blackmon Sanders died April 14, 1911 and was buried on Easter Sunday. Was he a psychic or a charlatan? He was investigated by the Boston Society for Psychic Research, and despite exhaustive research and interrogation of witnesses, they were unable to discredit his psychic abilities.

The believers saw the exit of the secondary personality as an act of God. Detractors thought otherwise. Some believed that the visitor left, not because of a pact with God, but with the devil from whom it had come.

Today it is impossible to determine the source of Reverend Sanders' power. For every doubter there is an avid believer. For every mystery that can be explained there is another one with no answer. He was, and still is, one of the most controversial ministers to ever serve Madison County.

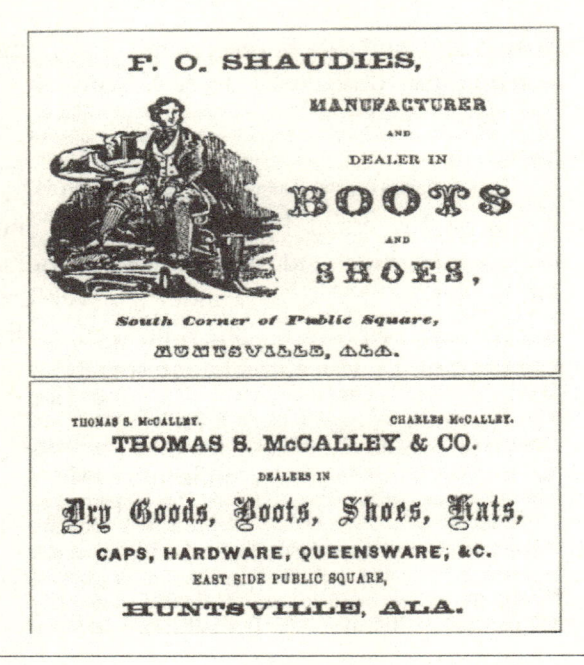

F. O. SHAUDIES,

MANUFACTURER
AND
DEALER IN
BOOTS
AND
SHOES,

South Corner of Public Square,

HUNTSVILLE, ALA.

THOMAS S. McCALLEY.   CHARLES McCALLEY.
THOMAS S. McCALLEY & CO.
DEALERS IN
Dry Goods, Boots, Shoes, Hats,
CAPS, HARDWARE, QUEENSWARE, &C.
EAST SIDE PUBLIC SQUARE,
HUNTSVILLE, ALA.

Chapter 40

The Monte Sano Railroad

Near the intersection of Tollgate Road and Bankhead Parkway in northeast Huntsville are several entrances into the western slope of monte Sano Mountain. Take any one of these trails and you will find yourself going back into another time, a time of long ago, a time when Huntsville was much simpler, and life was not the complicated reality that it is today.

Yet, people then, as today, had dreams and ambitions. The dream that once existed on these now quiet trails on the western slope of Monte Sano Mountain took the form of a railroad—the Monte Sano Railway.

The year was 1888 and with the ever-growing popularity of the grand hotel on top of the mountain, it became clear that better transportation up the mountain was needed.

The Huntsville Belt Line and Monte Sano Railway Co. employed engineer Arthur Owen Wilson to construct the railroad to the hotel. The line started from the Union Depot and ran south along Jefferson Street. At Clinton, it turned east towards the mountain and eventually down into Fagin's Hollow, where it began a circuitous route, gaining altitude all the time. Winding and circling to the rim of the mountain, the route rose so steeply that the grade seemed impossible for an engine to ascend. The remainder of the way lay directly across the top of the plateau to the back yard of the hotel. Half an hour was required for the entire journey when the line was finished.

In the construction of the Monte Sano Railway, more than 300 persons were employed on a regular basis. The weekly payroll was approximately $10,000. Mr. Wilson himself designed the three coaches that comprised the train and the St. Charles Car Co. manufactured them. The engine was of standard gauge, although smaller than those used on the trunk line. The size of the engine was the reason the line was called the "dummy line," as the undersized locomotive resembled a trolley car. Of course, some Huntsville wags called it the dummy line because "only a dummy would ride that steep and perilous route to or from the mountain!"

Sure enough, not long after the railway opened, there occurred an incident that seriously damaged the popularity of the railway. Returning from the hotel, the train's sand-pipes clogged as the engineer tried to check the speed of the locomotive down a steep incline. The train went out of control and left the tracks. Happily, no one was injured, but people were now somewhat nervous about taking this precarious path to and from the mountain.

Luckily, this accident had no lasting effect on consumer confidence and the Monte Sano Railway was successful in bringing visitors to the mountain, and business to the hotel continued to flourish.

Unfortunately, by 1895 the hotel was suffering financial problems and the railroad had to be shut down. Tracks were torn up and sold as scrap to pay off debts.

Now, with the passage of time the old railroad bed and stone foundations of the trestles are all that remain. Older residents of Huntsville say that as late as the 1950s there were still railroad ties stacked up near the area known as the "button hole."

Chapter 41

Underground Dancehall

Just a few miles up Pulaski Pike, well within the city limits, is a cave that was once heralded as the most popular nightclub in this area.

The early history of Shelta Cave is lost in the shroud of history, but some of the earliest stories tell of Confederate soldiers hiding in the cave to escape searching Union soldiers. One rumor that persists to this day concerns a bloody hand-to-hand battle supposedly fought in the depths of the cavern on the shores of a vast underground lake.

Like any other large cave, it has legends woven around it concerning buried treasure, ghosts, and eerie noises. These remained just legends with no basis in fact until 1888 when a Mr. Bolen James sold the land to a Mr. Henry Fuller.

Not much is known about the early life of Mr. Fuller, but judging from his actions he must have been a born entrepreneur.

Immediately after taking possession of the cave he hired a team of carpenters to install steps down into the main chamber. Next, he assembled a crew of craftsmen to install a dance floor in one of the great rooms with large stand-up bars at each end. He made no secret of the fact that he intended to open the grandest, fanciest, and most unusual dance hall in Alabama. Huntsville had seen its share of weird, wacky ideas, but a dance hall in a cave? Even by Huntsville's standards that was too much. Townspeople began to call the yet uncompleted dance hall "Fuller's Folly."

As is true in many a new business, Fuller soon found himself facing a slight problem—too many ideas and not enough money. Reluctantly he let himself be talked into forming a corporation called, appropriately enough, Shelta Cave Corp. With this new influx of money from investors came new opportunities and it wasn't long before Fuller heard of a new attraction in Nashville that he thought would be perfect for the business.

There had been much talk in Huntsville about a new invention called "electric lights." But while most people dismissed it as just another crazy idea, Fuller was determined to light his dance floor with the "marvel of modem technology." Within days of Fuller's visit to Nashville, workmen arrived to begin stringing wire throughout the cave.

Although few people realize it today, when Fuller pulled the switch on his new lighting system, he earned himself (and the dance hall) a place in Huntsville's history as having the first electric light bulbs in Madison County.

Even this was not enough for Fuller, for as he cast his eyes upon the vast underground lake he began to see another possibility for potential profits. Within the week neighbors watched in amazement as workmen unloaded three large boats from a wagon and awkwardly maneuvered them down the steps.

The citizens of Huntsville must have had a good chuckle when he announced his intentions of providing "Underground Boat Rides." And, as if that was not enough, he purchased hundreds of Japanese lanterns to hang overhead!

Finally, the day of the "Grand Opening" arrived, and true to Fuller's predictions, crowds thronged the cave to see the marvel of electric lighting, ride the boats and dance to the sound of a newly hired band. With the admission price of one dollar, Fuller should have been able to make a profit, but unfortunately, he was too deeply in debt. Also, the townspeople, after making one or two visits to the entertainment mecca, quickly lost interest.

Desperate for money, Fuller began to travel throughout the South promoting Huntsville and Shelta Cave as a convention center. Evidently he had some success, as the Huntsville Mercury in 1889 ran an article about a gathering of the press association:

"The entertainment of the Press Association by the citizens of Huntsville closed today with a grand barbecue in Shelta Caverns and nearly one hundred delegates and their ladies were in attendance. The affair was gotten up in a delightful manner and the beauties of the place were fully investigated by the astonished guests."

According to rumor, Fuller, or one of his cohorts, in another effort to stimulate business, (and keep down overhead) actually operated a moonshine still in one of the dark corners of the cave. Years later when it was discovered that Shelta Cave was the home of a rare species of blind shrimp, one local wag laughed and said, "Hell, that lickker made a lot of people almost blind, I reckon some of it could have spilled into the lake!"

Another story of the day concerns a duel fought over a lady's honor at the edge of the dance floor. The gentlemen, each slightly intoxicated, were pursuing the same girl at the same time when they happened to accidently meet at the dance. Harsh words were exchanged and to everyone's horror, they pulled pistols from underneath their coats. Both fired, and both missed. Fortunately, they let themselves be led away before real harm could be done.

The only casualty of the duel was a member of the band who was slightly injured by a falling stalactite.

As almost any nightclub owner can tell you, crowds are fickle, and within a few years the dance hall was again facing financial ruin. This time, even Fuller's salesmanship could not save it. On June 28, 1897, the cave was sold at a sheriff's sale on the steps of the courthouse to settle a judgement.

Although there is no documentation to support it, natives of Huntsville, who remember the 1920s and 1930s, swear that there was once a speakeasy located in the cave. Other sources claim that moonshine was produced in the cave at intervals all the way up to World War II. Another persistent rumor claims the cave was used as a liquor and beer warehouse during prohibition.

In 1968, after being neglected for years, the cave was purchased by the National Speleological Society. An iron gate has been placed over the entrance to prevent accidents.

1907 is the year to buy Huntsville real estate!

Big Bargains in city property

$5,500 2 story, 7 room brick, Smith residence on Randolph

$5000 The old Gordon property on Lincoln Street opposite church

$4,800 2 story, 8 room brick residence on Randolph with lot 108 x 200

$2000 buys 17 lots in Gists addition on Patterson Street

$2,700 4 room tenant house on Adams Avenue with large lot, 3-4 room tenant house in rear

$2,600 buys a nice 5 room cottage on East Holmes Street, hot and cold water

H.C. White
Halsey Building   Huntsville

Chapter 42

A Letter Home

To Mr. Robert Shirer, Meridian Road, Huntsville, Ala.,

Somewhere in California, 1889

Dear Papa,

I do not think I will be able to come home for Christmas. It is such a long way and not much money. I think about you and the family all the time. I wish you could be here to see the sights I have seen. California is truly a grand place. I have got a job at a sawmill now. I am throwing slabs. When I get some money ahead I am going to send you some picture cards of places I have seen.
 I went to San Francisco with the men I work with. The city must be as big as Huntsville and Decatur both. It is something to see the ocean. You can throw a fish up in the air and the birds will fight over it until one gits it and flys off with it. Some of the birds are as big as a turkey.
 Some of the men I work with are going to go off gold hunting. They want me to go but I said no. I don't think there is any gold left here.
 We did not find as much to pay for our beans this year past. There are men all over the hills and all the good places are gone. The way to get rich here is to open a cooking place. The food is bad and most of us would rather be hungry than

eat it.

I had to sell the horse. I had run out of money and no one to turn to. But don't worry—I will send money to pay you for it. I hope my letter gets to you by Christmas and tell everyone that I send my regards. I will surely be home Christmas next year.

Your dutiful Son,

Lee

Lee's father received one more letter from him postmarked Seattle, Washington. The family never heard from him again.

Chapter 43

The Wrong War

General Joe Wheeler, a Confederate cavalry general for whom Wheeler Wildlife Refuge was named, also served admirably in the Spanish-American War, but had a hard time remembering who the enemy was.

At the battle of Santiago, in Cuba, he insisted on being in the midst of the battle though he was very sick and had to be transported in an ambulance. When the battle seemed to be going badly, he bravely left the ambulance, dramatically leaped on a horse, and led a charge.

The charge was succeeding when Wheeler, slipping back into his youth, shouted exultantly to his men, "The Yankees are running! They're leaving their guns!"

"Oh, damn," he corrected himself when he remembered where he was and which war he was fighting, "I mean the Cubans, not the Yankees."

Later, when reminded of his slip of the tongue, he testily replied, "What's the difference? Anyone that shoots at me is a damn Yankee in my book!"

Chapter 44

Uncle Matt

No one is sure where Uncle Matt was born. One source claimed that he was born near Hazel Green, while another said he was from middle Alabama. But all agreed that he was born a slave. After the Civil War and emancipation, he settled in Huntsville near Spring Street. His home, according to a later account, was a ramshackle affair that would shake every time the wind blew.

In order to earn a living, he collected slop. A slop collector was probably the most despised job in Huntsville. With his makeshift wagon he would go from door to door, collecting the edible leftovers and scraps from people's meals, then haul the whole stinking mess out to some farm. The farmer would buy the slop to feed his pigs, paying Uncle Matt pennies for his hard work.

Uncle Matt made quite a sight, with his snow-white hair, ragged clothes, and flea-bitten hat. His wagon was a homemade affair pulled by two young calves. But regardless of how ridiculous he must have looked, everyone agreed that he was a proud man. According to one old-timer in Huntsville, whose grandfather lived during that time, the one thing that distinguished Uncle Matt was the fact that he was proud. Though many people had taken a liking to the old man and offered him charity, he always turned down the offers. "I am a free man," he said, "and not beholding to anyone."

In 1898, soldiers of the 69th New York were stationed in Huntsville. When they first saw Uncle Matt and his homemade wagon pulled by two calves, they thought it was the most hilarious and ridiculous sight they had ever seen. Every day Uncle Matt would drive his team to the soldiers' bivouac area and collect their slop. And every day he would be surrounded by laughing and jeering soldiers. Uncle Matt would just sit there in his wagon, holding his reins tightly, with his head held high.

Slowly over the next few weeks and months, the laughter and jeers began to subside. The soldiers began to respect the proud old man who was determined to make his own way. It soon became a common sight to see soldiers, off-duty, helping Uncle Matt load his wagon with slop. One story that has been passed down claims that the soldiers all chipped in and bought Matt a young mule to pull his wagon with.

The next morning, the mule was back in the soldiers' corral and Uncle Matt had his wagon hitched to the cows again. He never really gave an explanation, but the soldiers understood.

The Spanish-American War was just over in 1899 and the 69th was ordered to New York to march in the Victory Parade. It was the custom at the time for an important dignitary to lead the parade; someone whom all the men admired and respected, someone who could be held up as a hero, someone who was brave and courageous.

Look closely in your history books and you will read that when the 69th regiment marched down Fifth Avenue in New York, it was led by a man that fit all of the above criteria. Column after column of blue clad soldiers marched through the valley between the sky-scrapers that day, amidst the shouts and applause of tens of thousands of spectators. And in the lead, still driving his makeshift wagon pulled by two cows, was Uncle Matt, a free man, beholding to no one.

Chapter 45

A Bitter Legacy

No one in Huntsville, in 1902, was surprised when they learned the Rodgers and Ricketts families had been involved in a gun-fight. The families had been feuding for years—so long that most people had forgotten what the feud was originally about.

The latest incident began when the elder Rodgers was accosted by members of the Ricketts family while on his way to town. Harsh words were exchanged and both parties returned home to "gather their kin-folk."

Late that evening, Jim Ricketts and Halbert Rodgers met on the banks of the Flint River. Both were armed with shotguns.

Hatred between the two families was so great that both parties immediately began firing.

The first blast caught Ricketts full in the chest and neck. A second later Rodgers fell to the ground grievously wounded in both legs.

Although Rodgers and Ricketts would live many years after the gun-fight, they would both remain crippled for the rest of their lives.

Jim Ricketts and Halbert Rodgers were both only thirteen years old.

Chapter 46

Huntsville's Stone Warrior

Most of us are familiar with the statue of the Confederate soldier on the courthouse lawn, but some don't realize there's some interesting history behind him, too.

The idea of a memorial originated with the United Daughters of the Confederacy shortly after the turn of the century. They felt that the spirit of Southern fighting men during the Civil War should be preserved for the future, and what better way than a statue.

They sponsored many socials, rummage sales, teas, and parties in the Huntsville area to raise money for the project. Finally, they accumulated $2500 and began to put the plan together.

Today, $2500 doesn't sound like a lot, but in 1905, it was enough to buy an exquisite piece of Vermont granite and hire a sculptor to perform the work.

Huntsville had a pretty decent sculpting artist in 1905 by the name of Oscar Hummel, to whom the TDC wanted to give the job. However, since he was a local artist, some felt he wouldn't be able to do as good a job as other sculptors somewhere else. As a sort of test, he was assigned to sculpt an Indian head. If the Indian head was satisfactory, he would get the job. It was, and he did. Hummel set up shop on the site that is today a parking lot next to the Church of the Visitation in downtown Huntsville. As soon as the granite arrived, Hummel began his work. His model was Tim Mott Robinson, of Hazel Green, who posed while Hummel worked on with dedication and determination. In those days, a blacksmith shop was at the corner of Washington Street and close to Hummel's shop. People would watch the progress of the statue while they waited their turn to have their buggies and surreys repaired by the blacksmith.

Most were amazed and pleased with the progress as Hummel tirelessly continued.

At last, the statue was complete, and dedication plans were being finalized.

November 21, 1905 was a wonderfully festive day. Wagons, carts, horses, and people jammed the courthouse square for the dedication. Dignitaries, including the mayor of Huntsville, the county commissioner, and the governor of Alabama, were on hand with windy speeches and well-wishes. Thirteen pretty young ladies (one for each state of the former Confederacy) laid a large wreath at the pedestal base of the statue while Monroe's band played heart stirring music. There wasn't a dry eye on the square that day.

The years passed ... and the old soldier silently stood his ceaseless vigil as sentry, facing south in honor of those who fought for the Confederacy.

In 1966, plans were underway to tear down the old courthouse and replace it with a new one. Obviously, the statue had to be moved out of the way before the work started. A crane was called in to perform the task, which went well and without incident. The crane merely lifted the statue from the courthouse lawn, swung it across the street, and carefully set it down on the front lawn of the First National Bank.

This was to be the soldier's temporary home until the new courthouse was completed.

Before the completion of the courthouse, demolition of Cotton Row began in order to make way for the construction of the new State National Bank Building.

The fateful day was June 29, 1966. During the destruction of Cotton Row, one of the walls fell right on the warrior and knocked him down, breaking off his head, both hands, and his feet.

Since the UDC actually owned the statue, the Huntsville chapter president, Mrs. R.G. Moore, was notified. She came to the scene via a police car that picked her up at home, and she was both horrified and sickened by the sight of the old soldier, in pieces, before her. She absently tried to pick up the head for safekeeping before she realized it was too heavy.

Then began the long process of replacement, including insurance claims and legal actions.

At first, it appeared that molds could be made of the damaged parts for replacement, since the body of the statue was undamaged. However, that wasn't possible, and it was determined that a new sculpture had to be made, so the insurance appraisal was done that way.

The legal process took an unbelievable two-year period, but eventually, the courts found in favor of the UDC in March 1968. The re-sculpting process could at last begin.

The work was awarded to the Georgia Marble Works, one of only five granite sculptors in the U.S. The granite used was Georgia granite—good, but not as visually appealing as Vermont granite.

The original, undamaged pedestal was used, but the difference in the granites necessitated some re-sanding for a color match.

The new warrior's hands and face are exactly as the old one's were; the body is pretty close to the original except for some minor differences in the folds and creases of the uniform.

The original statue was surrounded by an iron picket fence, which has been officially "misplaced."

In case you're wondering what happened to the original statue, last word was that it is in the good care of Mrs. George C. Crome in Memphis, Tennessee. The next time you have business at the courthouse, you might pause a moment to reflect on the stone warrior who, like countless thousands on both sides during the Civil War, moved up to replace a fallen comrade.

Chapter 47

Alabama Birdman

An amazing part of Huntsville's early history can be found inscribed on a brass plaque at the Smithsonian Institute in Washington, D.C. Oddly enough, though millions of people a year see and read the plaque, few people in Madison County know the facts.

The inscription tells the story of how the first airplane flight in Alabama (and possibly the world's first monoplane) took off from a farmer's pasture in Madison County around 1909. This flight signaled the real beginning of the aviation industry as we know it today.

William (Will) Lafayette Quick was born near Shiloh, Tennessee, in 1859 and later moved his family to a small community outside present-day New Market which became known as Quick's Mill. An industrious man, he set up a grist mill, blacksmith's forge, saw mill, and machine shop in the late 1800s and began to dream of flying.

Quick had begun talking of what he called aerial navigation before the turn of the century. Although he had never heard of anyone trying to fly before, he decided to attempt to build a flying machine.

He was convinced by his study of the birds, bats, insects, and other flying creatures that man-made flight was possible. Although Quick had no formal education, he had the vision, skill, and drive needed to fabricate a machine that would fly. He was adept in carpentry and had a thorough knowledge of machinery and propulsion.

THE WAY IT WAS

Around 1900, Quick began what would become an eight-year design and construction project. With meticulous attention to detail, he built his first prototype of a monoplane, then chose his son, William, to fly the plane.

The flight lasted for only a few seconds. William achieved an altitude of a few feet, but then ran out of pasture. Unfortunately, while trying to turn the monoplane, he clipped the ground with a wing. The wing was damaged, the propeller broken, and the landing gear torn off, but the plane remained mostly intact.

Quick took the plane back to his shop and there it stayed for some 60 years, gathering cobwebs, forgotten by family and friends alike.

That event marked the beginning of the Quick family's career in aviation. Eight of Quick's children became pilots. Some were barnstormers and others were pioneers of the crop-dusting industry.

In 1970, the Experimental Aircraft Club discovered the remnants of the dilapidated monoplane in Will's old shop. After the club obtained the consent of the family, the plane was restored to its original condition with almost all original parts. It is now on public display at the Huntsville Space and Rocket Museum.

Although the flight lasted only a few seconds, it was a major accomplishment in aviation, and Huntsville history.

Chapter 48

Royalty in North Alabama

Royalty in North Alabama? Many people don't know it, but an Alabama native was both a countess and a marchioness. Her name was Grace Hinds Curzon, and she had a fascinating, almost rags-to-riches background.

Grace Hinds was born in the Hinds-McEntire home, located near the downtown area of Decatur on Sycamore Street in 1878. The home was built by John Burleson about 1835 and overlooked the Tennessee River.

The story goes that both Yankee and Confederate army chiefs used the house as headquarters during the Civil War. In fact, it was at the Hinds' home that the battle of Shiloh was planned by General Albert Johnston. The home was spared the flames of the Civil War fires, but several large, decorative balls which were atop the iron fence around the house were shot off during numerous battles.

After the war, Col. Jerome J. Hinds of Illinois and his brother were so taken with the house that they made it their home. Col. Hinds and his brother Monroe were both soldiers in the Union army. The two Hinds brothers made large purchases of property in a stricken but potentially rich valley and soon owned larger land areas on both sides of the Tennessee River near Decatur. Later, when Monroe Hinds married, he and his wife raised their children in the home, including their daughter, Grace.

Grace Elvina Hinds was born in 1872 in the upstairs room of the house in Decatur and was the third offspring of a family

~ 184 ~

of seven. Her father was a U.S. Marshal during Chester Arthur's administration and also served as a United States Minister to Brazil.

It was later said that when she became famous she forgot her old friends, but she never forgot the old Decatur home. In her book, "Reminiscences," she wrote: "Decatur, Alabama, as I remember it, was a quiet, sleepy town, although my older friends used to tell me, with great pride, of the wealth and dignity, of the vast entertaining and hospitality before the Civil War."

The Hindses moved to Huntsville when Grace was still a young girl, since her father was U. S. Marshal of the Northern District of Alabama. They lived modestly in Huntsville during his four-year term of office, in a house on Grove Street, almost opposite the Paul Davis home. While in Huntsville, the family attended the Episcopal Church and young Grace played in the area around Big Spring. Old-timers remember her as a bright child who appeared on the streets with long curls that her mother tediously wrapped.

While living in Huntsville, however, the family encountered some misfortunes. In April 1882, Grace's mother died and was buried in Maple Hill Cemetery. In February of the following year, her father died and later in November 1888, Lucia, Grace's sister, died also. Another unfortunate incident that befell the family was when the home on Grove Street burned and the family had to move to a smaller house on the corner of Madison and Gates.

In 1890, Grace and the remaining family moved back to Decatur. From then on, the story of this modest North Alabama resident reads almost like a fairy tale.

Five years after the family had moved from Huntsville to Decatur, Mrs. Hinds' brother, John Trillia, came to Decatur from South America to visit the family. He was fascinated by his young relative and offered to take her on a three-month journey with him. Grace jumped at the chance.

While visiting there, Grace met and married an

Argentinian millionaire and meat packer from London, Alfred Duggan, who kept herds in South America and was a native of Tennessee. Although she was never really happy with him, Grace gained experience, poise, and education in London and before long had captured the hearts of European society. They had three children—two boys and a girl.

After the death of Duggan, Grace was left with some $25 million. On January 2, 1917, she married George Nathaniel Curzon, a widower, in a private chapel of Lambeth Palace, outside of London. This was the second American heiress whom Curzon had married. The ceremony was attended only by eight or nine guests, including children, and Grace had only one attendant.

Following the wedding, the couple moved to London, where they bought the historic Bodiam Castle in Sussex. Built in 1386, this structure is considered the finest English example of medieval castles. There she lived with the splendor and pageantry of medieval royalty and became a world-famous hostess. Among her friends were King George V, Queen Mary, the Prince of Wales, the Churchills, the Queen of Portugal, Mrs. Cornelius Vanderbilt, and others.

Grace was an extremely beautiful woman. Sir John Lavey, the most famous artist of the time, painted her portrait. She was exceptionally youthful for her age, which was probably one reason she captured so many European hearts.

Curzon had a brilliant career behind him and was the idol of many women.

One of the ladies he eluded was Elinor Glyn, who later wrote a novel about a noble young aristocrat who was ruined and deserted by a scheming American heiress.

Lord Curzon became Viceroy of India, as well as Lord Viscount, Earl, Foreign Secretary, and Leader of the House of Lords. The King of England conferred Curzon with the title of Marchioness and Grace received that of Dame of the Order of the Grand Cross of the Order of the British Empire. All was not story-book perfect, however. Grace was extremely independent and as early as the first year of her marriage to Curzon, had a habit of living apart.

Curzon had a great dream of becoming the Prime Minister of England. He failed but did fill many important government posts. He was a controversial figure, attacked by some as a tyrant and a political turncoat and praised by others as a beneficent ruler of India and skilled negotiator and shaper of England's postwar policy.

He kept five or six mansions, country manors, and town houses and that included two or three castles. He was a collector of castles and was said to have artistic taste and a reverence for antiquities.

He died in 1925, literally in a harness, which he wore for 48 years because of the constant pain he suffered from a back injury. He was still making plans for his future on his deathbed.

Lady Curzon, Marchioness of Kedleston, a woman who won approval wherever she went, wrote her memoirs in 1955, something she had wanted to do for a long time. King George V knew that she wanted to do this but persuaded her to wait for a least 25 years after Lord Curzon had died. She wrote the book 30 years after his death.

Grace Hinds, the little girl who grew up on Grove Street in Huntsville, lived the rest of her life with the opulence and pageantry of medieval royalty.

It was a long way from the cotton fields of her North Alabama home.

Chapter 49

Legend of Lily Flagg

Even though not as old as some homes still standing in Madison County, the Watkins-Moore home on Adams Street bids strongly for a unique place among colorful local history. For this was the location of the only reception ever held for a cow.

In the 1850s the home was built by the Watkins family. James L. Watkins passed the land on to his son, Robert H. Watkins. At the time this home was built, Huntsville was renowned for having some of the most beautiful homes throughout the South. This started a building feud in Huntsville, and Watkins was not to be outdone. He was surrounded by stately dwellings and wanted his home to outshine them all.

As the building of his home began, craftsmen were called in from other states to create plaster of Paris molding. All the woodwork inside the dwelling was made of walnut, and frescoing was put together painstakingly in sections. Slaves were put to work making hand-pressed brick for its walls. Two stairways led to the second floor of the home, with a third going directly to the tower on the roof which consisted of two floors.

There was no other structure like the tower anywhere near Huntsville.

Those who traveled the world spoke of a similar one in Paris. On clear days, one could see as far as the Tennessee River from the lookout in the tower. Robert Watkins built this magnificent home as a gift to his beloved bride, Margaret Carter. She didn't live long in the home, however. Soon after the home was completed, the Civil War began, and the men went away to war. Margaret had just given birth to their first child when Yankee forces reached Huntsville. When the Yankees spread their tents all over the yard of the mansion, the alarmed servants ran in to tell the weakened mother the news. She was extremely agitated and died a few hours after being notified.

When Samuel Moore acquired the home in 1890 he continued to improve the interior of the home. Such rare items as bathtubs, lighting fixtures, and marble mantles from Italy were brought in.

Mr. Moore was quite a colorful character. As a renowned bachelor and member of the state legislature, he loved parties and people. Prominent visitors never missed a tour of his home, and many local celebrities were married there surrounded by flowers and gaiety.

Samuel Moore not only loved people, he loved his cow, Lily Flagg. This was not an ordinary cow but had just returned from the state fair in Chicago where she had taken top honors as the world's greatest butterfat producer. He was as proud of her as if a daughter had taken top honors in a world beauty contest. So, to celebrate her success, he decided to honor her with a grand reception.

He spared no expense in the preparations. He had the home painted a bright yellow for the occasion. A fifty-foot dancing platform was erected at the back of the mansion and was lit by one of the first electric lighting systems in the southeast. Lanterns were hung everywhere, flowers were in abundance.

On the evening of the event, guests dressed in formal attire formed a long line that wound its way to the small stable at the rear of the property where the little Jersey stood, almost hidden by roses. She was honored by people from as far away as Washington.

When the Italian orchestra from Nashville began to play, the dance platform quickly filled up. Special tables were set up all over the property to hold exquisite foods and pastries. Champagne flowed freely, and it is said that this was one of the best parties held in the Huntsville area, before or after. The party lasted until the early morning hours, and older residents said that they would never forget the party for the little cow.

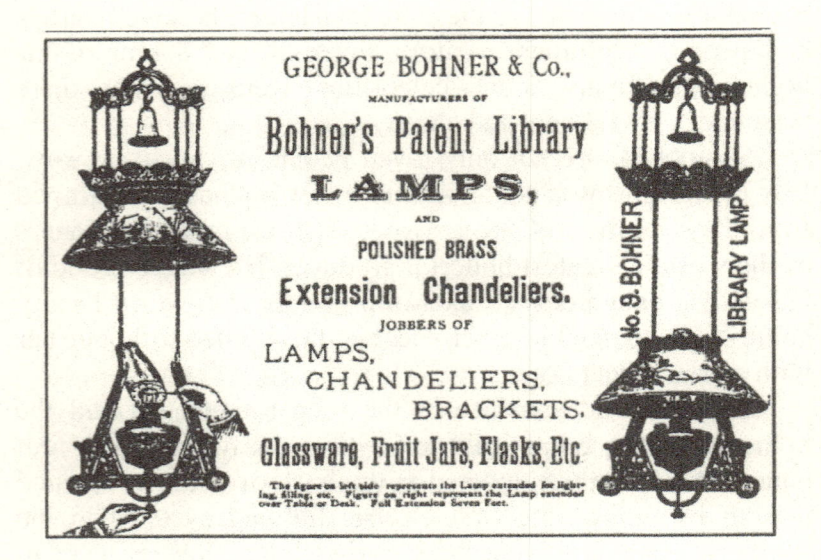

Chapter 50

UFO's Sighted in 1910

One of the great mysteries of Madison County that has never been solved are the reports of a UFO, here in Huntsville, on January 12, 1910. This was the era when airplanes and balloons were almost unheard of in the Tennessee Valley.

The following account comes from the January 13, 1910, *Huntsville Mercury* newspaper:

> Strange Airship
> Passed Directly over the City
> Yesterday Afternoon.
> Rapidly Passed Out of Sight,
> Going in a Northwesterly Direction

"An unknown airship passed almost directly over Huntsville at half past four o'clock yesterday afternoon coming from the southwest and continuing on its course on a straight line to the northeast. The craft appeared to be making a long journey and it passed on its course without making any signal or other demonstration and so swiftly did it move that it was out of sight over the crest of Chapman Mountain before many people on the streets had an opportunity of seeing it. It is believed to have passed on out of Huntsville territory as nothing more was heard of the ship during the evening.

"...Before anyone had time to obtain glasses, it had passed out of sight. The aircraft was not traveling with the breeze near the surface of the earth because the breeze on the surface was coming directly from the west. The speed appeared to be greater than any wind short of a hurricane would travel."

At first glance the preceding article appears to be speaking of an airplane or a balloon, except for the fact that a balloon could not travel against the wind and an airplane of that date, by no stretch of the imagination, could travel as fast as a "hurricane." Also, there were no airplanes in the Tennessee Valley in 1910.

If the whole event had a logical explanation, why did the *New York Tribune* think it was newsworthy enough to run an article about it on the front page of the same day?

Also on the same day, January 13, 1910, the *Chattanooga Times*, with a front-page headline, reported sightings of a "cigar-shaped vessel" traveling at a high rate of speed in a northeasterly direction.

The following day the strange airship appeared again in the skies over Chattanooga. The Chattanooga newspaper speculated that it was the same one that had appeared over the city the day before. The article went on to say, "Some are inclined to think the mysterious airship is the craft of a sky pirate who has sinister designs upon Chattanooga."

On January 15, the "cigar-shaped vessel" was spotted in the skies over Knoxville, Tennessee, headed south. This was the last reported sighting.

If this "airship" was some type of an airplane or a dirigible where did it come from and where did it go? It was in the area for three days, but there were never any reports of it landing anywhere.

Over a century later, people are still searching for an answer.

Chapter 51

Watercress Capital of the World

Almost lost and forgotten in our city's history is the fact that Huntsville at one time claimed the crown as "The Watercress Capital of the World."

Watercress cultivation began in New Market in 1907 when Foster DeWitt visited the area and became intrigued by the "wild" watercress growing along the banks of streams. This was one of the few places in the country where an abundance of fresh spring-water and limestone, combined with moderate winter temperatures, caused watercress to grow wild. DeWitt had spent much of his early life in Great Britain and while there was exposed to the plant as a culinary delight.

Greenstuffs in Great Britain were hard to come by in the winter months and watercress was one of the few plants available year-round. According to legend, an English officer started the custom of having watercress served in salads and within a few years it became a staple in every household. New York and Baltimore restaurants began serving watercress in salads in the early 1800s, but the cost of importing it from Great Britain was too prohibitive for it to become a widely used commodity in this country.

Foster hired local labor to dam a small stream on the land he had rented, creating a series of shallow ponds, much like rice paddies. By experimenting with water levels, he found that a level of six inches was the most favorable for cultivation. In cold weather the water would be raised, with the constant temperature of the water protecting the plants from damage.

Where at first the local populace had been skeptical about the whole idea, they soon became enthusiastic supporters as orders for the watercress began pouring in from Northern restaurants. Within a few short years, as other people began cultivating the plant, Madison County became the major supplier to the world's markets. Train-car loads of cress were shipped from Huntsville, sometimes as often as four times a week, to points all across the country. Many of these loads contained as many as one million bunches of watercress.

An interesting sidelight to watercress cultivation is that as the plants flourished, so did the snakes. Some of the ponds became so infested with water moccasins that laborers refused to work around them. John Derrick earned the dubious distinction of being the only "bounty hunter" of snakes in Alabama's history when he was hired by the landowners. An early account states that he was paid five cents a snake, with him keeping the skins.

Colder winters and the expense of shipping were cited as the two primary reasons the business declined here in Huntsville. With the advent of air freight, the railroads discontinued most of their express freight trains. Watercress became too expensive to ship by air and too perishable to ship by regular freight train.

As late as 1960, one could still see a sign at the edge of the city limits proclaiming: "Welcome to Huntsville, Watercress Capital of the World."

Chapter 52

Simp McGhee

Captain Simp McGhee was a fiery character whose nautical exploits were many, and about which legends abounded. He was a large man and sported an impressive belly.

Just before reaching Chattanooga, there was a treacherous three-mile area of the Tennessee River called "The Chute," known nowadays as Hale Town. It was dangerously rocky, swift, and narrow. This was long before the TVA widened and deepened the river so as to aid in flood control and navigation. Most boat captains dreaded "The Chute," but Simp McGhee saw it as a challenge. An adventure, so to speak. Unlike many boats, not once had his snagged a boulder, bumped the banks in the fog, or run aground in a storm. And he piloted the James Trigg with the grace and skill that only a veteran boatman could muster.

"Grab your shovels, hold onto to your britches, and kiss your girlfriend g'bye," he would yell. "We're gonna race the devil up the chute!"

On one such occasion he was navigating the chute while the passengers watched anxiously. The deckhands quickly manned their stations. Four of the men grabbed heavy shovels and began shoveling coal furiously into the vessel's furnace.

Others took up positions along the flanks of the ship, ready to call out if the treacherous rocks appeared too close. The chute had, between the time of the Civil War and the turn of the Twentieth century, become a veritable junkyard of wrecked ships as one captain after another misjudged the dangerous rapids and deep-sixed their ships, or at least sent them to dry-dock for major repairs.

It was almost impossible for a steamboat to navigate upstream through the chute. The current was almost as swift as the fastest ship, and any captain foolhardy enough to try it would find his ship standing still in the current, bouncing from one rock to the next.

In the 1800s, the government installed a winch at the head of the rapids which was used to pull steamboats safely through the dangerous waters. Unfortunately, there was usually a long line of boats waiting to be pulled through and Capt. McGhee was not a patient man.

McGhee, however, could navigate the chute in 30 minutes.

"Hold on, men!" he bellowed as the gushing water began to pummel the front of the vessel. "We're going in!"

While other boats waited in line, McGhee opened the throttle full-blast and barreled his way through the churning waters. The boat trembled. Every timber in its frame groaned in protest as it furiously battled the oncoming rapids.

When the boat was almost at a standstill, McGhee gave the order to "lay the fat on!"

Instantly, the deckhands began stoking the furnace with four sides of fat that had been reserved especially for this occasion.

With its boilers red hot and sweat pouring from the begrimed deck hands, the ship once again started making headway. The steamboat was quivering from the strain it was under, but not McGhee. He simply gritted his teeth, and ordered more coal thrown in the furnace. Then, with one final shudder, the Trigg shot through the last of the treacherous waters to safety.

And Simp McGhee swaggered up and down the deck, with his head thrown back, laughing at the cowardly riverboat captains still waiting in line. Once again, he had proved that he was king of the Tennessee riverboat captains!

No one knew much about Simp McGhee's early days. Some said he was born into a wealthy family who had lost everything during the Civil War, while others claimed that his family had kicked him out at a young age. Years later, when anyone questioned him about his youth, he would throw his head back and loudly proclaim, "My Daddy was a gambling man, my Mama was the Tennessee River. I'm too mean for dry land, too gentle for the river, but when I die, there's gonna be hell to pay ... cause hell ain't big enough for both the Devil and Simp McGhee!"

As a youth, Simp was a rambunctious devil-may-care lad who got his first job as a riverboat deckhand at the age of 13.

He supplemented his income by playing poker or by selling a few pigs that he just happened to find "running loose."

After he became a captain, his boat became known for serving the finest meals on the Tennessee River. Passengers never questioned why the pigs and chickens were always delivered late at night by suspicious looking characters.

With such shrewd business practices, it was little wonder that Simp became a prosperous business man. He spent much of his time, between river trips, in saloons around Huntsville and Decatur.

He opened his own tavern, which quickly became a success, where he served such culinary delights as S.I.T. beef (stolen in Tennessee beef).

He even opened a bordello in Decatur, rather than see Decatur's dollars spent in places like Huntsville and Athens. "It's my duty as a citizen to keep those dollars in Decatur," he reasoned when accosted by church people.

By this time, Simp's reputation had grown and there were few people who had not heard of him or his legendary exploits. One of his most famous escapades concerned a duel in the middle of the Tennessee River.

Simp's riverboat was running a few minutes behind schedule. Heading into Decatur, he saw another riverboat in front of him headed for the same dock. Rather than wait his turn, Simp called for more steam. With black smoke billowing from the smokestacks, he quickly gained on the boat and cut in front of it, reaching the dock first and almost swamping the other boat. The captain of the other boat was furious.

Later that night both of the captains ran into one another at Simp's favorite watering hole. Seeing Simp sitting there nonchalantly drinking his beer enraged the captain even more. He marched up to Simp and demanded satisfaction.

"Wait a minute. You're challenging me to a duel?" Simp asked.

"Call it what you like!" snarled the enraged captain. "Well, if you're challenging me, I reckon I have the right to pick the time and place," said McGhee. "We're both river men, so get your boat and I'll get mine and we'll meet in the middle of the river and shoot it out at 25 paces."

The bar emptied as news of the impending duel spread. Simp's boat left first, journeyed a few hundred yards and dropped anchor.

The other boat left shortly with the enraged and slightly inebriated captain standing on the foredeck, a dueling pistol in his hand. As the two boats approached each other, the fog began to clear, and what the captain saw then was enough to cause him to change his mind about dueling and to leave Decatur forever.

Standing unruffled on the foredeck of his boat was Simp McGhee, a mug of beer in one hand and a cigar in the other, casually aiming an old Civil War cannon.

Like so many other legendary figures, it was only a matter of time until Simp McGhee would meet his match. In his case, it would be the Federal Government.

After the Civil War, the government passed several navigation laws to ensure safety on the waterways. For years these laws were ignored, with the government having no way to enforce them. Finally, around the turn of this century, after hearing numerous complaints, the government decided to take action against Simp.

McGhee had been warned that government men were after him, so he was not surprised when a well-dressed "Yankee-sounding" gent boarded the boat and asked to be led to the captain. Simp, chewing on a cigar, told the agent he was sorry, but that the captain wasn't on board.

"Simp's at his summer home. But don't worry, we're going right by there and I will be glad to give you a lift."

The Federal man sat back to enjoy his trip and in about an hour the boat pulled up to an island.

"Right over there, "Simp said. "Just go through that brush and you'll be almost on his front porch. And he'll be glad to give you a lift back to town."

Witnesses said the Federal man stumbled around Hobbs Island for two days before he realized he had already met the legendary captain. He also became the first Federal agent to swim from Hobbs Island.

McGhee died at age 58 on June 16, 1917, just a few weeks after his riverboat piloting license was pulled by the government, citing "passenger endangerment" while running "the chute."

He was buried in a grave a few feet from the Tennessee River's northern shore near Guntersville. Black deck hands were his pallbearers.

HENRY DELP
MANUFACTURERS AND DEALER IN

PLAIN & FANCY FURNITURE

Clinton Street

Bet. Washington And Greene

Huntsville, Ala.

Chapter 53

La' Overture Toussaint

Teaching school was just about the worst job he could imagine. Confined in a class room for eight hours a day, it seemed to spell the end to his musical aspirations. For Willie Handy, however, it was a job. At least it put food on the table.

Born in 1873, as the son of a Methodist preacher, Willie decided at a young age he wanted to be a musician. But his family, all stalwart hell-fire and brimstone, God-fearing people, thought a musician was nothing but a blatant sinner in disguise.

In an effort to pacify his father, who wanted him to become a minister, Willie agreed to finish school and take the examination to become a schoolteacher. After graduation, however, he found the job opportunities in Birmingham to be much more profitable. He soon landed a job at one of the iron mills working as a laborer, making more money than he could ever expect to make as a teacher.

Willie had not lost his desire to be a musician, though. He quickly became friends with most of the black musicians in Birmingham and it was not long before he had formed his own group and was playing around town at night while still working in the mills during the day.

One of the first gigs he had in Birmingham, according to legend, was playing in a notorious dive. The owner, after listening to the audition, asked what the group's name was.

"Don't have one." Willie replied.

"Well, what's your name?"

"Willie."

"Sounds like a damn Uncle Tom name to me. What's your whole name?"

"William Christopher."

"Hell, that's even worse! We'll just call you by your initials."

W.C. Handy soon tired of Birmingham, though, and moved to Huntsville where he got a job teaching at Alabama A&M as a music instructor. Among his many duties as an instructor, Handy was also responsible for organizing recitals for his students.

Unfortunately, the headmaster at A&M believed that classical music was the only music that should be performed. He even insisted on personally approving the programs for every recital.

For his first recital Handy chose a piece he had written entitled, "La' Overture Toussaint." With a name like that, it was no trouble getting the headmaster to approve it. Handy diligently rehearsed the students, who were by this time enraptured with the new musical composition.

The day of the concert arrived, and it was an instant success. Even the staid headmaster was seen sitting in the front row tapping his foot to the music.

W.C. Handy's career as an instructor did not last long. He was still determined to make his mark as a musician. After leaving Huntsville, he moved to Memphis where he wrote the all-time classic, "Memphis Blues," which he sold for $100. Still a poor man, he next ended up in St. Louis, and after being forced to sleep in alleys and pool rooms, composed the song "Saint Louis Blues," a song that made him wealthy and famous and earned him the title of "Father of the Blues."

Ironically, he gained the most fame from the piece he had composed while teaching at A&M College, after he changed its name to "My Ragtime Baby."

Chapter 54

The Judge Lawler Murder

Murder, mayhem, blackmail, shoot-outs, bootlegging, election contests, and suicides were all part of the most scurrilous period in Madison County history, and before the turmoil settled, almost all of the county officials, Huntsville city officials, and judges were stained by it.

The most notorious political murder in the history of the state occurred in Madison County in the year 1916.

The weird beginning was on June 4, 1916, when probate Judge W.T. Lawler was attending a Chatauqua on the school grounds of East Clinton School, with Japanese lanterns everywhere, gas torches flaring, and mobs of people enjoying the entertainment brought to them by the Redpath Chatauqua Company. Witnesses would later claim to have seen Judge Lawler talking to someone on the phone at about 8 pm that night.

That was the last time anyone ever saw Judge Lawler alive.

Huntsville and Madison County, at the time, were a hotbed of corruption. There were allegations of prostitution, policemen hauling moonshine in police vehicles, gamblers paying city officials in order to operate, and court cases being dismissed because of political "pull."

There were reports of gun battles between rival bootleg gangs over territorial rights. One store in West Huntsville, a front for gambling operations, was dynamited when the operators refused to pay for "protection."

Depending upon which story you want to believe, Judge Lawler was either a reformer who was going to rid Huntsville of corruption or was as deeply involved in the graft as all of the other officials.

Judge Lawler's lifeless body was discovered the next day by ferryman Percy Brooks at the Hambric Slough Bridge on Aldridge Creek. The body was found to have been weighted down by heavy pieces of iron—later identified by Ed Green as having come from the Madison County jail. Gary Clinton, a 15-year-old, told of seeing bloodstains on the bridge. The body was brought to Huntsville for burial. Accounts of the day claim that over ten thousand people attended the funeral.

Feelings in Huntsville ran so high that the governor was forced to bring in three companies of National Guard to keep control in the area.

Upon being questioned, Brooks, the ferryman, told a story that implicated C.N. Nalls and David Overton. Nalls was the Madison County court clerk and Overton was an ex-police chief who had resigned to run for probate judge.

Nalls was indicted by the grand jury and arrested. Later, while searching his offices, officials found evidence in his desk, consisting of a revolver that had been recently fired.

The same day that Nalls was arrested, at exactly 4:45 pm, a shot rang out in the county jail and sheriff Bob Phillips was found dead with the alleged murder weapon at his side. A handwritten note stated that it was more than he could bear, just being suspected of involvement in the Lawler murder.

At this time, no one had even questioned his involvement.

Out of jail on bond, Nalls tried to get Shelby Pleasant to represent him as his attorney. Pleasants was an attorney who was also a former legislator and had represented Lawler in earlier political cases.

Pleasants refused to see Nalls. Then, to even further complicate matters, Pleasants committed suicide. No reason was ever given.

The grand jury, in its investigation, had condemned

conditions in Huntsville. The report claimed that a whiskey racket was responsible for much of the corruption in the county.

Chief of Police Kirby and patrolman George Blanton decided to resign.

Again, no reason was given.

Meanwhile, Overton had taken off for parts unknown. He was later captured in Smithville, Tennessee, on September 25th, and returned to Huntsville to stand trial. Two days earlier, a grand jury indictment was made public saying that Dave Overton and Charles Nalls killed Lawler with a pistol. The city and county were inflamed with the latest accusations.

B.M. Miller, later to become governor of Alabama, was appointed a special judge for the case. Assistant attorney general J.F. Thompson and Jefferson County solicitor Joseph R. Tate were placed in charge of the prosecution, assisted by local attorney Douglas Taylor. B.M. Allen of Birmingham and Huntsville's Charles Grimmett were the defense lawyers.

The defense entered a plea of innocent for both Overton and Nalls. A packed courtroom heard the state lay out a convincing case against Overton and anxiously awaited his appearance after the state rested its case on November 23, 1916.

On November 24th, Overton broke down. He said he had killed Judge Lawler in self-defense, to save his own life.

His story was that he met the judge in the courthouse basement that fateful night and drove with him in Overton's buggy down the Whitesburg Pike to a store building on the Tennessee River, stopping at the Aldridge Creek Bridge to talk.

Overton's claim was that Lawler wanted him to try and fix a grand jury investigation on election frauds. Overton said that he refused. Then, Overton said, Lawler became furious with him, grabbing him and slashing him with a knife across the temple, cheek, eye, throat, and chest.

At that point, Overton pulled a gun and smashed Lawler

in the head time and time again, testimony claimed. Overton said he went to see the sheriff at the jail and told him the whole story of what had occurred.

Sheriff Phillips told Overton to go back and stay with the ferryman Brooks and to return the next day with Brooks. Phillips said he would then look after the body of the judge. Overton said he later saw sheriff Phillips and that the sheriff said the body would never be seen again.

Despite the plea of self-defense, the jury found Overton guilty and rendered a verdict of death. Overton was removed to the Jefferson County jail on December 8, 1916. Nalls went free, totally exonerated.

The citizens of Huntsville thought that now, finally, the case was over. However, the following year, on Marth 20, 1917, seven prisoners including Overton escaped from the Jefferson County jail, reputedly using a wooden pistol. A waiting automobile sped off with the escapees.

On a tip, officers went to the neighborhood of J.R. Tate, who had prosecuted Overton, and a gun battle erupted with six of the escaped convicts. Two were killed, including Overton, who had earlier proclaimed, "I will never hang!"

Overton's body was brought back to Huntsville for burial.

The sheriff of Jefferson County had to face impeachment charges brought as a result of Overton's escape from jail.

Tragedy continued to follow the participants.

Percy Brooks, the able-bodied ferryman, met a horrible death two years later when he was run over by a freight train.

Former circuit court clerk Nalls died in 1918 from a flu virus. The son of Sheriff Phillips strangely committed suicide in Arkansas, also in 1918.

No one ever claimed to know the full story of how that bizarre case came about. Other theories exist today about who murdered whom, but the court record is the only documented evidence.

Part of the background undoubtedly dates back to the 1913 grandy jury recommendation for impeachment of the probate judge, the circuit court clerk, and county commissioners.

Over the years numerous tales and legends have popped up concerning the Lawler murder case. These are people who claim that Overton took the blame for other officials. These officials supposedly then reneged on the deal that had been made and let Overton be sentenced to death.

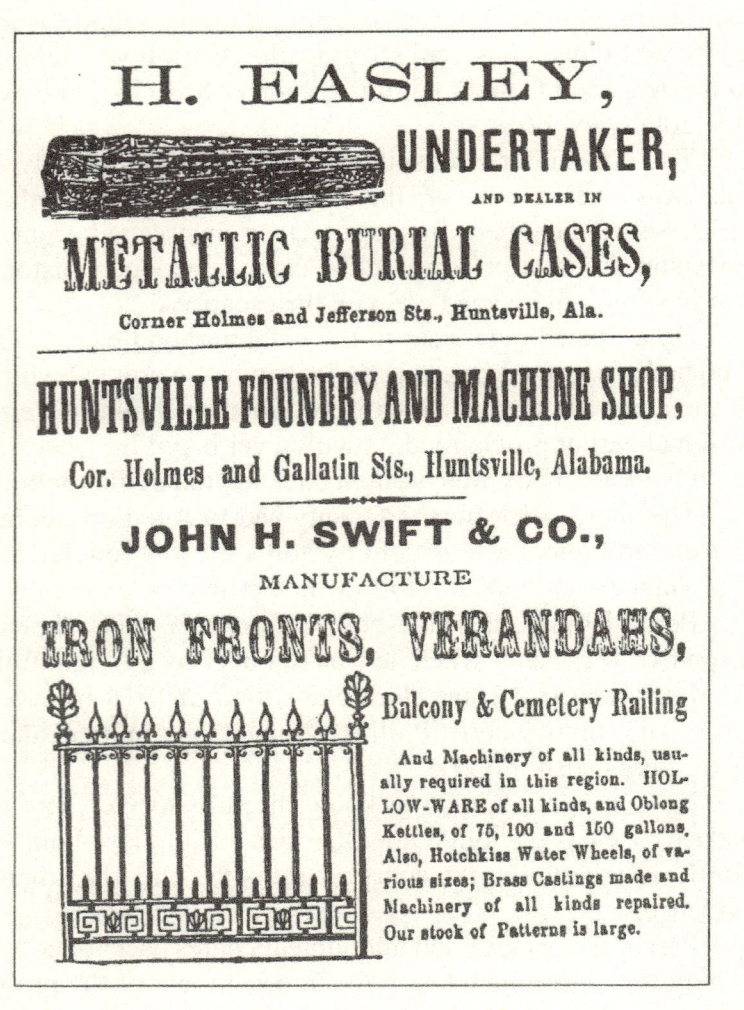

H. EASLEY,
UNDERTAKER,
AND DEALER IN
METALLIC BURIAL CASES,
Corner Holmes and Jefferson Sts., Huntsville, Ala.

HUNTSVILLE FOUNDRY AND MACHINE SHOP,
Cor. Holmes and Gallatin Sts., Huntsville, Alabama.

JOHN H. SWIFT & CO.,
MANUFACTURE
IRON FRONTS, VERANDAHS,
Balcony & Cemetery Railing

And Machinery of all kinds, usually required in this region. HOLLOW-WARE of all kinds, and Oblong Kettles, of 75, 100 and 150 gallons. Also, Hotchkiss Water Wheels, of various sizes; Brass Castings made and Machinery of all kinds repaired. Our stock of Patterns is large.

Chapter 55

The Life and Times of J. Emory Pierce

His name was Jacob Emory Pierce. With nothing but a dream he founded a newspaper that would forever change the lives of thousands of people.

If he had been alive today, many people would have called him a con man. Others would have called him an egotistical eccentric.

He was all of these things. He was a newspaper man.

Emory Pierce was a vindictive man, and shrewd. He was controversial around the turn of the century, and still is in some circles. There was one thing for sure and disputed by none—nobody messed with Emory Pierce.

The publisher of one of Huntsville's early newspapers learned that lesson the hard way in 1909. Exact details have been lost with the passage of time, but it appears that the publisher made the mistake of writing an editorial with which Pierce disagreed. It had to do with whether livestock should be permitted inside the town limits. When Pierce, whose parents owned a small dairy on Meridian Street, showed up at the newspaper office to voice his displeasure, the publisher, instead of trying to placate him, added insult to injury by giving him the bum's rush out the front door.

A second such article, even more strongly worded, appeared in print the following week. To say that Emory Pierce was angry would be an understatement. The whole matter was a small thing, the kind of thing that most people would have forgotten in a few days. But Pierce was not like most people. During the next several months he tried many ways to heap revenge on the publisher.

I.E. Bradshaw recalls hearing his father tell the story: "Everybody in Huntsville watched the feud. The arguing went on for most of the summer and then all of a sudden Pierce stopped his efforts. This kind'a dumbfounded everybody cause that wasn't in character with him. What nobody knew was that Pierce had lined up a couple of investors and was going to open his own newspaper. It's hard for people today to understand, but Pierce could talk the horns off a billy goat.

"He would say, 'Boys, y'all put the money up and I'll be your partner. Together we'll get rich!'

"Well, it seemed like a good deal. Pierce would be the working partner and these other boys would pay the bills. He figured their finances would be in the black in a few months. They rented this building down there on Washington Street, right up from the old Yarborough Hotel, bought a press and hung out a sign. A couple of weeks later he came out with his first issue."

That was the start of the *Huntsville Daily Times*.

"Everyone was excited about the newspaper and thought Pierce had forgotten about his feud with the other publisher. They should have known better.

"Pierce didn't have any advertising salesmen, so he did it all himself. You have to remember that all the businesses in town were used to advertising with the other paper.

"My father told me that Pierce called on every business in town and offered free ads if they would not run in the other paper. Sure enough, it didn't take long before the *Times* was jammed full of advertisers and the other paper was hurting financially. They had also learned not to mess with Emory Pierce. The bad thing about this whole thing was that the *Times* was in a bad financial way, too. All the ads were free and no money was coming in. The investors called a meeting with

Pierce and told him that they could not afford to put any more money into the paper.

"Pierce agreed to buy out his partners for a few pennies on the dollar, rather than let the paper fold."

The following week Emory Pierce became the founder, sole owner, and editor of the *Huntsville Daily Times*. He immediately stopped the free ad practice, after having almost bankrupted his competition.

Furthermore, he raised his ad rates far above those of his competitor. The new paper became an instant success and Pierce, despite his sixth-grade education, quickly became an effective editorial writer. He blended into the journalistic ilk perfectly, considering that worthwhile writers are an eccentric breed.

He had always worn his hair longer than the norm for the era, so as it began to turn gray, he let it flow to shoulder length. He bought a black Stetson hat and it became his trademark. Edmond Duffy, who went to work for the *Times* in 1924, recalls going to work each morning and seeing Pierce walking down Holmes Avenue.

"There used to be a streetcar line running down the middle of Holmes and sometimes Pierce, wearing his ten-gallon hat and swinging his cane, would purposely walk in the middle of the track. The streetcar conductor would have to almost stop the car and ring the bell furiously before Pierce would step out of the way. This went on for several months and finally one morning Pierce, in an agitated mood, turned to the exasperated conductor and said, 'Would you stop ringing that damn bell! If I'm not moving fast enough you can get out and walk, too!'

"When I first went to work there they were still on Washington Street. Huntsville was just starting to build up at that time and it was his dream to have the tallest building in town. He bought land for a new building and had already dug the basement when his financial backers changed their minds. That big hole in the ground was there for several years and everybody called it 'Pierce's folly.' He finally went to

Nashville to find new funding for the building.

"Anyway, he got the money and they started construction. Things were going along real good with Pierce boasting to everyone he met that he would soon have his office on the top floor of the tallest building in town.

"The construction was almost finished when a major bombshell hit, taking the wind out of his sails. Another skyscraper was under construction, the Russel Erskine Hotel. Plans called for it to be the same height as the new Times building.

"Pierce was livid. Angrily he ordered the workmen to add another floor on his building. The elevator shaft was already in place and couldn't accommodate the extra floor, so a stairway provided the only access to the top floor. The Times Building was finally completed and, true to his boast, Pierce had his office on the top floor of the tallest building between Nashville and Birmingham."

Unfortunately, big bills come with big buildings and they kept coming in every month. Advertising revenue was down and expenses were up. Everyone knew Pierce was having trouble financially, but he refused to admit it to himself. Pierce was a tyrant to his employees. "We used to get paid every Saturday morning," says Duffy. "One such payday morning we were all waiting when Pierce walked in. 'Boys,' he said, 'I'm going to do you a favor. If I pay you today, all you are going to do is spend it ... so I'm not going to pay you today.'

"He abruptly turned and walked out. We were speechless! Of course, we eventually got our money, but after that we lived in fear from week to week."

But even with this type of tactic, Pierce still could not generate enough revenue to pay all the bills that piled up.

Within a few years his business bit the dust.

With the foreclosure of The *Times*, Pierce lost everything. Although everyone agreed that he was an eccentric, egotistical character, he was also an exceptional newspaperman and had become a prolific writer.

Too proud to remain in Huntsville, he moved to Memphis where he started a small regional paper called the *Tennessee Valley Booster*.

The whole nation was in the throes of the Great Depression and newspaper revenues were hit hardest of all. With Pierce's small quarterly paper floundering, there was no way he could compete against the big dailies for the few advertising dollars available.

Ever the consummate salesman, Pierce decided to create his own market. President Franklin Delano Roosevelt had already announced the TVA program. To the small farmers it was seen as a salvation. Pierce, instead of calling on businesses for advertising, called on these small farmers.

Pierce was a sharp dresser and an eloquent speaker. Calling on a farmer he would spend a few minutes talking about hogs, weather, or whatever. Eventually the conversation would always turn to the TVA and invariably the farmer would begin praising it.

This was Pierce's cue.

"Friend," he would say, cleverly choosing his words and their timing. "This is your lucky day. I am here to make sure you get your shares of *Tennessee Valley* ... Authority has been given to me by the state of Tennessee and I am the only man living that can legally sell these shares. Now for the small sum of..."

The farmers, illiterate for the most part, would gladly shell out their savings for what they thought were shares in the TVA project. What they got in reality was advertising in the *Tennessee Valley Booster*.

It wasn't long before Pierce's new-found prosperity attracted the attention of a young ad salesman with the *Memphis Appeal*. "How," he wondered, "can Pierce be selling so much advertising." The young salesman got several copies of Pierce's paper and decided to call on the accounts and try to sell them advertising himself.

"Advertising?" the farmers angrily spat. "We ain't bought

no advertising. We bought stock in TVA!"

The next day Emory Pierce, the former *Huntsville Daily Times* publisher, was a resident of the Memphis jail. A top floor cell, ironically. He had become fairly affluent by this time, so it came as a shock to everyone when he refused to post a mere thousand-dollar bond in order to gain release. "I have committed no crime," he announced, "and I refuse to refute that fact by posting bail. I will stay in jail until I am tried." After ordering that his typewriter be brought to him, he settled down in his new home for the next few months. Strange as it may seem, he continued to sell "advertising" and publish the paper from his jail cell.

When his case was finally called, the courtroom was packed with angry farmers, reporters, and salesmen. The first person to be called was the young trouble-making salesman, who related his findings. Next, the prosecutor asked one of the farmers:

"Did you buy what you thought was stock in TVA?"

"Yes sir."

"Can you identify the man who sold you this stock?"

"Yes sir," he said, pointing at Emory Pierce.

"May I see the stock certificate?"

The farmer reached into a pocket of his overalls and pulled out a crumpled piece of paper. "Your Honor," the lawyer said triumphantly, "I would like to enter this into..."

He froze in mid-sentence as he stared at the crumpled certificate. The judge, sensing that something was wrong, asked to see the paper. The judge slowly put his glasses on, and smoothing the paper in front of him, began to read. The certificate was an expensive, beautifully engraved piece of work. But, it was also a receipt for one month of advertising in the *Tennessee Valley Booster*.

The case was dismissed and Pierce never explained why he chose to spend the summer in jail. Not long afterwards, Emory Pierce died of a heart attack in Tupelo, Miss. A friend said that losing the Huntsville newspaper was what really killed him.

"One of his proudest possessions," the friend said, "was an old calling card that read: Jacob Emory Pierce, Publisher, Huntsville Daily Times."

Chapter 56

The Mill Strike

In mid-July of 1934, after months of mediation and agitation, nearly 4,000 Huntsville cotton mill workers went on strike as part of a nationwide walkout that quickly ensnared America's entire textile industry.

The strike brought violence to the streets in the form of killings, kidnapping, assaults, shootings, and bombings.

A cloud of fear hung over Huntsville like poisonous vapors seeping into the hearts of the populace. No man, woman, child, home, or business was safe. Living here was dangerous. Mill owners across the nation refused to negotiate, threatening to hire strike breakers to quell any riotous activity by the strikers.

Then on July 17, the Fletcher Mill opened at the regular hour of 6 am but was forced to close within three hours. Noisy strikers were clamoring in the street outside the mill and it appeared that major violence would erupt at any second. Sensing the severity of the situation, the nonunion employees chose to leave their jobs rather than confront the raucous pickets.

Police and deputies armed with tear-gas rifles and machine guns were called to the scene as the strikers grew more unruly, but the crowd dispersed when the officers arrived.

Merrimac was the next mill to close as strikers, under the leadership of state union organizer Albert Cox, went through the building telling workers to leave. The mill emptied in minutes.

Lincoln and Dallas mills closed that same morning when the night shifts came off duty.

John Dean, representing the United Textile Workers of America, urged strikers to maintain picket lines and prevent the mills from running.

Carloads of strikers, armed with shotguns, pistols, knives, baseball bats, and anything else that could serve as weapons, cruised the streets shouting and waving their weapons, intimidating anyone who might have had thoughts about going to work.

A meeting of the Dallas Mill workers was held at the old Methodist church on Humes Avenue. Monroe Adcock, president of the Dallas local union, presided and urged that no destruction of mill property take place during the strike. He also pleaded that all union members refrain from using intoxicating liquors while the strike was in progress.

The following day reports of trouble sent police racing to the Admiral Braid Company. A crowd of a few hundred men had gathered outside the plant when it was reported that an attempt was going to be made to move a load of merchandise. The report was false, and the crowd dispersed without incident. On July 30, special deputies guarded the Tennessee River bridge between Decatur and Huntsville as rumors indicated that a motorcade of more than 500 striking textile workers from Huntsville were enroute to Decatur in an effort to urge the textile workers there to join the strike.

The deputies managed to turn the strikers back, but everyone knew that it was just a matter of time before violence would explode.

Earlier in the day, three union men were attacked on a street comer near the Goodyear fabric plant in Decatur. The aforementioned union local head, Monroe Adcock, was shot in the leg, and Isaac Bullard and Burnice Rigsby were injured in an altercation with three unarmed men. Special guards were placed around the Goodyear plant.

Early Sunday morning, August 6, John Dean, leader of the strike in Alabama, was kidnapped from his room on the sixth floor of the Russel Erskine Hotel by four men and taken at gunpoint to Fayetteville, Tennessee. During the ride he was beaten about the head with a pistol. His abductors, in a bizarre move, then registered him at the Pope Hotel where he managed to, according to the porter, initiate a call to his friends in Huntsville. In less than an hour a dozen automobiles, filled with armed men, arrived in Fayetteville to rescue their leader.

Instead of returning to his hotel, Dean went into seclusion at the home of George Davis on F Street in Merrimac Village. Armed guards were placed around the house to prevent further kidnapping.

During the time of Dean's abduction 400 angry men, most of them carrying guns, gathered near the Russel Erskine Hotel. They had heard of the abduction and were seeking the men responsible. The mayor sent a large contingent of police to the hotel, preventing the mob from getting out of hand.

Strikers set up roadblocks at each road leading into Huntsville. Automobiles going in and out of the city were stopped by strikers brandishing weapons who said they were looking for the kidnapped man, not knowing that he had returned and was in hiding.

The situation was becoming serious. Many citizens were afraid to leave their homes. Gangs of armed men roamed the town looking for would be strike breakers and terrifying everyone with whom they came into contact. Sometimes as many as eight carloads of strikers would slowly caravan through downtown.

With strikers demanding that the city take action, solicitor (district attorney) James Price announced that the Grand Jury would meet the following Monday and that a warrant had been issued in the kidnap case. Fearful that the crowd would take the law into its own hands, the sheriff refused to name the persons involved until the arrests had been made.

Monday morning found a large crowd assembled downtown awaiting the day's events. In an act of bravado, Dean drove in from Merrimac and casually breakfasted at the Central Cafe downtown while armed bodyguards patrolled the sidewalks out front.

Meanwhile, the Grand Jury returned an indictment against James Conner, a mill worker. When word spread that the owners of the cotton mills might have been responsible for Dean's kidnapping, the pent-up fury of the strikers exploded.

Rumors that downtown stores were going to be dynamited caused additional deputies to be brought in, but the day passed without incident.

Threats against the indicted Mr. Conner caused guards to be placed at his home. They were called off that same afternoon when it was realized that Conner had left town for parts unknown.

Cars were not permitted on streets where union leaders lived, unless permission was first obtained from the strikers. Armed guards were maintained throughout the night and augmented the following morning by additional strikers.

The Thomas Mill, forced to shut down when the strike began, reopened despite threats from the strikers.

Before the plant could begin operating at full capacity it was invaded by a gang of strikers from Merrimac Mills and Erwin Mills, despite protests by the foremen. The workers were quickly assembled and ordered by their leaders to quit work and leave the building by the spokesman of the strikers. William Fraser, manager of the Thomas Mill, later identified the leader as Henry Parmlee, the union leader at Merrimac. Fraser said the strikers ignored the "posted" signs displayed at the entrance to the mill.

On August 13, the kidnap charge against Conner was stricken from the docket of the Grand Jury and a lesser charge of "whitecapping" was entered. Whitecapping was defined as "loan act to prevent and punish the formation or continuance of conspiracies and combinations for certain unlawful purposes." Trial was set for Nov. 28, but was continued until

Feb. 19, 1935, when the matter was dropped.

Random acts of violence continued. No one was safe. On Sept. 3, three charges of dynamite damaged the grocery store of Mrs. R.W Atkins on Pike Street in Merrimac Village. The explosion brought a crowd to the scene.

Shortly before daybreak, strikers were brought out of their beds by bugle calls and gunshots. Armed strikers rushed into the city from Lincoln Village after being told of trouble at the Fletcher Mill. They returned home when everything was found quiet.

A group of young women decided to ignore the picket line and return to work, but they were pushed to the ground by the angry strikers. Ignoring the girls' screams of protest, the strikers produced a pair of scissors and proceeded to roughly cut their hair.

A short while later, residents of Lincoln watched the strange sight of four bald-headed girls being paraded down Meridian Street.

The same day, gunshots were fired into the store front windows of businesses downtown who were suspected of being sympathetic to the mill owners. An automobile belonging to a union organizer was burned while it was parked in front of the courthouse.

City officials, frantic by this time, asked that a federal mediator be brought in. Something had to happen. Huntsville could not continue living under a cloud of terror.

Judge Petree, mediator, and his staff arrived in Huntsville and immediately went into a conference with union leaders. After the meeting at the Davis house, where John Dean had established his headquarters, Petree then conferred with the officials of the Erwin Mill, which had been trying to reach an agreement for several days.

On Sept. 22, before the mediator could work out a compromise, the great textile strike ended. National Union leaders had reached a settlement.

Almost as quickly as it had begun, the violence ended.

Thousands of Huntsville textile workers responded to the union leaders and returned to work. Peace had returned to Huntsville.

No charges were ever filed against anyone for the hundreds of acts of lawlessness committed during the strike. "It was," as one old-timer remembers, "as if Huntsville just wanted to forget."

Chapter 57

Obsessed Love

"We was just poor working girls. We had got laid off at Margaret Mills and there weren't no work here in town so we caught a freight to Chattanooga to look for work. We spent the night in a boarding house and the next day caught another freight back to Huntsville. While we were on the train these black boys got in a fight with some white boys on the train and threw them off. Then they started waving knives and a gun. There was nine of them and one of them held a gun on me. Anyway, they held us down and took turns ravishing us. I hope they all burn for what they did to me."

With these words, Victoria Price and Ruby Bates sat in motion a chain of events that would have worldwide repercussions. The case, known as the "Scottsboro Boys Case," would become the most notorious series of trials ever held in Alabama.

By most accounts, Victoria was a good-looking girl. She was raised in the cotton mill villages where she first went to work at the age of thirteen. The victim of a drunken father who beat her mother, Victoria married when she was only fifteen. This marriage didn't last very long once she found out that her new husband was addicted to drinking "canned heat." The second husband, a year later, just kind of drifted away; afterward, she would claim not to know whatever happened to him.

By the time Victoria was in her late teens she had become known as a hard-drinking, devil-may-care woman to whom casual sex meant as much as a friendly handshake. Ben Giles, sheriff of Madison County, would later describe her as a "quiet prostitute who didn't bother nobody, so we didn't bother her much."

If Victoria had one weakness, most people would agree it was married men. Single men, she could take her pick of, but a married man was a challenge.

It was in early November 1930, when Victoria first saw Jack Tiller. He was a handsome, well built, hard-drinking and hard living guy. He was the type of man that Willie Nelson would sing country ballads about today—and he was also married.

Within a week they were living together. Both Jack and Victoria had been laid off at Margaret Mills, and in the true American spirit, they decided to open up their own business.

The section of the mill village they lived in was known for its gambling dives, houses of prostitution and bootleggers, so it was no surprise to anyone when they opened up their own "shot house."

Things seemed to be peaceful for a while until Jack, always a lady's man, began to cast his eyes elsewhere. Coming home one night, under the influence, Jack was met at the door by a screaming Victoria waving a butcher knife. "If I can't have you, no one else will!"

Jack settled the argument by locking her in the coal shed until she calmed down.

It wasn't long before everyone realized Victoria had met her match. She still liked to drink, raise hell, and even have a couple of sugar daddies on the side, only now she was careful not to let Jack know. One elderly person still living in Huntsville recalls, "It was kind of sad. That girl wanted to be in love only she didn't know how, And Jack ... well, he liked her all right, but he liked all the girls all right."

With all the screaming and fighting going on, it wasn't long before Jack and Victoria had come under the scrutiny of the Huntsville police department. Our fair city was undergoing one of its periodic "cleansings," and the H.P.D., after raiding their home and not finding any evidence of bootlegging or prostitution, decided to arrest Jack and Victoria on the charges of "Adultery."

Jack and Victoria were both given sentences of ninety days "at hard labor."

While in jail, Jack befriended a young vagrant by the name of Lester Carter. Lester didn't have a girlfriend, so Jack promised to fix him up once they were released.

The first night out of jail, Jack and Lester went to call on Victoria. It was obvious Victoria had something else on her mind when, grabbing Jack by the hand, she pulled him into the bedroom, leaving poor Lester to pass the time with her mother.

Jack made arrangements to meet Victoria and her friend, Ruby Bates, the next evening at the entrance gate to Margaret Mills and introduce Lester. After stopping at a shot house and having a few drinks, Victoria suggested going someplace where they could have some privacy. Slightly tipsy, the two couples made their way to a group of trees located next to the railroad tracks known to locals as a "hobo jungle."

As Lester would later testify, "I hung my hat on a limb and went about having intercourse with Ruby Bates while Jack was doing the same with Victoria Price." During the night, their lovemaking was interrupted by a rain-shower. Getting up from the honeysuckle bushes, the four sought shelter in an empty railway car where they continued drinking and carousing.

No one knows how the argument began, but sometime during the early morning hours Jack and Victoria got into one of their legendary fights. "I'm tired of this whole damn city," Victoria cried. "I'm leaving and if you don't want to come—the hell with you!" Jack, by now, was tired of arguing. "Go on," he said. "I'll meet you in a few days."

After just getting out of jail for adultery, there was no way he was going to cross the state line with her.

Victoria was furious. If Jack wasn't going, she would go by herself, just to prove her point. That afternoon Victoria

Price, Ruby Bates and Lester Carter met in the train yards and hopped a freight to Chattanooga. As is the case with most people in love, Victoria started missing Jack before they had barely left the Huntsville city limits. They arrived in Chattanooga and after spending a fretful day, Victoria talked Ruby into heading back to Huntsville.

As the train approached Paint Rock, Alabama, it began slowing down. Lining the track on both sides were armed men, flagging the train down and ordering everybody off.

No one can say for certain what was going through the girls' minds, but we can be sure they were aware they were breaking the law and could be arrested for "hoboing" and vagrancy. And Victoria also knew that if she got locked up, Jack might find himself another girlfriend.

One of the posse members told the two girls to have a seat under some nearby trees. Sitting there, the girls watched as the armed men took nine black males, who had also been on the train, into custody. A deputy told Victoria there had been a fight on the train, with the blacks throwing a group of white men off.

Later, trial testimony would show that when the men finished arresting the prisoners and had secured them by tying them together with a rope, a deputy approached the girls and asked what they were doing on the train.

Victoria evaded the question by crying, "It's their fault," while pointing to the black prisoners. "Those boys held me and my friend down and raped us. All nine of them."

By the time the truck carrying the prisoners reached Scottsboro, word of the vile accusation had spread like wild fire. Within twenty-four hours the courthouse resembled a military camp, with armed soldiers guarding the entrances and a crowd estimated at ten thousand filling the square.

The good citizens of Scottsboro took up a collection and purchased for the girls, who were wearing overalls, new dresses.

When the trial was held a few days later, Price and Bates

both identified the boys and swore they had been raped. All nine boys were tried and sentenced to death in a matter of hours. The youngest of the boys was only thirteen years old. Within days an appeal on the boy's behalf had been filed.

Unfortunately for the accused, the case was about to take on a new dimension.

People all across the country had become interested in the case, and offers of help for the defense started pouring in. None of the families of the accused had money to hire lawyers, so the boys were at the mercy of whatever organization that chose to offer help. Although most of the organizations meant well, some of them were not exactly the best choice to represent a defendant in an Alabama courtroom in 1932.

It was the most absurd scenario anyone could dream up. Nine black boys on trial for their life in Alabama, accused of raping two white women, represented by a Yankee Jewish lawyer who was being paid by the N.A.A.C.P., and with the backing of the Communist Party.

It quickly became a case of Alabama versus the World. "Even if the girls were common prostitutes and even if they were lying," according to one old-timer. "The Blacks, the Jews, and the Communists were still wrong and had no business messing in Alabama affairs."

Returning to Huntsville as a martyred woman, Victoria once again set her sights on Jack Tiller, and within a matter of days they were back living together.

In May of 1933, Victoria indicated to the defense that she might be willing to change her story if she was bribed with "the right price." After much negotiation, two attorneys from New York chartered a plane and flew to Nashville, Tennessee. Upon landing, they were arrested by the Nashville police. In their possession was the $1,500.00 they had agreed to pay Victoria for changing her story. At the same time in Huntsville, police arrested J. T. Pearson in connection with the bribery attempt. According to one source, Jack and Victoria had gotten into a big fight when Jack found out about her offer. In an attempt to pacify Jack, and at the same time remain the martyred woman, Victoria went to the Huntsville police and informed them of the bribery attempt—neglecting to say, of course, that it was she who made the first overture.

Jack had always taken pride in being a truthful person and expected the same of others. He was also highly protective of anyone that had been wronged, and it was this weakness that Victoria played on.

Meanwhile, Ruby Bates was having her share of trouble, too. Myron Pearlman, alias Danny Dundee, was arrested by the Huntsville police on a routine charge of public drunkenness. While searching him, the police found a letter that Ruby had written to her boyfriend. The letter read:

Huntsville, Ala. 215 Connelly Alley Dearest Earl,
I want to make a statement too you. Mary Sanders is a....lie about those negros jazzing me. those police man made me tell a lie. that is my statement because I want too clear myself...

I hope you will you believe me. The law don't. I love you better than any Body else in the World that is why I am telling you this thing. I was drunk at the time and did not know what I was doing. I wish those negros are not Burnt on account of me....

P.S. This is one time that I might tell a lie. But it is the truth so God help me.
Ruby Bates

When Pearlman, under intense pressure from the Huntsville police department, realized that this letter did not coincide with the police department's public statements, he quickly came up with a story about being paid to get Bates drunk and getting her to write the "confession."

A visit by the Huntsville police produced a statement from Bates to the effect that she was drunk at the time the letter was written, and that it was all a lie.

A later investigation would point to Bates and Pearlman

being coerced by the police into signing false statements.

Several days after signing the statement for the police, Bates disappeared.

The second trial of the Scottsboro boys was scheduled to be held in Decatur with Judge Horton to preside. Leibowitz, the defendants' attorney, quickly began to make a shambles of the whole case, or so he thought.

Medical evidence was presented to prove the girls had never been raped. It was ignored by the jury.

One witness for the state testified to seeing Victoria assaulted by the boys. When asked how he knew it was Victoria, he replied, "because of her dress."

Victoria was wearing overalls at the time.

When questioned about her actions in Chattanooga, prior to the alleged rape, Victoria testified she had spent the night at a boarding house while seeking work.

The boarding house did not exist, except in her imagination. Witnesses testified she had spent the night in a hobo jungle.

During this whole time, Jack Tiller had remained loyal to Victoria. Many times he had doubts, but in the end she was always able to make him believe her. Now, as he heard testimony unfold, he began to have doubts again. Witnesses later recalled seeing him standing in the back of the courtroom shuffling uneasily from one foot to another as he listened to evidence that seemed to indicate his girlfriend was lying.

Victoria would probably have been able to talk Jack into believing her again if it had not been for a surprise defense witness. Just when it seemed as if everyone had forgotten about Ruby Bates, she walked into the courtroom.

Only this time she had a different story to tell.

The rape had never happened, she testified. Victoria had made her tell the story. As Ruby Bates continued her testimony, she portrayed Victoria Price as a cold-hearted woman who was willing to send nine innocent people to the electric chair. The whole story was a lie, told to keep from being arrested for vagrancy.

There was shocked silence in the courtroom. Jack Tiller, Victoria's strongest supporter, looked across the courtroom to where she was sitting, a look of disgust on his face. Slowly he stood up and made his way out of the crowded room, shaking his head in bewilderment. He never looked back.

Victoria ran out the doors trying to catch Jack, but it was too late. He had already gotten in his car and was pulling away from the curb.

"Damn you," cried Victoria, as she stood there on the courthouse steps with tears of rage and frustration running down her cheeks. "You'll never find another woman like me." That afternoon when Victoria returned to Huntsville, Jack had already moved out.

Epilogue:

Even though few people believed Victoria's testimony, Alabama authorities insisted on continuing to prosecute the case. The defendants would spend a total of almost a half century behind bars until the case would finally be closed and all the defendants released.

Ruby Bates was forced to leave town after changing her testimony. She became active in the Communist Party and toured the country as a speaker. At one time she even met with the Vice President of the United States and presented him with a petition asking for the boys' release. Eventually her notoriety died down and she moved to Union Gap, Washington where she died in 1976.

Jack Tiller never again had any contact with Victoria Price. Despite notes and telephone calls that continued up into the 1950s, Tiller steadfastly refused to talk with her. For the rest of his life he would condemn Victoria Price for her infamous lies. He remarried in 1938 and made Huntsville his home until he died here in 1966.

Victoria Price, feeling bitter at the way the state had abandoned her after the trials, offered to change her testimony in 1940, but only for a substantial price. The defense attorneys, having heard this once before, wisely refused the offer. After giving contradictory evidence in eight different trials, her credibility had reached an all-time low. At first, Huntsville's citizens tolerated her, but as time passed and the truth began to come out, sentiment began to turn against her.

Six months after the last trial, she moved across the state line to Flintville, Tennessee.

She died in a Huntsville hospital in 1982.

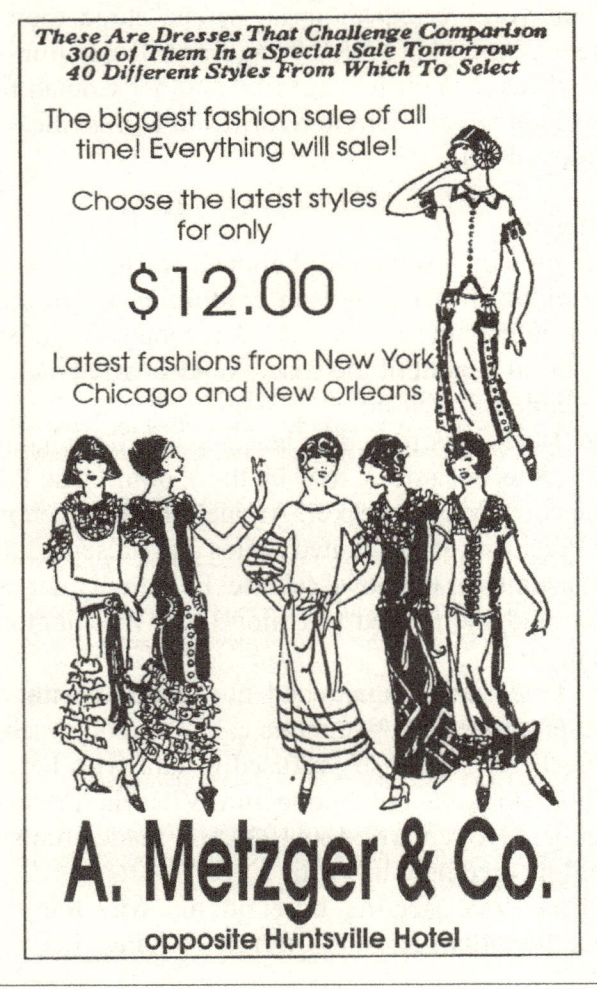

These Are Dresses That Challenge Comparison
300 of Them In a Special Sale Tomorrow
40 Different Styles From Which To Select

The biggest fashion sale of all time! Everything will sale!

Choose the latest styles for only

$12.00

Latest fashions from New York, Chicago and New Orleans

A. Metzger & Co.
opposite Huntsville Hotel

Chapter 58

Moonshine, The Law, and Sugar Tits

The courtroom was silent as the judge shuffled his papers. Finally, after taking a long look at the man standing in front of him, he asked: "Well, what do you have to say for yourself?"

The defendant, remembering that his lawyer had told him to be honest and tell the truth, replied: "Your Honor, my name is Jim Brasemore and I make moonshine. Matter of fact, I make the best white whiskey in Madison County!"

Jim Brasemore was a moonshiner and he talks freely about it, now that the statute of limitations has run out.

He learned the art of whiskey-making from his father, who had learned it from his father. Young Jim started feeding a firebox when he was only seven or eight years old.

"We had this groundhog still out next to the Flint River," he says.

A groundhog was a still built into the side of a hill or cliff. Such distilleries were hard to detect.

"Every morning Mama would pack us a lunch of biscuits and fatback and we would set out walking. We had to walk about three or four miles to the still, but back then it didn't seem like a long way," he remembers.

The Brasemores had a reputation for making some of the best liquor in the county and, of course, that made a lot of people jealous.

"There was this family, Ricketts I believe the name was,

that used to live close to us. The old man was what you would call shiftless, never did a hard day's work in his life. He used to come around and buy liquor from us and then sell it to the field hands," he recalls.

"Of course, before he sold it, he would cut it down 'til it didn't even taste like good whiskey. Everybody knew it was Brasemore whiskey, so they didn't question it too much. When Daddy heard about what Ricketts was doing, he wouldn't sell him anymore. We had a reputation to maintain, you understand."

Not long after that, the Brasemores got to noticing that someone was stealing from them. Some culprit would sneak into their "holding areas" in the woods, where they stashed their whiskey until it could be picked up by the haulers. Whiskey started disappearing, a couple of gallons at a time.

They put together a plan to catch the thieves.

"One morning just after sunup, Daddy comes and wakes me up. We were ready to put our plan into action. We headed for the stash place and took along this old shotgun, a rabbit ears Parker. After we got to the stash, we made us a hideout under some brush.

"On up in the morning, here comes old man Ricketts, just lumbering along like some ol' fat hog. We watched and sure enough, he goes straight to the whiskey and helps himself to a couple gallons.

"Ricketts was just about the fattest man I ever knew, and when he bent over his hind end looked like the broad side of a barn. I reckon it was more than Daddy could resist, 'cause he cut loose with that old Parker and when he got done it looked like termites had gotten hold of the rear end of Ricketts' britches!

"Fortunately, the gun was loaded with saltpeter and the shot wasn't very dangerous, although Ricketts had to eat his meals standing up for a few weeks."

When the younger Brasemore was born in 1902, homemade whiskey was a respectable and thriving industry in

Madison County. Although many people today would frown on the practice, at that time many families depended on it for a living. The alternative was to work in the mills (if they were lucky enough to find one that was hiring) or try to survive as a dirt farmer.

"Daddy got caught the first time in about 1916 or '17. The law was paying informers to tell on people. They put his bail bond at fifty dollars. That was on a Friday, and we didn't have any money, so the next morning Mama gets me to hitch up the mule and we loaded up the wagon with what whiskey we had left. Back then, Saturdays was the big trade day downtown and the streets would be so busy you could hardly walk.

"We tied the wagon in front of the courthouse and just sat there all day, selling whiskey. Everybody knew what Mama was doing, so a lot of people who didn't even drink would stop and buy some. For medicine, they would say.

"On up in the morning a deputy came by and asked her what she thought she was doing.

"'I'm gettin' my man out of jail,' she replied. Back then no one messed with Mama. 'Anything else you want to know?' she asked the deputy.

"'No ma'am,' the deputy replied sheepishly, 'but I reckon I'll take a gallon if you got any left, my croup has been acting up lately.'"

They got their dad out of jail that day, but he didn't stay free long. When his trial came up, he was sentenced to 12 months on the county farm. Pickin' peas, he called it.

"I was a pretty good size boy by then and with Daddy in jail it was up to me to run the business," the younger Brasemore recalls. "Before he got caught, Daddy had hid the worm (copper condensation coil) and I got a neighbor to build me a pot.

"It wasn't but just a couple of weeks 'til I was back in business. When I run off my first batch they said the sheriff thought my father had escaped."

"Nobody makes whiskey that good," the sheriff said,

"except for old man Brasemore!"

"I hadn't forgotten about the cur dog that had informed on Daddy, though. Giles was his name. Him and the deputy that arrested Daddy were big drinking buddies. This deputy lived out next to Chase Nursery and every Sunday like clock-work, those two would pitch a big drunk.

"Some of my cousins helped me and we took this old worn-out still, it only had a ten-gallon pot, and we set it up out back of his house in a brush patch. First thing Sunday morning we loaded it with mash and started cooking. If you have ever been around a still, you know you can't hide the smell, and sure enough, on up in the morning the deputy gets a strong whiff and decides to investigate.

"Well, here we are, me and my cousins are hiding in the brush, and the deputy and Giles are stretched out in front of the still sipping free whiskey and acting like they are in hog heaven.

"Next thing you know, there's this big ruckus and when the deputy opened his eyes, there was the sheriff pointing this big pistol at him."

"You and Giles are under arrest for making whiskey," the sheriff said.

Seems as if someone had sent the sheriff a note.

"Like I said, while Daddy was in jail I was running the business. One of the first things I did, after I got a little ahead, was to buy me a truck. Daddy wouldn't have nothing to do with automobiles, he had worked with a mule all of his life. Well I was bound and determined to impress him, so the day he was to get out I took the truck and loaded it down with as much whiskey as I could put on it. It had not been picked up in a while and we had a sizable load.

"Things didn't work out the way I figured, and the truck broke down a couple of miles from the house. I got the mule, hitched it to the truck and began to pull it on home.

"Daddy was sitting on the front porch when I pulled up in front of the house. He took a long look at that truck I had bought and then took an even longer look at his mule that was pulling it. Finally, after spitting out a long stream of tobacco juice, he asked me, 'Well, what else can it do?'

"He never did like that truck. Every time I got stuck in mud or whatever, he was always there to tell me that with a mule it would not have happened."

Young Jim got married in the fall of 1925 to a city girl who wouldn't have anything to do with making whiskey. One of her uncles got him a job in Merrimac Cotton Mill.

Jim wanted to quit the whiskey business but working in the mill was not for him. He would come home at night spitting up lint and cotton dust. His wife, Laurie, could tell by his look that he wasn't happy.

"Finally, 'bout a year later I come home from work one day and she's packing our things in boxes. She told me we were moving back to the country.

"Kenneth Abbott and I set up a still down next to Byrd's Spring where there was this hunting club. We ran it most of one year and then we put another one down next to the bridge at Whitesburg.

"That was the biggest one I ever run, a 2,500-gallon groundhog.

"By this time we had two stills running and plenty of whiskey to sell, so we figured we would expand our business. Normally we would sell the whiskey to a tripper or hauler who would distribute it to the bootleggers. We figured that instead of paying the middle man we would take the money ourselves."

Many people have sought Jim's advice about the whiskey business: "I tell all of them the same thing. Have lots of kinfolks. They are about the only ones you can really trust.

"Anyway, we got Mickey, my second cousin who owned a Ford coupe, to start hauling for us. That went real good. Then George, another cousin, decided to come in the business. He was driving a milk truck and had a regular route at the time. Once a week we would load him up with whiskey and he would make home deliveries all over town."

It appeared that the Brasemore crowd was making all the money in the world and that's what caused the trouble.

At that time there was another family in Huntsville that was big in the whiskey business, too. They were connected to a bunch of moonshiners over in Cloud's Cove. Unfortunately, they began to get angry when they realized the Brasemore outfit was cutting into their profits.

"The first we knew about it was when they shot Abbott, my partner, at the Whitesburg still. He had been tending it along with some hired hands when someone shot him from behind with a shotgun. It didn't kill him, but he was crippled for the rest of his life.

"Next, they started going after the boys who hauled the whiskey. They shot at them, ran them off the road, and they even set Mickey's house on fire.

"The law knew something was going on and they started to really crack down on whiskey making. This hurt us bad, as we couldn't keep a still running more than a month without it getting raided.

"I don't think it bothered that Cloud's Cove bunch, though. There was only one way in there and one way out. If you weren't kin you didn't get in!

"I was sitting in a shot house in West Huntsville when they shot me. It was Oct. 23, 1934. I had delivered some whiskey and had stopped to watch a dice game. When I walked out they were waiting for me.

"I knew exactly what was fixing to happen when I saw that car window roll down and I started to reach for my pistol. I never had a chance.

"Claude Murphy had been shooting dice inside and when he heard the gun shots he ran outside. When he saw me laying there, he said, he thought I was dead.

"After I got shot, we pretty well shut the business down. We laid low and just decided to let bygones be bygones."

Three months later, two of the assailants were ambushed

near Meridianville and severely wounded.

When questioned about this, Brasemore's only comment was, "I reckon that's what you call bygones."

Things weren't the same after that. There had been too much trouble and the law was now watching every move the moonshiners made.

"I remember one time when Cousins, a boy we had driving for us, was stopped downtown. He was hauling a load of whiskey and was right in front of the movie theater when the law spotted him. Traffic was backed up for a red light and Cousins knew he couldn't get the car away, so he just jumped out and took off running.

"The police jumped out of their cars and started chasing him on foot. Mickey was standing on the sidewalk and when he saw what was going on, he jumped in Cousins' car and when the light changed, took off.

"It didn't take the police long to catch Cousins, but when they got back they discovered the evidence was gone! They roughed him up a bit, but finally had to let him go.

"Was the law honest back then? Let me ask you a question. How many policemen did you know that never took a drink? All of them knew what was going on, but you got to remember—back then, most everyone was kin to one another. We never worried too much about the city or county police unless there was an election coming up, and even then they tried not to bother us too much. They never came right out and asked you for money, but you knew you had to give. I remember one election back in the late 30s when the judge was making speeches. He'd be up there talking about getting rid of the bootleggers and I would be outside passing out free drinks to everyone who would vote for him. One time the judge's car broke down up around New Market, so he hitched a ride with us. All day long, we drove him around while he was spitting hell and brimstone about whiskey and the whole time he was sipping the white whiskey that we were giving him. When we got back to town that night, he was so drunk his wife made him sleep on the front porch."

By the time the Second War came around, it had become difficult for an independent whiskey operator to make any money. There were too many "big" family names in the business.

A hardware store owner downtown manufactured various size stills in the basement. For an extra twenty-five dollars a nearby furniture store would deliver the distillery to its intended site. When sugar became rationed during the war, a downtown grocery wholesale house sold sugar under the counter. Often, when they would receive a large shipment, the wholesaler would sell it off to moonshiners at a private auction to the highest bidder. One prominent family in Huntsville even financed moonshine operations—at a high interest rate, of course.

Many successful businesses in Huntsville today were founded with the profits of the whiskey business.

"They didn't have sense enough to come in out of the rain back when their grand-daddies was making whiskey, now they got fine houses and put on airs like they are blue-bloods or something!

"Now look at this," he said, pointing to a recent society page from *The Huntsville Times*. "That girl used to sleep on the back seat of a Ford coupe, sucking a sugar tit while her daddy delivered whiskey for me."

Chapter 59

Feeding the Kids

The Great Depression was devastating for Huntsville and Madison County. Times were hard and jobs were scarce. Many people, with no other way to support their families, began manufacturing illicit whiskey.

Sheriff Frank Riddick had received several tips about a moonshiner by the name of Tyler Moore making whiskey out on Hurricane Creek. When he went to check it out, sure enough, there was Moore fixing to run off another batch.

Mr. Riddick knew that Moore had a large family and would be in dire financial straits without the money from that whiskey, but he had no choice but to make the arrest.

Tyler appeared in court and was sentenced to six months. Sheriff Riddick, feeling sorry for Moore's children began stopping by their home every week or so to carry them groceries and to loan them money.

Six months went by and Tyler was released. Unfortunately, he went back to his old livelihood and was promptly arrested and sentenced again, this time for another six months.

Again, Sheriff Riddick provided food and clothing for the children while their father was in jail.

Another six months go by and Moore is released. Less than a month later, the sheriff received another tip and found Tyler back at his still working on another batch.

The following week, Moore appeared in court and was again found guilty. The judge was about to announce the sentence when Sheriff Riddick spoke up and said, "Your Honor, could you make it thirty days this time? I don't think I can afford all those kids for another six months."

Chapter 60

The Russel Erskine Hotel

More than nostalgia, the Russel Erskine Hotel still stands as a monument to a bygone era, a time when Huntsville was young and growing. Now that there are other and newer monuments and skyscrapers, the Russel Erskine Hotel has taken a lesser, but still significant, role.

Albert Russel Erskine was the onetime president of the Studebaker Corporation. Although he did not have an important financial interest in the hotel, it was named for this local person of national prominence.

According to local folklore, the hotel ran into financial trouble before it was ever completed. In an attempt to raise more money, the owners came up with a plan to name it after Erskine, a local hometown boy made good, hoping to interest him in investing in the venture. When the hotel was dedicated, Erskine came to Huntsville, listened to the speeches honoring him, ate the free food, drank the free liquor, stayed in the free suite, and then went back to Detroit without spending any money!

As each city has its prominent hotel, the Russel Erskine was, "the place to go" in Huntsville, Alabama. Officially opened on January 3, 1930, in the midst of the Great Depression at a cost of 1.5 million dollars, it was and still is a splendid building—12 stories high and 132 rooms. It became one of Huntsville's leading attractions and immediately became a popular spot for conventions and travelers. Besides the convenience and availability of a large hotel in Huntsville, visitors noted the "completeness" and "exquisiteness" of the furnishings in 1930. It was also noted that such modem conveniences of the day as an electric fan and an RCA radio were in each room. One satisfied guest, Dr. George Alden of Massachusetts, wrote the hotel saying that the Russel Erskine was the best appointed and gave the best service of any hotel during his trip. The Russel Erskine became the shining jewel of Huntsville.

It was Huntsville's best advertisement and many balls and gatherings were held in its splendid ballroom and banquet rooms.

In the decade of the 1940s, the Russel Erskine grew and prospered with the development of the Army's newly founded chemical warfare arsenal. Rooms during the war years were easily filled and the guests were more than adequately served by a staff of over 100 persons. High ceilings, chandeliers, an inviting comfortable lobby with scurrying bellmen, entertainment, fine dining on tables with white linen tablecloths, and a barber shop on the premises seem uncommon to the average traveler today, but the Russel Erskine was the premier hotel in North Alabama. It was before the widespread use of motels, "no frills," and budget accommodations.

After the War, as the Nation's economy sputtered, the Russel Erskine was merely changing gears. In 1949, with the advent of the Rocket Center, the hotel again had no problem filling rooms. The hotel continued its success throughout the 1950s, and in 1955 the Russel Erskine commemorated its 25th anniversary with a week-long celebration. From 1937 until its closing, the hotel turned a profit each year.

But as motels began to be built on the perimeter of the city, the hotel not only had to deal with competition, but also a change of taste and choice of potential guests. In the 1960s, the movement of commercial activity away from downtown areas in many American cities hastened the demise of many hotels and businesses. The stately Russel Erskine Hotel, so proudly rooted on Clinton Avenue, could not move with the new development and economic opportunities outside its downtown site. Measures to revive the hotel were short-lived. In March of 1971, the Russel Erskine Hotel closed its doors to transient guests. It's only business thereafter was to cater to conventions, civic clubs, and special accommodations.

Many well-intentioned plans of a succession of owners to revive the hotel were unsuccessful. Consequently, the hotel was auctioned off to the First Alabama Bank in 1975 for $300,000, which included the furnishings. Interestingly, this was far less than the construction cost of $1,500,000 in 1929. If this was not indignity enough to the landmark hotel, in May 1979 its contents went on sale. For thirty days the hotel was opened to the public to buy whatever they wanted. The First Freewill Baptist Church bought the ballroom's main chandelier and the lobby's four metal chandeliers within the first half-hour of the sale. Visitors and buyers rummaged through the halls of the once-proud hotel, looking at price tags on the furnishings, and eventually removing the trappings of the hotel. Perhaps they bought for their own use, to resell, or to obtain a precious keepsake of the place that held for them a fond memory of a "Cotton Ball," an unforgettable evening for a debutante, or honeymoon. By any account, it was the wake of the hotel.

Ironically, in 1978, the Russel Erskine Hotel was considered as a county-state work-release center for the Department of Corrections. Reportedly, a proponent of the idea said that, "It looks like the building was just built for this purpose."

Finally, and happily on September 15, 1983, the Russel Erskine reopened its doors as a high-rise complex for the elderly and disabled. Renovated for $3.6 million by local business people, working with the Huntsville Preservation Authority, the memory, the brilliance, and the hotel building itself has been revived. Huntsville's premier landmark of the 30s and 40s remains, except now it serves to house its residents permanently—not as temporary guests. While the new tenants still share much of the same ambiance of this venerable building as the former occupants, still there is a distinction between a hotel and a high-rise apartment house. But two facts are indisputable: the new residents still have magnificent views from their windows, and residents of any time have lived in a part of Huntsville's history.

Editor's note: Since the writing of this article, the hotel was extensively renovated in 2006 into 69 modern, affordable apartments for the elderly.

By Chris Pruitt [CC BY-SA 3.0 (https://creativecommons.org/licenses/by-sa/3.0)], from Wikimedia Commons

Chapter 61

Get a Real Job

Baseball history in Huntsville, like much of our history, is full of irony and untold stories. Perhaps one of the best tales of baseball is one of a young man who grew up over in Georgia and made his way to Huntsville in pursuit of a career.

The young man was born near Royston, Georgia, in 1886. At a young age he discovered the sport of baseball and immediately it became the passion in his life. This was in the days when every city, town, and mill village had its own teams, and professional players were almost unheard of.

At the age of nineteen, the young man left home to pursue his new career. Walking and hitching rides on wagons, he made his way across the Southland, looking for the "Big Time," or so he thought. According to one report of the day, there were so many baseball teams that the scores were no longer listed in the newspaper.

The young man sought out every sandlot team in town trying out for a position but was repeatedly turned down. One team offered him a position as an unpaid player, but he had to furnish his own uniform and glove. The young man had a glove but did not have the money to buy the uniform.

The manager of a local team, a mill village team, listened to the young man and then burst out laughing. "Son, you better go on back home and get a real job. If you think you can make a living playing baseball, why, you're crazier than you look!"

Probably a large part of it had to do with the exorbitant salary he was asking—$65 a month.

Disappointed, he left Huntsville after only a few days and eventually ended up in Detroit where he landed a job with a local baseball team.

This team went on to become one of the best-known teams in baseball history and the young man, Ty Cobb, became a legend in his own time.

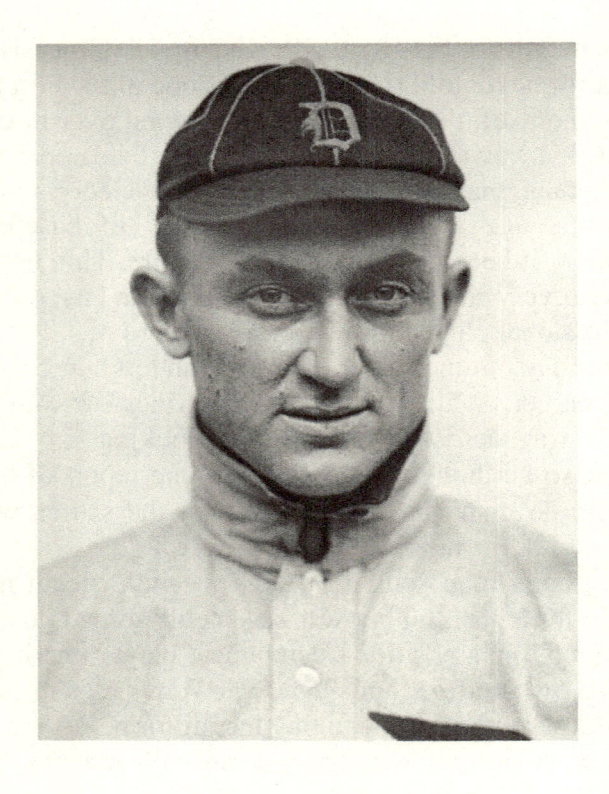

This work is in the public domain in the United States because it was published (or registered with the U.S. Copyright Office) before January 1, 1923.

Chapter 62

Army Birdmen Lose Their Way

Heavy storms on the night of March 15, 1938, almost caused a major tragedy at Huntsville's new airport.

The airport, located on Whitesburg Drive, was in reality nothing more than a meadow with a wind sock and a small office. With no lighting, it was woefully inadequate to meet any type of a night time emergency.

The first sign of impending danger came as Huntsville's citizens began to hear the drone of airplanes circling overhead, searching for a place to land. With no lights, any attempt at landing would result in a catastrophe.

The group of planes, flying a training mission, had been caught by a pulverizing rainstorm and were miles off their course, when they were drawn to Huntsville by a huge electric arrow atop the Russel Erskine Hotel, and the lights of the city. The roar of their planes brought alarm from the citizenry.

At least one family thought a tornado was coming, and took refuge in the basement of their home, staying there until a radio announcers voice informed them otherwise.

Quick thinking by the two state highway patrolmen stationed here played a major part in the safe landing.

Patrolmen S.T. Barrett and Franklin Moore heard the roar of motors, and, looking aloft, saw the cloud-laden sky filled with the circling planes.

Hastening to the local radio station, they had an appeal

broadcast for citizens to drive swiftly to the unlighted landing field and turn their automobile lights onto the broad open expanse, which was little more than a pasture.

Hundreds of automobiles, loaded with passengers, dashed to the field that night to help break the darkness, and to aid the fliers in their precarious attempts to land.

The Army birdmen, one by one, commenced to land while breathless citizens looked on. The first plane taxied back up the field late that evening.

Finally, after two very tense hours, the last plane landed. It was this pilot's escape that provided the biggest suspense of the entire event. Just before touching earth, the ship was caught by a strong gust of wind. It whirled completely about, but the pilot kept his mind alert and settled to safety. He dropped a flare before circling to come in.

"The boys did something proud," said their commander, Captain D.M. Allison. "But it certainly was a great relief to see the last ship land and start back up the field—right side up.

Immediately after the planes had landed, Capt. Allison was surrounded by Huntsvillians offering assistance.

The Army fliers spent the night at the Russel Erskine Hotel having experienced what could have been a tragic landing, but for Huntsville's speedy answer to a distress situation. Throughout the dark hours, multitudes of spectators visited the field. Still more suspense came during a heavy rain storm, accompanied by thunder, lightning, and gale-force wind. Again, quick thinking by concerned citizens saved the day when the winds threatened to wreck the fragile aircraft.

Capt. Allison was liberal in his praise of the cooperation given the birdmen by Huntsvillians.

"On behalf of myself and my men, I want to express our heartfelt appreciation for the quick response and the splendid cooperation we have received all the way through."

The aviators, already behind schedule, were forced to depart Huntsville early the following morning, amidst the well wishes of an admiring population.

In 1972, one of the pilots returned to Huntsville on a visit to the Space and Rocket Museum. While here, he toured the site of the old airport and reminisced about the arrow on top of the Russel Erskine Hotel that had guided him to safety.

"Thank God for radios and Tin Lizzies," he was quoted as saying. "They saved a lot of lives that night."

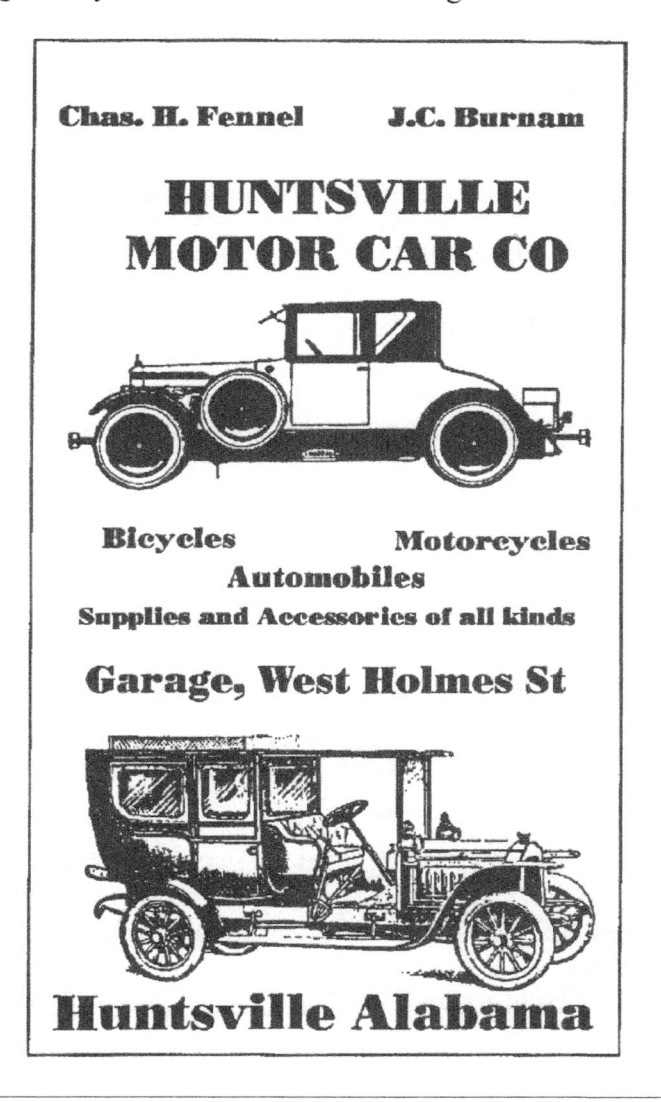

Chas. H. Fennel   J.C. Burnam

HUNTSVILLE MOTOR CAR CO

Bicycles   Motorcycles
Automobiles
Supplies and Accessories of all kinds

Garage, West Holmes St

Huntsville Alabama

Chapter 63

The Courthouse

When Huntsville's early settlers first started arriving, they discovered a large mound of stones directly above the Big Spring. This mound of stones was infested with rattlesnakes and was considered worthless.

In 1809, the Mississippi territorial government decreed that Madison County was to have a system of circuit and county courts and that the appropriate buildings be erected. This mound of stones, known as the public square, was deeded to the local government and in 1811 the first courthouse was built. The first floor was used as offices and courtrooms. The basement was also completed and was open on the north side. The first city market was located in the basement. A small wooden jail and pillory was constructed on the northeast corner of the public square.

The incomplete courthouse became the nucleus for civic, religious, and commercial activity. In 1817, arrangements were made to complete the building of the first courthouse. Arrangements were also made for a more substantial jail and pillory to be built on the east side of the square.

During the 1820s and the prosperous 1830s, Huntsville and Madison County continued to grow. By 1835, it was evident that a new courthouse was needed. Plans were drawn up and the firm of Mitchell and Wilson was hired to construct the new courthouse at an approximate cost of $31,000. The building was built in the popular Greek Temple style, being constructed of brick and stone and having two full stories in addition to a full basement. The old courthouse was sold at auction for $494. After it was removed, the ten-foot elevation it sat on was graded down and the rock was used to pave the surrounding square. As work progressed, changes and additions were made to the original plans, necessitating additional revenue. In 1840, the commissioners, in an attempt to raise more money for the building of the courthouse, ordered taxation on a variety of things including land, town property, slaves, free males, horses, watches, clocks, playing cards, and billiard tables.

The new courthouse was completed in 1840 and provisions were made for a new jail in 1846. The new jail was a brick structure located at the northeast comer of Washington and Clinton streets. During this time the square began to take on the appearance of a thriving business center. The yard in front of the courthouse became a place where cotton could be bought or sold, slaves could be auctioned off, and punishment would be administered by flogging or even sometimes hanging.

At the outbreak of the Civil War, when it was realized that the courthouse might be occupied by Yankee troops, most of the public records were removed and sent to Blount County for safekeeping. When indeed Huntsville was occupied by federal troops in 1862, the courthouse was taken over by military officials. A blanket of depression and hardship descended upon Huntsville during the occupation. From the courthouse, signed passes and loyalty oaths were extracted from any citizen entering or leaving town, buying supplies from the commissary, or when protection was needed by Union troops.

After the war, the grounds of the courthouse had deteriorated badly due to lack of money and upkeep. Many newspaper articles of that time spoke of the "overgrown courthouse yard."

One of the more interesting stories of the late 1800s concerns that of pet deer kept in the courthouse yard. No one today is sure where they came from, but for years they were a common sight to anyone having business downtown. According to one old-timer, the deer were taken from a bootlegger when he was arrested. The sheriff, not knowing what else to do with them, turned them loose in the courthouse yard. When the courthouse was torn down, they were moved to the McCormick estate on Meridian Street.

The original plans had called for that courthouse to be remodeled, but when work began it was found to be in much worse shape than anyone had expected and had to be torn down. The third courthouse was completed in 1914. Certain items were retained, such as the town clock, the massive "Doric" columns, the D.A.R. plaque listing the names of all the Revolutionary soldiers buried in Madison County, and the statue of the Confederate soldier, which was a memorial to the Confederate dead.

As Huntsville continued to grow, the third courthouse was renovated in 1940 to help accommodate this growth, but during the boom of the 1960s it was found to be woefully inadequate.

In 1964, $37,050 was awarded to the Bama Wrecking Company to demolish the old (third) courthouse which had stood for fifty years. The contents of the 1914 cornerstone were saved and the twenty massive stone columns were salvaged to be used elsewhere. The weather vane atop the old dome was transferred to the First Alabama Bank on the west side of the square.

The current courthouse was completed in 1967 at the approximate, cost $5,301,500. For the first time since 1846 the jail was located on the square.

There is one interesting footnote. One of the things that all of the courthouses have in common is that none of them were ever completed in time allowed by the contract, and they all cost more than originally thought.

Editor's note: A new $110 million-dollar federal courthouse will soon be built in Huntsville.

Chapter 64

The Futility of Man

In 1935, sixty-five percent of the cotton farmers in Alabama were sharecroppers. These people became the forgotten history of our land.

Under the hot, broiling sun, scorching everything its rays came in contact with, a wizened old man, with skin burnt like aged leather, labored tirelessly between the cotton rows. In the next row, his wife, wearing an odd apparel that had long ago lost any resemblance of a dress, knelt on lacerated knees and desperately plucked at the ripened bolls.

Sun up to sun down; 200 pounds at 1/2 cent per pound. Pay the man at the store for the sack of flour you bought yesterday. That takes all the money, but you can buy again on credit tomorrow. Go home and rub liniment on your tired aching muscles and try to forget they will be sore again tomorrow.

There is no other choice. This is your only way to survive in the bleak existence that nature has so cruelly bestowed upon you.

There was no hope of escaping the vicious cycle of tenant farming. Bound by debts to the land owner and untrained for other types of work, all they could expect was a pair of cheap shoes for the children to wear to school, or maybe a few store-bought groceries to supplement their standard diet of beans, fatback, and corn bread.

In another few weeks the rains would begin, and following that would come the cold, frigid blast of winter, spreading its gloom on the now exhausted fields. Young boys and old men would pace the floor like caged animals, pausing every so often to stare out the windows of the broken-down hovels they called home, and curse the fate that made them slaves to unseen cotton moguls a thousand miles away.

Keep the fire going, ration what meager food there is, and wait for the frozen ground to thaw. Walk down to the store. Maybe they will let you add some tobacco and a bag of flour to the long overdue bill. Stop and talk to Lem Wilbanks over on the next farm. His daughter is expecting any day and her husband is up north, in Chicago, trying to find a job. Talk and kill time and wait. Wait for the warm showers of spring to thaw the frozen earth and bind you to another year of servitude. "Maybe next year," they would say, year after year.

"Maybe next year will be better."

Spring jumps out suddenly across the barren land. The sopping red clay is now dry to the touch, waiting to embrace the seeds of a brand-new cotton crop. It will be a new beginning, the start of new dreams. Tonight you will sleep the slumber of a conquering warrior, for tomorrow you will prove your manhood.

You stand and look at the fields through the early morning twilight, daring and challenging the gods up above to anoint you; let you pay off your debts and maybe have enough left to buy your wife a new dress.

But as you pick up the hoe and begin trudging silently toward the dismal fields, a truth begins gnawing at you, deep inside. And no matter how hard you try to suppress the thought, it keeps coming back and coming back, until it envelopes you in its overwhelming reality. And then, with your body shaking in convulsions, you hold your head in your hands and cry like a new-born baby.

This year won't be any better and there won't be a new dress.

Cotton will still be King ... But not for the people working in the fields.

Years later, when the man talked about not being able to buy his wife a new dress, his eyes began blinking, and in an effort to hide the tears, he pulled out an old, worn handkerchief and loudly pretended to blow his nose. After regaining his composure, he refused to talk anymore about sharecropping.

Chapter 65

King of the Snuffdippers' Ball

Stories have been written about most of the historic places in Huntsville, but one you will never see in the history books is a place that carved its own niche in this city's history for over a quarter of a century. It was a place that a lot of people will never forget—and some people would like to forget. During this time Monte Sano Crowder reigned supreme, as King of the Snuffdippers' Ball.

Monte Sano Crowder was born on the mountain that he was named for in 1914. When Monte was only six years old his mother died, leaving his father with a whole house full of kids, with very little money. Monte's father was a natural musician and often, when times were especially hard, would wrap his Sears and Roebuck fiddle in an old flour sack and "take off fiddling for a week or two, in order to keep food on the table."

Monte began fiddling when he was about ten years old. His dad kept his fiddle lying on the bed and while he was fixing supper, Monte would slip into the bedroom and saw very quietly on the fiddle. His dad came in one day and told him to "go ahead and play it, only don't break anything." From that day on, Monte was a fiddle player.

Like his father, Monte and his brothers were all-natural born musicians. In 1928, Monte and his brothers began playing together as the Crowder Brothers. The oldest brother, A.R., was the manager of the band. A.R Crowder later moved to Illinois where he became known as the top fiddle player in the state.

Monte recalls that back in those days people would plan barn dances sometimes a year in advance. There would be cold drinks and ice cream and the street would be roped off with sawdust spread down for people to dance on. Sometimes the dancing would go on till the wee hours of the morning. The band tried to charge $15.00 a night for the entire group, three or four dollars apiece was pretty good money in those days. "Times were gettin' kind of lean back then and I was getting tired of chopping cotton, so one day I tell Leon, my brother, I say, let's go to Texas or someplace where we can make music and make a little money, too. Leon, he looked at me and laughed and said, 'we can't play that good!' Well, by Golly, we can at least try, I told him. The next day we took off for Texas.

"We were hitchhiking and didn't have no money so we carried our cotton sacks with us. We figured that if we didn't make no money-making music, we could still pay our way by picking cotton. It's a good thing we had them sacks, 'cause when we got to Texas, they had mosquitoes as big as birds and we had to crawl into those sacks to sleep, otherwise they would have eat us alive.

"Well, we got to Texas and we started making music on the sidewalks. We would stand there and play all the tunes that we knew and if we were lucky someone would put a little spare change in the hat, and then we could eat again. We had been doing this for a couple of days when this guy with a medicine show hires us to play for his show. We would make music, people would gather around, and then this medicine man would sell his goods. We spent that whole summer in Dallas making music. That's when we got to thinking that we were genuine musicians."

Monte returned to Alabama, convinced that he could make a living playing the fiddle. In 1937, Slim Daniel gave Monte his first job in Huntsville. Word of the young man and his fiddle playing spread throughout the Tennessee Valley, and it wasn't long before he was in great demand.

"Those were the days when a man put his heart and his soul into his music. I remember back in 1939, or maybe '40, when some guy by the name of Hank Williams called me and wanted me to make music with him. I played with him for a while, but he wanted to go to Louisiana and make some records. I told him that I didn't care nothing about being famous, I had everything I wanted right here in Huntsville."

Hank Williams went to Louisiana where he auditioned for the "Louisiana Hayride," the show that was to propel him into worldwide fame within a few years.

In 1941, a man appeared at Monte's door and asked him to take a job playing for a square dance. The man told Monte that they weren't making much money and couldn't afford to pay anything except a percentage of the gate. The square dance was commonly known as the "Snuffdippers' Ball" and Monte was to play there for the next thirty-two years.

The Snuffdippers' Ball was located upstairs at the old Temple Theater, in a room normally used for union meetings, on Jefferson Street. The lot on which it stood is now a parking lot for the Heritage Club. Walking down the street years ago, the only evidence you would see of the ball was a narrow doorway and a long, steep set of stairs. No signs, no neon lights. You had to know what you were looking for in order to find it.

"You had to climb the steps, pay a fifty cents admission, and then you'd be in this big room. The room itself wasn't much to look at, it was just a big room with a few chairs on the side, had a place to sell potato chips and soft drinks, and yes, back in the old days it even had spittoons for people that dipped snuff or chewed tobacco.

"But it wasn't the room that made the ball, it was the people. Use to, most everyone lived out in the country and they had to work hard for a living, and Saturday night was the only night they had to have a little fun and let off a little steam. There would be people dressed in their Sunday best, their hair slicked down, and a Sunday-go-to-meeting shine on their shoes. And over there, against that wall, would be the boys that picked cotton all week, still dressed in their overalls. Grandpa would be back in a corner holding court with all the other men while the missus would be sitting there clapping her hands to the music. There'd be so many people packed in that smoky room that it was a wonder that the old wooden floor didn't just cave in with all that stompin' and dancing going on.

"Lord, if that old building was still there, and if those walls could talk, there would be a thousand ghosts in that room, and they would all be tapping their feet to the memories of all the music that was played there."

With the new fiddle player taking the lead, the Snuffdippers' Ball became an instant success, with throngs of people lining up in front of the door hours before it opened. Its success created a new entertainment district downtown. No alcohol was served on the premises of the Ball, so bars began to spring up around it to cater to the thirsty crowds. An old-timer claims that "you could always tell when Monte took a break. When the music stopped, the people would swarm out of the Ball, like bees on honey, headed for the bars, but when Monte picked that fiddle up again, the bars would empty out and the sidewalks that were crowded with noisy people a few minutes earlier would grow silent."

By this time the Snuffdippers' Ball had acquired such a reputation that it was posted "Off Limits" to military personnel as far away as Nashville, Tennessee. Ironically, this was one of the few places of entertainment downtown that did not serve alcohol, but a lot of people had bottles of "cough medicine" in brown paper bags, sticking out of their back pockets.

Monte recalls, "There was never no trouble inside my place. It was all outside. I would tell those boys that if they wanted to fight they could go outside and do it. I wouldn't put up with that in the Ball. Why, there were folks that would drop their kids off with us while they took off to the bars!"

The fact that Monte was a professional wrestler, undoubtedly helped persuade some of the local rowdies to keep the peace. He first stepped into the ring in 1937 and over the next 15 years would wrestle as a professional in over 200 matches, under the name of "The Breakdown Wrestler." Asked if he was any good, Monte replied, "I didn't win very much, but I made me a little money."

Earl Frazier, a retired Madison County deputy sheriff, recalls working Jefferson Street in front of the Ball every Saturday night. "We never had no trouble in the Ball itself, but whenever the band took a break we got ready. A lot of those boys would go outside and try their best to see how fast they could get drunk. Most Saturday nights, we would arrest forty, fifty or maybe sometimes even sixty people on the sidewalks in front of the Snuffdippers' Ball. It wasn't really as bad as it sounds, most of them were the same people every week. The sheriff's department had regular customers back then.

"One night, me and Bulldog Daniels was working the sidewalks in front of the Ball. We had already arrested one drunk and had him in the car and we were putting the handcuffs on another one, when a third drunk staggered by. When I saw the third one, knowing that we didn't have any more room in the car, I reached over and tapped him on the shoulder and told him that he was under arrest. Just walk on down to the jail, I told him. We'll be down there directly to take care of you.

"Sure enough, in about 15 minutes, when we got to the jail to drop off another load of prisoners, there the guy was, sitting on the curb waiting for us to put him in jail. Something like that would never happen today."

Life was treating Monte pretty good in those days. Monte recalls, "I was married and had a son. I was making a little money and only had to work one night a week. Somewhere around 1947 or 1948 some guys come to me and asked me if I wanted to do a radio show. It was WHBS and was down there where we pay our utilities at now. So I asked these guys, what was in it for me?"

They told Monte, "We are going to sell twelve sponsors at $3 apiece, and you'll get $12 and we'll get $24."

"That didn't sound like too bad a deal to me so I became a radio announcer. I'm making twelve bucks an hour for sitting there talking just like I been doing all my life for nothing. I had this show called 'Crowder's Corn Crib' and I talked and played music. Only thing I didn't like was doing the weather. Most of the time the weather forecast back then was wrong, so they would give me this sheet of paper with the weather on it and I would go on the air and say, 'I don't believe a word of it, but this sheet of paper says that the weather is gonna be.' Only thing was that this job was interfering with my fishing. Got to where every time they wanted me at the station, the fish would be biting. Well, anyway, they call me in the office one day and tell me that I have to choose between fishing and doing radio. That was a dumb thing for them to do, 'cause I had my fishing rod in the car all ready to go."

In 1972, progress caught up with the Snuffdippers' Ball. Nightclubs began selling drinks over the bar, a practice not allowed until the late sixties, and most had free entertainment. People who had been going to the Ball for years slowly began to drift away, and Monte was forced to close it down.

Monte Sano Crowder, the King of the Snuffdippers' Ball, became one of the most well-known fiddle players in the Southeast, recording numerous tapes and records, with his music being used in two movies produced here in Alabama.

The man who claims to be able to play six types of music on his fiddle says, "There still ain't no music like mountain music. Most of the young kids coming up today, they make a lot of noise, but they don't make much music. You got maybe one or two others that can still play good music like my Daddy taught me, but there ain't many of us left.

"When you get old, there ain't much to do except sit under a shade tree and drink Double Cola and remember. You try to remember all the things you've done and all the people you've met.

"And I've loved every minute of it."

POST OFFICE INFORMATION.

POST OFFICE EAST SIDE MADISON BETWEEN PUBLIC SQUARE AND GATES. WM. I. WINDHAM, POST MASTER.

Eastern Mail, by M. & C. R. R., arrives 8.42 p. m., departs 2.06 a. m., closes 6.30 p. m.

Western Mail, by M. & C. R. R., arrives 1.58 a. m., departs 9.02 p. m., closes 6.30 p. m.

Fayette Mail, arrives Mondays, Wednesdays and Fridays at 5 p. m., departs Tuesdays, Thursdays and Saturdays at 8 a. m.

Montevallo Mail, arrives Tuesdays, Thursdays and Saturdays at 10 p. m., departs same days at 5 a. m.

Athens Mail, by the way of Centre Hill, arrives Saturdays at 5 p. m., departs Wednesdays at 5 a. m.

Claysville Mail, arrives Thursdays at 8 p. m., departs Wednesdays at 5 a. m.

Office Hours.—Sundays from 7 to 9 a. m. The above will be strictly observed.

Chapter 66

The Last Soldier

"Hell, that's a great idea. Dress the old man up in his uniform and we can make him a grand marshal or something. We can play up the Old South, make the parade a success, and get all kinds of free publicity."

They picked him up in one of those fancy convertible cars. They told him all he had to do was sit back and wave at people. He wasn't much to look at. The old gray uniform was threadbare and soiled from years of neglect. The shoulders it rested on were hunched with age. Watching the old man, you had to wonder what was going through his mind. The once proud soldier of a hundred battles, long ago, now sat perfectly still, silently watching the crowds.

The biggest crowd was around the reviewing stand. When the band saw the convertible approaching, they paused, and then began a loud stirring rendition of "Dixie." The old man removed the tattered campaign hat from his head and held it against his breast, while the crowd whooped and hollered.

The car started moving again as the last strains of the Confederate battle song died away. After a brief pause to catch their breath, the band broke into a slow, sad rendition of the old Union standard, the "Battle Hymn of the Republic."

"Stop," yelled the old man to the driver of the car. People grew silent, every eye was on the old man as he struggled to pull himself erect. Holding onto the back of the seat to give himself support, he raised his other hand to his forehead in salute, and held it there, trembling, as he turned to face the

American flag.

John A. Steger was born on December 7, 1845, the son of Kennon H. Steger. The elder Steger had moved from Virginia and settled in Ryland, a few miles north of Huntsville, where he became a prosperous farmer.

When Alabama seceded from the Union in 1861, John, like all young men everywhere, was anxious to enlist. He was attending school in Ryland at the time and his father reminded him that 15 was too young to go off and be a soldier. The war became a reality early the next year when General Mitchel and his hated Yankee troops invaded Madison County, burning, looting, and terrorizing at will.

These were dangerous times. The Yankees automatically suspected any young man as being a rebel, while the Confederates assumed any young southern man not in uniform was a deserter, or even worse, a traitor.

On May 24, 1863, John Steger was sworn in as a private in the Confederate States of America army. He had heard of Confederate forces camped at Brownsboro, and after receiving permission from his father, quickly made his way to join them. The group he joined was Company G of Colonel William A. Johnson's 4th Cavalry Regiment, which was then passing through Madison County after a raid into Tennessee. Johnson's regiment served in the brigade of General Philip Dale Roddy, the famous "Defender of North Alabama."

Steger's army life was filled with adventure, and the teenage soldier quickly rose through the ranks to sergeant. He served mainly in North Alabama and Mississippi, though he also saw combat in Tennessee and Georgia. His closest call came on June 10, 1864, at the battle of Brice's Crossroads, Mississippi. Roddy's men had ridden all day in the hot sun to reach the battlefield, but General Forrest ordered them into action almost immediately. When the cavalry dismounted, the soldiers counted off and every fourth man was assigned as a horse holder. Steger was fortunate enough to be so designated. However, he traded places with another and charged with his comrades. As the Alabamians were driving back the Yankees, a bullet struck Steger's cartridge box and cut the strap holding it to his side. A fraction of an inch closer and it would have seriously injured him.

Another of Steger's encounters took place quite close to home. In the fall of 1863, Roddy's horsemen had been sent to North Georgia. When they returned to Alabama, they found the Yankees in force at New Market. Steger and several others were sent to scout. Unfortunately, they were cut off by the enemy for several days. Steger suggested the men head for his father's house near Ryland. They reached the house late in the afternoon. Steger was about to approach the house when he was stopped by one of the family's servants. The old black woman warned him that four Yankees were already there. Steger and his companions waited until early morning, then they surprised the sleeping Yankees and captured them, without firing a shot.

After General Lee surrendered at Appomattox, word was slow to reach the scattered remnants of the Confederate army still struggling in North Alabama. It was more than a month later, May 17, 1865, when General Roddy finally surrendered at Pond Springs (now Wheeler, Alabama).

For John Steger, like hundreds of thousands of other men, there was nothing else left to do except begin the long walk back home. Returning to Huntsville, he found a land that was completely devastated, with people starving and no way to earn a living.

Luckily, parts of his father's farm was still intact and he was able to return to farming. On January 19, 1870, he married Mary Simpson and with both of them working in the fields, was able to rebuild the rest of the farm.

When the United States went to war with Spain in 1898, there were reservations in parts of the South about putting on a Yankee uniform and fighting a Yankee war. Most people were content to sit back and see what would happen, but when General Joe Wheeler and General Fitzhugh Lee (late of the

Confederate army) joined the hostilities, the mood changed in a hurry. Young men everywhere joined in droves.

When John tried to enlist, he was told that he was too old. There were no openings for 53-year-old soldiers. Disappointed, he returned home and sent his two sons in his place. Around the turn of the century, Steger became active in veteran's affairs. He served several times as commander of the Egbert J. Jones Camp, United Confederate Veterans, in Huntsville. Later he was elected Commander of the Third Alabama Brigade, and was often called by his honorary title of General, which went with the position.

Too old to serve in another war, John was forced to fight the war sitting on a bench outside the old courthouse, swapping old wartime stories with his comrades.

Time began to pass by quickly. When automobiles became popular on Huntsville's muddy streets, John Steger was already too old to obtain a driver's license. The first war came and went with its bloody trench warfare and deadly machine gun nests. Every year would see fewer of John's comrades returning to share the bench and swap stories with him.

Prohibition was voted in, and then out. Our country was in the midst of the depression when a group of men went to visit John and give him the news.

A friend of John's had died and now he was the only surviving Confederate soldier in Madison County.

It became harder for people to get him to talk about his service in the Confederacy. When war with Japan was declared in 1941, John Steger raised an American flag in his front yard. Every day, morning and night, it was raised and lowered for the duration of the war.

At the age of 99, no longer able to take care of himself, he was forced to move in with his daughter in Birmingham. Shortly before his 100th birthday, he returned to Huntsville one last time, by airplane. Years before he had walked much of the same route, as a defeated soldier.

THE WAY IT WAS

On Saturday morning, February 28, 1948, John Alexander Steger died. While the rest of the world worried about the Iron Curtain and atomic bombs, a few people gathered at Shiloh Church in Ryland to pay their respects. Among the people gathered that day were veterans from the Second War, the First War, and the Spanish-American War. There were none from the Civil War.

John Steger was the last soldier.

This picture was apparently taken around 1927 during a Confederate Veterans Reunion in Huntsville. By this time most of the old soldiers had died and the few left were highly revered by a population who had begun to eagerly embrace "the lost cause." The last Confederate veteran from Madison County died in 1948.

Chapter 67

Huntsville Hospitality

It was a hot day in June 1941, when Colonel Charles E. Loucks and his assistant checked into the old Russel Erskine Hotel. In the past month they had spent time in Florence, Tuscaloosa, Kansas City, St. Louis, and Memphis. Anyone who has traveled much can imagine how tired they must have been.

After taking a shower and changing clothes, Colonel Loucks walked down to the hotel's restaurant. Deciding he wasn't very hungry, he ordered a cup of coffee, when, to his mortification, he discovered he had left his wallet in the room. When the waiter returned with the coffee, the Colonel explained his predicament, promising to return with the money.

"Aw, don't worry about it. Sit back down and drink your coffee."

Amazed, not used to Huntsville hospitality, the Colonel sat back to enjoy his coffee when the waiter reappeared with a slice of apple pie.

"This ought to go good with your coffee, sir."

The whole story might have ended with that free cup of coffee, if Colonel Loucks had not been so impressed by Huntsville that he went back to Washington and recommended the city to his superiors.

One month later the War Department announced that Huntsville had been selected as the site for a chemical weapons manufacturing plant, upon Colonel Loucks' recommendation.

THE WAY IT WAS

This plant would become Redstone Arsenal.

Of course, many other factors affected the choice, but for years afterwards, Colonel Loucks would tell the story about the free cup of coffee that so impressed him.

Redstone Arsenal building 7101.

Chapter 68

The Keller Automobile

It's difficult to imagine that, but if history had taken a different course, automobile manufacturing could have meant more to Huntsville than the space industry.

But that's exactly what might have happened, if the Keller automobile had achieved the success that it could have. The story began thousands of miles from Huntsville, in San Diego, California. As World War II was drawing to a close in 1945, many defense positions were being phased out. John Lefield recognized that, and decided he'd better get involved in something else before he was out of a job.

Together with S.A. Williams, and Studebaker executive George Keller, he developed a fiberglass compact car called the "Bobbi," in California.

Although still in the prototype stages, the "Bobbi" seemed to fill a niche in the auto market for smaller cars. It weighed only 800 pounds, very light even by today's standards. After some refinements and development, the men were ready to go to work on phase two—marketing the car. The advertising and promotions were handled by Williams, with considerable success. The media was interested, and published articles hawking the car's virtues and advantages. Williams also bought advertising space in newspapers and magazines to further push the wave of favorable response.

Potential investors displayed interest and the press continued to be helpful.

Things were going just fine until California officials dug

up some dirt in Williams' past that threatened the entire project. Apparently, he'd been involved in some questionable business dealings before, including a stock swindle and counterfeiting. Not exactly the kind of reputation needed to launch a business venture. The press turned the "Guns of Navaronne" on Williams personally, speculating that this venture was probably a scam and referred to his prison record as proof.

What the project needed was a significant geographical change. The operation was moved to Alabama when the Birmingham Chamber of Commerce contracted Keller to find civilian use for an empty aircraft manufacturing facility there. Investor Hubert Mitchell, of Hartselle, was impressed with the idea of the "Bobbi" and its potential. He joined the firm and bankrolled most of the early operation.

It didn't remain long in Birmingham, as Mitchell wanted it closer to home, and Redstone Arsenal was just the place. The year was 1947, and the Arsenal was also welcoming postwar industrial development. The old Betchler-McOne airplane plant was chosen as the site, and the Huntsville Chamber of Commerce was elated.

The name was changed to Keller Automobile Company. About 130 workers were employed and things geared up toward a promising future. Keller had been a respected and successful executive with Studebaker, so the name change was significant—and helpful for market recognition.

Plans and production forged ahead. Painstakingly, early models called the Keller Super Chief were assembled, mostly by hand, at the Redstone Plant.

The Super Chief, a subcompact station wagon, was really ahead of its time. The cabs of these cars were all wood. In addition to the station wagon, plans were in the works for convertibles with options such as front or rear-mounted engines. It seated five people and claimed 35 M.P.G., with engines manufactured by Hercules (known mainly for tractor engines).

Keller Automobile Company even had an engineering office in Detroit for the purpose of obtaining parts for the car while it was being developed and prototyped. The Hercules engines were contracted from the Detroit office, as well as other miscellaneous parts. (The Super Chief used Buick hubcaps, for example.)

The Super Chief was to have sold for about $900. The production line on Redstone Arsenal was slated to produce 16,000 cars the first year, then 72,000 the year after that. George Keller used his contacts in the automotive business well to propel the project along. The car appeared in some significant auto shows in New York and Detroit and was well received by the public. Financial backing was positive, too. Keller successfully sold $2.5 million of the company's $5 million stock offerings obtained franchise commitments totaling $450,000 from all around the country and was one day away from hundreds of millions of dollars of additional backing—when he died suddenly of a heart attack in October of 1949.

At that point, the wheels fell off, so to speak. The big financial investors choked, stalled, and backed out, convinced that the company couldn't successfully produce the automobile without Keller.

Mitchell couldn't find an individual to replace Keller in the 90 days granted in the stock option contract. The stock was removed from sale and the company had no choice but to dissolve operations and go out of business.

Only 25-30 cars were actually produced on Redstone Arsenal during the firm's brief life span, and the dream of thousands of "made-in-Huntsville" Kellers on America's roadways never materialized.

Chapter 69

Delivering the Mail

It may be hard for Huntsvillians to believe, but as German rocket scientists were preparing to move here to set up an arsenal that would change the world, our mail was still being delivered by horse and buggy!

A mail carrier for the Huntsville Post Office for over 30 years, Clarence Celia Powers refused to change to the automobile and delivered mail to his customers by horse and buggy until he retired in 1948.

Clarence was a familiar sight to all on his route. He knew all his mail recipients by name and would often carry candy to the young children along his route. The children especially liked to run alongside his buggy until he would get out of their neighborhoods. On several occasions he had stopped to help people in distress and was known to have a kind heart and a good sense of humor.

Clarence served several territories throughout Huntsville. His last route covered the area of Pulaski Pike and West Clinton Avenue. One of the few black men working for the post office at that time, Clarence was born in March of 1878 and was the youngest of five brothers. His father was a farmer and a Methodist minister, and Powers had always taken an interest in church work. When he wasn't delivering mail, he was usually found at the church. Powers' high school education was received at Central Alabama Academy, located on Franklin Street. Clarence became a mail carrier on June 1, 1917, after working for Chattanooga, Memphis, and other

Huntsville employers. He especially liked carrying the mail, he said, because he liked seeing the same people every day. The fact that ladies along his route often times would have pies and cakes waiting for him just provided an extra incentive. For all the eating he did, Clarence was a tall, slim man.

The last day that he served, January 27, 1948, was one of the most difficult he had ever experienced, due to the severe icy conditions of the Huntsville streets. His horse had gotten quite old by this time and found it very hard to maneuver the slick roads. There were very few days that Clarence was not able to deliver the mail to his customers. He had many friends, both black and white, among the people who knew him and respected him. Powers was recognized by the post office for all the years of dedication he had given by a dinner in his honor, and the gift of a beautiful pocket watch.

The new man who was to take over Clarence's route, when asked if he was going to use a horse and buggy, replied he was going to use a "gas burner, not a hay burner!"

Clarence Powers was 70 when he retired.

Upon his retirement, the horse and buggy were consigned to the county barn. Two months later, a group of people led by farmer Ben Lucas, bought the buggy and horse and presented it to the retired mail carrier in appreciation of his years of dedicated service. For several years thereafter, Clarence and his horse remained a familiar sight to Huntsvillians.

Chapter 70

Suicide

"A man is on top of the Russel Erskine Hotel and he's gonna jump!"

Within minutes all the citizens of downtown had heard the news. Eagerly, almost morbidly, they rushed to the scene of the impending tragedy. The street in front of the hotel became a mass of swirling humanity as crowds jostled for a better look. "Someone said he works at the Arsenal and he just got a letter from his wife saying she is leaving him."

This news, by some unidentified source, was quickly consumed and spread by the four winds to the crowds who were now grasping at every morsel of new information.

Suddenly the still night air was rent by the screeching sounds of police cars arriving on the scene. Emerging from their cars, the policemen began pushing the crowds back with night sticks, trying to establish some sense of order.

"Be careful. He's got a gun," yelled a voice from out of the darkness.

The crowd ran scurrying for cover and the policemen quickly ducked behind their automobiles for safety.

When a few minutes had passed with no shots being fired, the throng, now prompted by the latest developments, began surging forward. The crowd now numbered in the hundreds and was growing larger by the minute.

The police were frantically working to regain control, the sounds of a woman screaming emerged above the noise of the mob. The crowd had inadvertently pushed her into a storefront window, breaking the glass, and now she was running hysterically down the street with blood streaming down her arms. Before the police could reach her, another woman began screaming. This woman had been knocked down by the crowd jostling for a better look.

Sensing that something had to be done, and quickly, the brave officers of the Huntsville Police Department drew their pistols and resolutely began making their way to the front entrance of the hotel where the unseen assailant lay in wait. There was no hesitation in the purposeful stride of the policemen on that cold day in 1942. This was their town, and this was their job. Someone had to take charge and they were the ones.

Cautiously, with their guns drawn, they took the elevator to the top floor. The men were silent, probably thinking of their loved ones and the danger that lay ahead.

History does not record the name of the first policeman to exit onto the roof, ready to do battle with the fiend lurking in the shadows. Nor is there the name of the man who, after receiving the dear John letter, tried to commit suicide.

You see ... it never happened. There was no Dear John letter and there was no man on top of the hotel.

Some unknown person in that year of 1942 had started the rumor and within minutes downtown Huntsville had been caught up in a frenzied state of anticipation. Every rumor became fact and every fantasy became reality.

And with every passing year the story became even more exaggerated. To this day there are people who will point at a spot on the sidewalk in front of the old hotel and tell you that it is where the "Dear John" jumper ended his life.

Chapter 71

The Bon Air Restaurant

The old Bon Air Restaurant was noted for its down-home atmosphere and its delicious home-cooked meals. It became a favorite place to eat for all kinds of people. One day, Dr. Wernher von Braun and two other German scientists who worked for NASA were having lunch there when a couple sat down at the next table. They were obviously Yankee tourists, with their Bermuda shorts, cameras slung around their necks, and two handfuls of guidebooks.

The Yankee lady, upon hearing von Braun speak, leaned over as far as she could. After intently eavesdropping for a few minutes, she turned to her husband and said, "I just love these Southern accents."

Chapter 72

The Last Slave

The following interview with Tom Moore was conducted by Kenneth Marsh in 1948. Shortly afterwards, Tom Moore died at the age of 105. At that time, he was the last surviving person in Madison County to have been born into slavery.

"If my body had to suffer all the misery that my eyes have seen, I would have been dead a long time ago. I don't remember too good the things that happened yesterday, but the old things, the things that happened when I was young, I remember good.

"I was born on April 28,1843. Mr. Ben (Benjamin Tyson Moore, his master) wrote the date down in an old family Bible. My mama, she was bought in Mobile when she was a little girl and brought to Mr. Ben's place. Mama said they paid $700 for her. I never knew my daddy, don't even know what happened to him.

"Mr. Ben, he was a cotton man. The first thing I remember is pulling bolls. After all the cotton was picked, we'd go through the fields again and pull all the cotton bolls that had opened late. That winter, when it would get cold, we'd sit in front of a fire and pick the cotton out.

"I remember we had this boy on the place, his name was Buck, and he kept running off. The paddy-rollers caught him clear up next to Nashville one time. His mama did the cooking for the big house. When they caught this boy, they brought him back and tied him to a big tree out next to the cabins. When

Mr. Jim started whipping this boy, they had to lock his mama in the smoke-house, she was carrying on so much.

"Before then, sometimes if we went to the door of the kitchen, she would give us a bite of whatever she was cooking. After they whipped her boy and we saw the look in her eyes, we never asked for no food that she fixed for the white folks!

"When the war (Civil War) came along, all the men got ready to go off and fight. Mr. Ben, he sent me and my uncle to take care of his kin. It was just like we were in the army. We took care of the horses, cooked for them, and fixed their clothes and stuff. 'Course, we didn't have to put up with all that marching back and forth and yelling.

"After 'bout a year, the war heated up real good and the Captain sent us back to Alabama. He had this big, red horse that he had took from a Yankee soldier and we rode that horse all the way back to Alabama, Yankee saddle and all!

"We were working in the fields when we heard the war was over. Mr. Ben, he came out to where we were working and told us that he had orders to tell us all that we were free. He said that anyone that wanted to stay could, but everyone else had to be off the place by sundown. Most everyone, after Mr. Ben left, just threw down their hoes and started walking to town.

"They had this place in town where all the colored folks had to go to, to get registered. We got there, me and Sally, my wife, and they asked us what my name was.

'Tom,' I said.

'What's your last name.'

'Don't have none,' I said.

'Who was your master?" they asked me.

'Mr. Ben Moore.'

"So they wrote me down as Tom Moore and I been a Moore every since then!

"I took up with this Yankee soldier and started working for him. He was a good man and when he got out of the army he carried me home with him to Indiana. I lived up there for about two years working in a stable, but I was miserable the whole time. You wouldn't think a man could miss cotton fields, but I sure did. Finally, I got Mr. Foster to write a letter asking (the Moore family) if I could come back home.

"I didn't wait for no answer, me and the family just started walking toward Alabama. When we got here, Mr. Ben, he told me that we could stay in the old quarters, but he couldn't feed us. We'd have to take care of ourselves.

"It was too late in the year for anything but turnip greens. We lived most that whole winter on turnips and rabbits. Didn't have no gun, the Ku Kluxers wouldn't let us have none, we trapped the rabbits in boxes.

"Those were hard times and not just for the black folks. Every day you could see men and women and children, black and white, walking down the road with no place to go to. The war just tore this country up good.

"I seen a lot over the years, but times ain't really changed that much.

"People hate more now than what they used to. Trouble is, people ain't got nothing to be scared of no more. Everybody has to be scared of something, even if it is his wife or God or whatever.

"A man that ain't never been scared, he ain't lived much of a life."

Chapter 73

Vance Morris and the Alabama Playboys

People in Huntsville knew him as the gentle, philosophical grandfather who operated Vance Morris Motors, a garage out on Oakwood Avenue.

But travel a few miles north, to Nashville, walk through the Country Music Hall of Fame, talk to some of the older stars of the music industry and you will hear tales of a living legend.

They will tell you stories of a time, over a half a century ago, when Vance Morris and the Alabama Playboys thrilled audiences and dance crowds in giant dance parlors and ballrooms all across the eastern United States.

Others will laugh and remember stories about times when they dodged flying beer bottles while performing on stage. But regardless of who you talk to, they all remember. "I would never have gotten into music if it hadn't been for an old mule," recalled Vance Morris.

"We had this old plow mule on our Oklahoma farm and one day I was following along behind it and I got to studying it. It never looked ahead to see where it was going, nor did it look off to the side to see what it was missing. He just plowed ahead for 12 hours a day with nothing to look forward to.

"That's when I decided that I didn't want to go through life hooked to the wrong end of a mule."

His father was an avid lover of country music and was friends with the legendary country star Bob Wills. It was Wills who influenced Vance in his choice of a musical career.

Determined to be a musician, he bought a guitar for five dollars and spent hours trying to emulate Wills' style.

Unfortunately, the Great Depression and the dust bowl put Vance's budding career on hold.

"My father had been a prosperous man, but when the Depression hit, it just about wiped him out. A few years later the dust bowl came along and took what we had left. My mother had kin in Mississippi, so we moved there. If we were to be poor it may as well be around family."

A few years later he came to Huntsville to visit a friend. "I took a drink of spring water, bought a pair of shoes, and decided to stay," says the amiable guitarist.

Another inducement to staying here, according to a niece, had something to do with a Mississippi sheriff who was not very understanding of young people and their street-screeching hot rods.

The sheriff had attempted to put a halt to racing in the city limits by harassing everyone who owned a hot rod. Angered by the sheriff's high-handed actions, the spirited young men planned their revenge.

Creeping into town late one night, they attached a length of chain from the rear axle of the sheriff's car to a nearby tree, then raced their noisy hot rods past the jail. The sheriff, livid by this time, ran out of the jail to give chase. Unfortunately, his patrol car only went the length of the chain. The county got a large repair bill, the sheriff got a warrant and Vance got a sudden interest in Huntsville.

Vance grew up listening to a type of music which was unfamiliar to many Southerners. It was a combination of Dixieland jazz, black man's blues, and country sounds. After moving to Huntsville, he began experimenting with this new sound, which was called Texas swing.

"Our music lessons consisted of listening to the radio and trying to copy the same sounds," he recalled.

In 1943, Morris organized the "Alabama Playboys." With

13 members, it was one of the largest bands in this part of the country.

Among the members was young W.C. Williams, whom everyone called "Hank." Years later he had to change his moniker because a young upstart named Hiram Williams from south Alabama began using the same name and became famous.

"At first we just played at store openings and street dances," recalled Williams. "But then we started getting invitations to play out of town, and not from the sheriff, either." A local radio station featured the swing orchestra. It was during World War II and for a country accustomed to daily doses of depressing news, the fresh sound of the "Alabama Playboys" was just what the doctor ordered.

Offers came from all over the country asking the band to perform.

"We would pack ourselves into a couple of cars, like sardines in a can and drive like the dickens to Arkansas or wherever we were playing. Often, when we finished playing, we'd load up and drive back home the same night. Most of the boys had families and day jobs here in Huntsville."

Vance had also established himself as a pretty good race car driver. Enroute to dance gigs in faraway cities, band members said, he often slid the car around curves at 90 miles an hour, a practice which certain members of the band found upsetting. A few years later he would win the Tennessee State Championship for stock cars, driving a 1933 modified Ford with, as he described it, "a few goodies under the hood."

The "Alabama Playboys" continued to gain in popularity. Within a period of five or six years they had become the most popular swing band east of the Mississippi River.

Vance and his band traveled continuously, making personal appearances on radio stations all across the country and playing to overflowing crowds at every stop.

In 1948, the "Alabama Playboys" were offered a contract with the Saturday night Grand Old Opry.

"I had already opened up my garage by this time and we were still playing major Saturday night gigs all over the country. It didn't seem like a good thing to do at the time, to give everything up just to work on the Opry. Most of the boys felt the same way.

"Besides," Vance said as he grinned, "they only offered me $60 a week."

Hank Snow, during the same period, was paid only $46 a week as an Opry regular.

Versions of several of Vance's songs such as "Faded Love," "Crazy About the Boogie," and "Some of These Days" were well on their way to becoming classics.

With the band's popularity growing by leaps and bounds, record companies began to take interest. In 1952, the band signed a contract to cut a series of records for a Nashville recording company. Several of the songs became big hits nationally, as well as in Asia, Europe, and elsewhere.

Unfortunately for Morris, fame was all he got. The record companies, after discovering he had not copyrighted the songs, released them under another artist's name.

Disillusioned by Nashville and stardom, the "Alabama Playboys" returned to Huntsville, where Vance began spending more time in building up his automotive repair business. He quickly earned a reputation for building "custom" cars that were in great demand at the time.

"This was back in the whiskey running days," recalled one old-timer. "His cars looked just like any other car on the road, but there wasn't a police car around that could stay up with them. And if the police did catch them they couldn't find the whiskey! Vance had secret compartments built all over those cars. Why, he even had the headlights fixed where you could unscrew them and hide a case of whiskey in the fender behind each one of them."

Music was in his blood, though, and it wasn't long before the band was performing again. This time, instead of traveling, they chose to play in area night-spots.

Among these night spots, and probably the most infamous, was the White Castle, which was located at the intersection of Winchester Road and Meridian Street. It was illegal to sell alcohol in those days, but the management of the White Castle had made "certain arrangements" with the local authorities.

The White Castle was a rough establishment, but the owner, Laurel Hardin, had her own way of keeping order.

When a fight would break out, "Aunt Laurel" would wade into the fracas, pushing people right and left. Grabbing the offenders by their shirt collars, she would shove her .45 caliber pistol in their faces.

"Boys," she would say, "you can fight in here or you can go outside, but if you fight in here you better call yourselves an ambulance. 'Cause when I get done, you'll need one!"

W.C. "Hank" Williams remembered playing at the Castle during its heyday. "You could say it was good exercise. If they ever had a contest for dodging flying beer bottles we would have won easily. One night they had a fight and several beer bottles came flying on stage. I managed to get out of the way, but when I looked down I saw that one of the bottles had hit my bass and was sticking out by its neck!"

"We had a good time playing there," Morris said. "But we couldn't take any breaks. Every time a fight would start, Aunt Laurel would holler at us, 'Play, boys, play!'"

By the mid-1950s the band members started drifting their separate ways. Guitarist Malcome Buffaloe moved to Chicago where he continued to perform until recently. "Hank" Williams opened a small gas station that has today grown into a chain of Williams Oil Company service stations. Other members moved away and never returned.

In 1981, twelve recordings by Vance and the "Playboys" were placed into the Country Music Hall of Fame at Nashville. In 1986, the band was reunited in Chicago, where they played their last public performance to a standing ovation.

Chapter 74

The Man Who Would Be Sheriff

He was a tall, gangly man, the kind of man who always looked uncomfortable in new clothes. He drove a 1949 Ford and wore a pistol at his side.

He was Oliver McPeters, and in 1952, he was the "high Sheriff of Madison County."

Most folks knew Oliver McPeters as a sharecropper who lived out around New Hope in an old wood-frame house with no running water or electricity. Sharecropping was a hard life; you would work hard all year long and when the crops were done, if you were lucky, you might have enough money to live on during the winter. Unfortunately, most of the time, after the seeds and the fertilizer bills were paid and the owner of the land got his share, there wasn't anything left over. But still, for people like McPeters, it was the only way of life they had ever known.

His short political career began, as many others have, in a local barber shop. The barber shop was a popular place for the local prominents and the "good ol' boys" to congregate. Almost everything that wasn't worth talking about would become a topic of conversation there. On this day in particular, about the only thing they could find to talk about was the fact that Jimmy Record, down at the courthouse, was thinking about buying a new car. After exhausting that conversation, the crowd grew silent for a moment, until one person, searching for a new topic, mentioned the upcoming sheriff's election. Immediately, speculation began as to who would be running and who would be the winner. Again, the conversation died down after a few moments. Oliver McPeters had been lounging against the front door frame and when he said that he was of a good mind to run for sheriff himself, all eyes were upon him. "Yep," said McPeters. "If I had the money, I believe I'd run for the sheriff's office myself."

There was dead silence in the barber shop. Of all the men in Madison County, you could not have picked a more unlikely candidate. The man sitting in the barber chair, a local prominent businessman (who shall remain nameless for obvious reasons), stood up and asked McPeters if he was serious. "McPeters," he said while reaching for his wallet, "if you want to run for sheriff, I'll pay the $10 qualifying fee." No one really thought McPeters was serious, but he was. He took the money, turned around, and walked out of the barber shop. As soon as he left, gales of laughter broke out from the "good ol' boys." This had to be, declared the men, "the best joke of the year."

No one had any idea how serious McPeters was. After leaving the barber shop, he quickly walked over to the old Elks building, where a kindly clerk showed him how to file the necessary papers. By the time the sun went down in Huntsville that evening, everybody in town knew that "sharecropper McPeters" was running for sheriff.

Oliver McPeters hit the campaign trail running. It was said later that he called on every home in Madison County, asking for folks to vote for him. He was a man of little education and was known for speaking his mind, so it was not surprising that he ran a colorful campaign. In Hazel Green, when asked about recent allegations of corruption in the sheriff's department, he replied that if folks would elect him, he would promise not to hire anyone who has ever worn a badge or a gun.

While speaking in Gurley, he promised the people "you men folks won't have to worry anymore; if your women folks get locked up in my jail, I promise you they ain't gonna get knocked up." He was speaking in reference to an alleged rape that had taken place in the jail the previous year.

Most old-timers in Huntsville today contend that people voted for him solely as a protest vote. People were turned off by the other candidates. But, whatever the reason, on election day when the votes were counted, Oliver McPeters was the new Sheriff of Madison County.

One of his first acts was to call on every bootlegger in the county and tell them they had to close up. Everybody who knows anything about our county's history will tell you that bootleggers were a part of our heritage, and to close down every one of them ... well, that was almost unpatriotic.

Needless to say, he made a lot of enemies, immediately.

Next, he went after the juke joints. Everybody knows that "good ol' boys" had to have a place to blow off steam, and if you take that away from them, they're going to get mighty upset. Many of these boys had been going to the same joints for years, and it was really hard for them to break the habit. One local fellow tells the story about the time Sheriff McPeters raided the White Castle, a honky-tonk out on Meridian Street, and closed it down. Several weeks later, J. Otis King, a local Baptist preacher, made arrangements with the owners to use the building for a revival. On the night of the revival, they turned on all the neon lights out front, and had all the lost sinners sitting around the tables with Preacher King up on the dance floor doing his preaching. Unfortunately, a lot of people did not know what was going on. Every few minutes the services would be interrupted because people driving down Meridian would see the bright neon lights, stop their cars, go in and line up at the bar, and loudly demand a "setup."

Within days of being elected, the "High Sheriff" of Madison County was striking terror into the hearts of would be lawbreakers. He arrested the commanding officer of Redstone Arsenal for driving six miles over the speed limit. A local prominent automobile dealer was arrested for jay walking—on a rural county road. A well-respected, church-going lady found the sheriff knocking at her door after she had inadvertently given the sheriff's office a bad check. Her account was overdrawn by 16 cents.

The boys down at the barber shop realized, by now, that their joke had backfired. Calling a meeting with the sheriff, they tried to explain that he needed someone with experience to guide him, because his actions were causing a lot of ill feelings in the community.

Some people claimed that it came from walking behind a stubborn mule while sharecropping, but for whatever reason, he was one stubborn man. Looking at the assembled group, he told them that he was the "High Sheriff of Madison County" and he reckoned that he would just keep on enforcing the laws the way that he saw fit.

Next on his list were those vile dens of inequity, the private clubs. Everyone knew that these clubs were bending the law, and McPeters decided it was time to do something about them. Calling his trusty deputies together, he set out to enforce the law.

Before the night was over he had raided the Elks Club, the Eagles Club, the black V.F.W, the American Legion, the New Hope chapter of the American Legion, the Moose Lodge, the Disabled American Veterans Home on East Holmes, and last but not least, the Huntsville Country Club. Almost half the prominent people in Huntsville were arrested, all on the same night.

There was no joy for the "good ol' boys" down at the barber shop. They all agreed that something had to be done. The "joke" they had elected had turned into a "law-enforcing monster."

Several weeks later, allegations begin to spread that Sheriff McPeters was taking payoffs to allow certain juke joints to operate. Complaints reached the governor's office, and within weeks W.L. Allen, a veteran criminal investigator working for the state, arrived in Huntsville to investigate the charges. Allen had made his reputation while investigating the Ku Klux Klan in Jefferson County and was known to be a thorough investigator.

Normally in an investigation, it is difficult to find people willing to talk, but in this case it was different. Allen had people lined up at his door, all with complaints. Of course, a lot of these folks had newly acquired jail records.

On November 13, 1952, eleven months after taking office, the state supreme court voted to remove Oliver McPeters from office. The most damning evidence against him was a canceled check that he was supposed to have received as a bribe. McPeters claimed the check was given to him as a loan. The check, supposedly, came from a local private club and was in the hands of the investigators within hours after McPeters cashed it.

After being impeached and removed from office by the state supreme court, McPeters took the train back home from Montgomery, a broken man. Witnesses say that when McPeters got off the train, he was immediately grabbed and thrown into the back seat of a car by three unidentified men. Hours later his wife and children were awakened by the sound of a car door slamming shut. Rushing outside, they found the bruised, bloody form of the ex-sheriff lying face down on the side of the road.

Oliver McPeters, the man who would be "High Sheriff of Madison County" was out of office.

After a slow, painful recovery, McPeters became a foreman for a construction company, pouring concrete. He never pressed charges against the men who brutally assaulted him that night.

No one was ever prosecuted for the alleged bribery.

Chapter 75

The Birth of Huntsville

Many people will argue that Huntsville had its beginning when John Hunt founded our fair city way back in 1805, while others will claim the cotton mills were the actual beginning. But for the people that lived and grew up here, the start of prosperity began with the launching of our first space satellite.

While the rest of the nation's economy was booming, progress had bypassed Madison County. There were few jobs, and even fewer opportunities. Outhouses were still common in many homes and a large percentage of people still cooked on wood-burning stoves. The county schools closed for two weeks in the fall so the children could help pick cotton. Without their labor, it would have been impossible for many small "cotton farmers" to survive.

In 1950, the government had started transferring the German rocket scientists to Redstone Arsenal. A few companies started opening up offices in Huntsville to take advantage of the government contracts that were being awarded for research and development. While this created new jobs, the majority went to people who had been transferred here.

A few natives were lucky enough to secure "good paying" jobs on the Arsenal. J. B. Tucker, and his wife Margaret felt like they had struck gold when he was hired. On Hurricane Creek, their home, they were considered "well-off," especially when they bought a new car and began building a new home. Mr. Tucker had been hired at 80 cents an hour.

Huntsville continued its slow growth up until the late fifties when the Soviet Union, under Nikita Khrushchev's leadership, launched the first satellite into space. World attention was focused on Huntsville, Alabama, as the rest of the world held their breath to see what we would do. The sleepy cotton town would never be the same.

On the night of January 31, 1959, a Jupiter-C rocket was launched at Cape Canaveral carrying an 18-pound satellite. The citizens of Huntsville and Madison County anxiously stood by their radios as word was relayed from Mission Control. Finally, late at night, the word was received. "The satellite is up."

Instant bedlam broke out downtown. Folks from all over the county began congregating on the square, with more people arriving every second. Car horns were blaring, and firecrackers were set off.

One resident, caught up in the excitement, even showed up in his pajamas.

Huntsville's representatives at the annual Decatur Chamber of Commerce banquet left in a mad rush when a waiter whispered the news to one of the members. The banquet hall was empty in a matter of minutes as the representatives formed a convoy to Huntsville, noisily blowing car horns the whole way.

Telephone switchboards were jammed as reporters from around the world relayed word of the celebration going on downtown. The next day *The London News* carried a picture on its front page of Mayor R. B. (Spec) Searcy setting off fireworks as jubilant bystanders cheered him on.

The Huntsville Times had sent its staff home and was shut down for the night when J. M. Langhorne, the publisher, received word. Immediately he ordered an "Extra" and employees began streaming in. A linotype operator was pressed into duty as a proofreader while another employee was assigned the task of making enough coffee to keep everyone awake through the night. Huntsville Times photographers, without even contacting the office first, rushed downtown upon hearing the news in an effort to capture the historic celebration on film.

Barely two hours after *The Huntsville Times* received word, the first "Extra" copy rolled off the presses.

Within days, Huntsville became the focal point for the United States space program. High-technology businesses began pouring into town, setting up offices in converted cotton mills and anywhere else they could find room. Men, who had made a living picking cotton the year before, suddenly found themselves helping build rocket components. One man, a house painter at the time, later boasted that he was offered seven jobs in one day, with each employer outbidding the other.

Of all the stories told to describe Huntsville's explosive growth after the success of the satellite, probably the best one is given by Leroy Hodges.

"There used to be this big cotton field up there in North Huntsville, surrounded by briar patches. Place was covered up with rabbits. About a month before rabbit season opened I went up there to look around, walk the fields and kind'a get a feel for it.

"Opening day of rabbit season, I got up way before daylight, loaded my dogs on the truck, and went on up there. Well, it was still dark, so I had to sit there and wait for a while before I could see anything. 'Bout the time the sun starts coming over Monte Sano, I got a good look at the cotton field only it weren't no cotton field no more. In the past month they had done built a subdivision, complete with roads and all."

Chapter 76

A Tale of Two Friends

Earl Frazier and J. B. Webb had a strange relationship. They were good friends and spent much time in one another's company. They shared the same friends and had even once talked about opening up a garage together. Unfortunately, J. B. Webb was a bootlegger and Earl Frazier was a deputy sheriff whose job was to put bootleggers out of business.

Needless to say, Huntsville in the 1950s and 60s was a much different place than today. It was still a small rural community, where everyone knew everyone, and a man's word was his bond.

J. B. Webb's bootlegging enterprise operated out of an old frame house off of Monroe Street. It was reported that he began the first "curb service" in Huntsville. A customer could pull into an alley next to J. B.'s house, blow his horn and someone would take his order. Webb stocked a wide variety of beers, whiskeys and an occasional jar of moonshine, all of which found a ready market among Huntsville's citizens.

Webb and Frazier had been friends for years when Webb heard the new sheriff was looking for another deputy. Immediately he sent word to the sheriff, recommending Frazier for the position. Earl Frazier was well qualified for the job. He was honest, a native of Huntsville and above all, a man whose physical size demanded instant respect from any would-be law breakers.

The same day after being sworn in as Madison County's newest deputy, Earl stopped by to express his thanks to J. B.

After exchanging greetings, the two men sat down at the kitchen table to enjoy a drink and talk of old times, much in the same manner they had done for years.

Their conversation was interrupted however, by the loud blowing of a car horn in the alley next door. Webb disappeared outside, took the order and then came back in the house to get the merchandise.

"I wish you hadn't done that," drawled the deputy as he watched Webb retrieve two bottles of whiskey from the cupboard. "Why?" replied Webb, not really paying attention. "Cause now I got to arrest you for selling."

Strange as it may seem to people today, Earl had sworn to uphold the law regardless of his personal friendships. Even stranger was the fact that J. B. respected him for it.

Arriving at the jail and preparing to make bond, Webb realized he had no money with him. Frazier immediately loaned him the required amount.

Periodically, just before elections or holidays, Huntsville's finest would stage raids on the community's bootleggers. Though it was a nuisance, J. B. Webb accepted it as the cost of doing business. One time however, he received a tip about an impending raid that worried him. He had just received three cases of an expensive Scotch, part of his Christmas stock and could not afford to have it confiscated.

Hurriedly placing the liquor in the back of his pink convertible, he drove to Earl's house where he hid it inside of a shed behind the house. If the neighbors saw him they paid no attention as Earl and J. B., were continuously borrowing lawn mowers and tools from one another.

Just like clockwork, the police arrived the next week and raided the premises. After they left, Webb sat down at the table to have a drink when Earl walked in carrying a package.

"J. B.," he said, "I just wanted to come by early and give you your Christmas present."

The old bootlegger, after expressing his thanks, opened the package to reveal a bottle of expensive, aged Scotch.

Touched by his friend's generosity, Webb asked, "Where did you ever find such good Scotch?"

"Oh, it's nothing," the deputy replied. "I was cleaning out my woodshed the other day and I found a few cases I must have forgot about, so I figured I'd give them for Christmas presents."

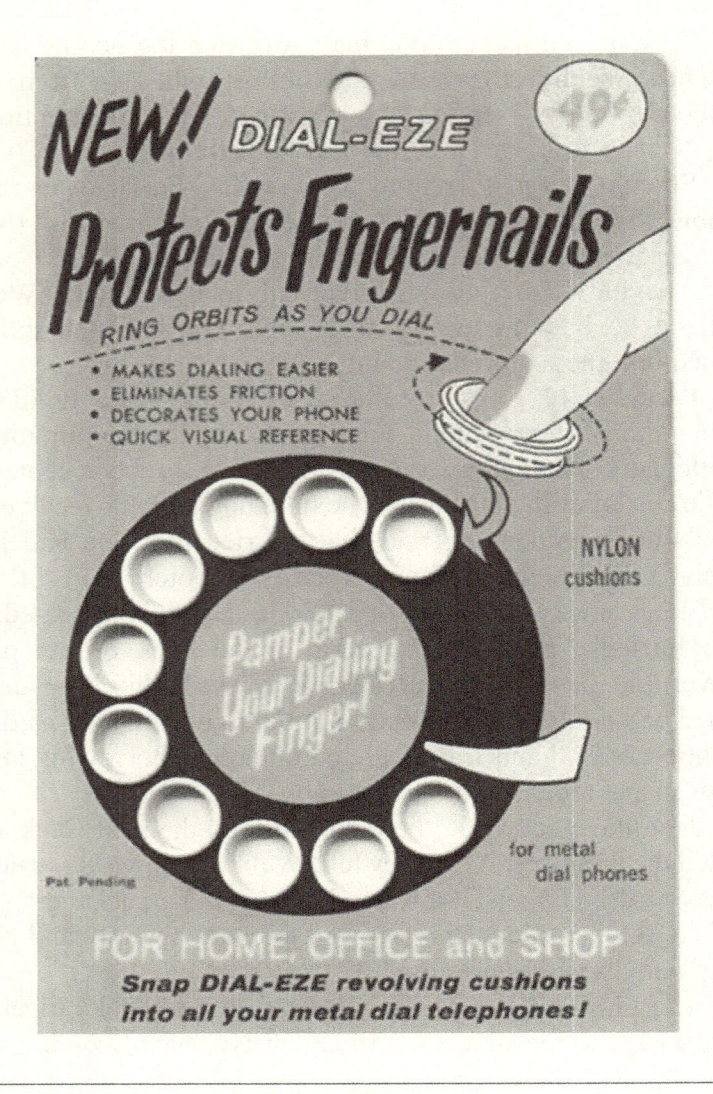

Chapter 77

The Old Man and His Violin

The night was cold and blustery, with a touch of snow in the air. It was a night unfit for mortal or beast, so when the old man with the beat-up violin case walked in and sat down in front of the wood-burning stove to get warm, no one paid much attention. On a night like this, everyone was welcome to share the warmth of the old bar.

It was a week before Christmas and everyone was feeling low. Joe and Laura, sitting at the table in the corner, were depressed. No money, no gifts to give their relatives. It didn't look like it would be a very cheerful Christmas. Benny, who had just lost his job, was sitting at the bar, carefully trying to nurse one beer to make it last as long as he could. Even Cathey, the bartender, was lost in thought, wondering how she would buy presents for her children and pay rent at the same time.

The old man might have sat there forever without anyone paying any attention to him if he had not picked up his violin and begun playing. Softly and quietly he began, so low that it took the customers a few moments to realize where the music was coming from.

It was obvious to everyone that the old man and his violin had seen many years together, maybe a concert stage or maybe even a symphony orchestra.

Hushed and hauntingly the music poured forth, filling the room and finding its way into every dark corner and crevice. With his head bowed and his fingers dancing softly on the strings, the old man and the instrument seemed as one. It was the music of the gods—music that would make an angel cry.

The customers stared at the old man as his music began to envelop them with its warm, haunting melodies. The music seemed to gently beckon to them until finally, unable to resist, they were caught up in its magical harmonies and transported to a time and place where everything was perfect and the only tears shed were those of joy. Riding on a crescendo of love and passion, the violin carried the customers to a place where time had no meaning and Christmas was in your heart forever. Maybe it was because of the tears in the patrons' eyes, but for whatever the reason, no one saw the old man leave. ...

Just a short story about an old man, his violin, and Jay's Lounge. A completely meaningless story—unless you had been there.

Howes Music House
F.A. HOWE, PROP'R
Huntsville   **Alabama**

Complete stock of MUSICAL GOODS, string and trimmings of all kinds. Everything Musical. Special prices for summer trade

"My Sweetheart," by F.H. Howe Jr., latest popular song. 40 cents

Chapter 78

Earthquake

On August 6, 1961, a radio station disc jockey, in Birmingham, interrupted his programming to broadcast news of an earthquake. The amount of damage was not yet known, but there were reports of windows rattling and dishes being knocked off the shelves all across North Alabama. Within minutes, other radio stations began broadcasting the same news and civil defense sirens began blaring across all of North Alabama.

Robert Snider, a newspaper reporter, was on his way to Birmingham when he heard the news. Immediately, he stopped at the next phone and called the radio station that had first broadcast the report.

The radio announcer repeated the information released over the air.

Playing a hunch, Mr. Snider next called the Marshall Space Flight Center in Huntsville. "Yes," said the space flight official, "there was a test firing of the Saturn today. It took place at 1:00 p.m."

There had never been an earthquake. The earth tremor that had been reported was the test firing of the Saturn rocket, the most powerful engine in the world. It had been felt, and heard, all the way to Birmingham.

Even today, there are still people who remember the powerful "earthquake" of 1961.

Chapter 79

The Church with its Own Beer Cooler

One of the stories of old Huntsville that has almost been forgotten is the one about Faith Presbyterian and Cambron's nightclub.

As Huntsville began to grow in the late 1950s, so did the need for more church space. A recently formed congregation of the Presbyterian church had been meeting in members' homes and anywhere else they could find space to worship. As the membership grew, so did the need for a permanent meeting place.

The answer to their dilemma came one Sunday evening when Charley Motley, a member of the congregation, was driving down Whitesburg Drive. Noticing a nightclub by the name of Cambron's, Charley paused and took a long look at it. Due to the Sunday Blue Laws of that time, nightclubs were not permitted to open on Sunday. "What a waste," Charley thought. "All that space not being used on the one day of the week when we could really use it."

Due to the nature of their business, it's hard to shock most nightclub operators but when Mr. and Mrs. Motley walked into the darkened club and asked permission to use it for a church gathering, Cambron was flabbergasted. "Ruby, come here," he said to his wife. "You gotta hear this."

As Mr. Motley explained their needs, Cambron shook his head and decided, "Why not? If you are willing to help clean the place up on Sunday mornings, it will help me out, too."

Over the next several months, a routine was established by the Faith Presbyterian Church that had to be unique in the annals of church history. Church members would arrive early on Sunday morning and begin sweeping the floors. One person was assigned to empty ash trays, while others would clean tabletops and carry out trash. One member was even assigned the task of unplugging the juke box and turning off the neon sign that proclaimed Budweiser as the "King of Beers."

The membership continued to grow with Cambron's being the only nightclub in Huntsville with Bibles and textbooks stored in the back room. One old-timer tells a story about a man who was in the habit of drinking too much on Saturday nights. After much persuasion, his neighbor finally talked him into going to church. One Sunday morning, as he got out of the car in front of Cambron's, the man paused, as if in reflection and said, "I've heard that guilty people always return to the scene of the crime, but isn't this just a little ridiculous?" When Mr. Cambron offered to sell the property, (for one million dollars with no money down) the church quickly accepted the offer, becoming the only Presbyterian church to ever purchase a nightclub.

The nightclub has long since been replaced by modem facilities and the church continues to flourish, only now without the neon Budweiser sign.

Chapter 80

The Parkway

By the early 1950s, downtown Huntsville was becoming so congested with traffic that our city officials realized a bypass was a necessity. After looking at various plans, they leaned toward a plan that would have a four-lane bypass built on the mountain ridges, east of the city. Hannes Luehrsen thought the route for the proposed by-pass absurd. Luehrsen was one of the original von Braun team members, brought here from Germany where he had helped design rocket facilities. He was presently busy redesigning Redstone Arsenal for the work on rockets that would eventually take place there.

In a conversation with *The Huntsville Times* editor, Reese Amis, Luehrsen explained what he thought was wrong with the proposed route, and also offered an alternative that he thought made better sense. Amis, a typical editor, was willing to listen, but insisted on seeing plans before he ran a story. Unfortunately, Luehrsen had no plans.

No one has ever accused our Germans of not being resourceful, and Hannes Luehrsen was no exception. Taking pencil in hand, he sat down and drew the plans for what would later be known as the Memorial Parkway—in two hours.

Years later, when asked about it, he replied, "What do you expect in two hours?"

Chapter 81

Tombstone for a Monkey

On May 28,1959 two monkeys (a squirrel monkey named Baker and a rhesus monkey named Able) were strapped into the nose cone of a Huntsville built Jupiter ballistic missile and blasted into a fifteen-minute suborbital space flight to test effects of this new environment on mammals before man would risk himself in his quest for the stars. Although both monkeynauts survived the historic flight, Able died soon after reentry when medical instruments were being removed from his body. Miss Baker, the sole survivor, would go on to live an incredible twenty-five more years while becoming one of the world's most famous and adored monkeys.

Miss Baker was born in a Peruvian jungle in 1957. She was taken from her habitat shortly thereafter and was subjected to an intense preflight program to condition her to being strapped into a miniature couch during her flight for mankind. She was a spunky little squirrel monkey all her life. Her first response to humans after the flight was to bite her handler. Her last act before her death, in 1984, was again to bite her handler.

In between, she became the cornerstone and prime attraction of the Huntsville Space and Rocket Center in Huntsville. She was in no small way responsible for the museum's growth and popularity that today has reached international proportions.

Miss Baker was beloved by children all over the world and in her lifetime received thousands of letters and appeared on twenty network news shows over the years. Typical letters to

Miss Baker usually inquired of her health and would ask her if she needed or wanted a new friend. Children also were curious if Miss Baker saw any Martians while in space and one child wrote and wondered if she had seen Jesus during her celebrated journey.

The care, love and attention Miss Baker received from the Space and Rocket Center was outstanding and deeply felt. The little monkey (14-ounces) was under meticulous medical care during her entire life in captivity. Besides her Huntsville veterinarian, the Yerkes Primate Center's monkey specialists in Atlanta were always on call in case of any dramatic change in Miss Baker's condition.

Unfortunately, nothing is forever, and in the late fall of 1984 Miss Baker passed into legend. Her death was mourned worldwide, for she was the little squirrel monkey that blazed a trail into space that men and women would later follow. Her tombstone at the Space and Rocket Center reads:

MISS BAKER
SQUIRREL MONKEY
BORN 1957
DIED NOV 29, 1984
FIRST U.S. ANIMAL
TO FLY IN SPACE
AND RETURN ALIVE
MAY 28, 1959

Chapter 82

Clinton Avenue Archaeology

On December 15, 1968, North Alabama was riveted by the news of a possible major archaeological find in Huntsville. William Thomas Young, a resident of 507 East Clinton Avenue, was working on replacing a floor in his home, and upon finding a pile of loose bricks underneath, decided to remove them. What he discovered next would earn his home a spot in Huntsville trivia for all time to come.

A skeleton, the biggest that anyone had ever seen, was uncovered. Everyone agreed that the bones were of some type of animal, but no one could imagine what kind of a creature could be so huge.

Immediately, speculation began about the bones. As the word spread, gawkers began lining up on the street trying to get a view. Old history books, with pictures of dinosaurs, were hastily retrieved from dusty attics and neighbors began talking of the Tyrannosauruses, and Trachodons that once stalked this region. One person who lived on Clinton even suggested calling the Smithsonian Institute to have them fly in experts. Unfortunately, the puzzle was quickly solved, and Huntsville missed the opportunity of becoming the site for an archaeological dig. A local historian remembered hearing tales of an elephant being buried somewhere on Clinton Avenue and by putting two and two together, solved the mystery.

It seems as if a circus had come to town in the fall of 1893 and erected its tents about a half-mile outside of town in a location now known as Five Points. As the circus was packing up and getting ready to leave town, one of its elephants died. Circuses and traveling carnivals were notorious for leaving sick and dead animals behind, so when Sheriff Jere Murphee heard of the dead elephant, he quickly informed the circus that they could not leave town until the carcass was buried.

Mr. Bradshaw, the manager of the circus, then hired a local man by the name of Gentry to bury the carcass for the sum of ten dollars. Although some people may think that ten dollars was a large sum of money, it was also a large elephant. Mr. Gentry hitched his team of mules to the carcass, the circus left town, and everyone was happy.

In retrospect, it seems as if Mr. Gentry might have been a bit on the lazy side, for instead of digging a hole to bury the carcass, he took the easy way out. In the 500 block of East Clinton, there had at one time been an old brickworks, and adjacent to the works was a large hole from where the clay for the bricks had been dug. It was here that Gentry dumped the carcass and finished filling in the hole with old bricks and rubble.

And it was here, years later, that homes were built, with Mr. Young eventually buying the one with the secret.

So, the next time you go by 507 East Clinton, take a long look. It's probably the only house in America with an elephant buried underneath it.

Chapter 83

Music Appreciation

Probably no man in Huntsville's recent history was admired and liked by more people than Grady Reeves, a noted radio and television personality.

He had so many friends that once when he asked a local politician to appear on his television show, the politician replied, yes, on the one condition that Grady promised to never get into politics and run against him.

Grady Reeves was a storyteller. He could keep an audience enthralled for hours, spinning yarns about people he had met and things that had happened to him. And like all good storytellers, he was not above poking a little fun at himself.

Most people don't know it, but back in the mid-1950s Grady was booking entertainment at the old Coliseum on University Drive. He was always being besieged by entertainers, all wanting a chance to perform. One young man kept calling constantly, until finally Grady agreed to give him a chance.

On the night of the performance, the young man showed up with his band, after driving from Nashville in his beat-up old car. The car had guitars tied on top, drums sticking out of the truck and most of their dirty laundry in the backseat. Grady wasn't too impressed with the boy. He had long, greasy, black hair, a pale complexion and wore clothes that even a blind man wouldn't buy.

But Grady, being the nice guy that he was, told the boy to go ahead and get on stage. There were almost 100 people in the audience that night and Grady carefully watched their reactions to this young unknown.

The audience was restless, not at all impressed by the new singing sensation.

Meeting the young man backstage, Grady, who was always known for his honesty, had a talk with the young performer. "Son," he said, "I been watching those people out there, and your stuff ain't gonna work. You might ought to go back to Nashville and get that truck-driving job back."

The young man didn't take Grady's advice, though, and a few months later he recorded his first song — and Elvis Presley never drove another truck again.

Chapter 84

The Governor Goes to Breakfast

During Fob James first term as governor, he had occasion to spend several days in Huntsville attending a series of meetings. The second day he awoke early with a ravishing hunger. Quite naturally, he remembered Eunice's Country Kitchen, a place he had visited several times before, and which was well-known for its ham and biscuits.

Quietly getting dressed, so as not to awaken anyone, James slipped out of the hotel room and, after sneaking by the guards stationed in the hall, caught a ride with a car that was waiting out front.

Eunice's had not changed very much. Autographed pictures of many famous people were still on the walls and the coffee pot was still brewing.

Trying to be as incognito as he could, the governor slipped into a back booth and ordered breakfast. He was halfway through his second biscuit when he noticed an elderly gentleman staring at him. Every few minutes the man would turn excitedly to his companions and, after pointing at the governor, would engage them in a spirited conversation.

"Oh well," the governor thought. "I should have known I would be recognized."

Deciding to make the best of it, James hurriedly finished his breakfast and walked over to shake hands and introduce himself.

"I'm...," he began.

"I know who you are!" The old gentleman exclaimed, with a grin stretching from ear to ear. "You're that TV fellow who announces the wrestling programs on TV every Saturday night! Can I have your autograph?"

Needless to say, the gentleman got an autograph.

Chapter 85

Account Paid

When Bragg's Grocery, on Hurricane Creek, closed in 1993, it was the end of an era. The old store had at one time been the center of the community, with house-wives gathering inside to trade gossip while their husbands sat outside on the bench talking endlessly about the weather and whittling on ever-present pieces of cedar.

With the store closed, the only thing that remained was a stack of old ledgers from a bygone day, when people would charge their purchases and pay when their crops came in, or maybe when times got better. These yellowed account books contained, in many cases, the life stories of many people who called Hurricane Creek home.

There was Bob Ashbourn. He charged a pair of shoes that cost $2.65. That same day, he purchased a shirt for 75 cents. Looking back at an old calendar, we see that the day was a Friday.

Had he just gotten paid? Or, maybe he was buying new clothes in order to court someone special.

Bill Matthews, the following day, bought 12 yards of cloth and 10 cents worth of snuff. Wonder if the same person used both?

Charlie Fears must have been a hard-working man because most of his purchases were for farm implements and seed. Two days before Christmas, in 1937, he was back in the store buying apples, candy, and oranges, probably for Santa Claus.

Henry Tucker stopped at the store for 50 cents worth of gas on Christmas Eve. Louise Jolly was in the store the same day settling her account. Bob Langford seemed to have not been in the Christmas spirit that year as the only purchases he made on December 24, were tobacco, snuff and coffee for a total price of 65 cents.

The first of the month must have been a busy time at the store.

Old-timers called it "check-cashing day," as that was when they received their government checks. That must have been a popular day for the children too, as almost everyone purchased candy when cashing their checks. Among the people cashing checks was Bill Smith, who also paid his insurance premium (51 cents) at the same time.

Gus White must have been a carpenter, or maybe he was adding on to his house. In January of 1938 he purchased 500 feet of oak boxing, 50 posts and 25 feet of lumber. The lumber was 2 cents a foot.

Macaroni was obviously a popular food. Besides tobacco, coffee, and candy, it was the product sold most often. The Walton family purchased macaroni four times in three weeks.

Alvin Blackwell probably didn't travel very far when he was young. His average purchase of gas was only 50 cents. That summer he also charged 19 cents worth of fishing tackle. The community didn't need a restaurant. On almost every page were listings such as "Logan Honey, lunch—20 cents."

You would have to guess that the Robert Harris family suffered from sickness that winter. Among their purchases were aspirins, salve, iodine, Black Drought, castor oil, alcohol, and salts. The week before Christmas, Mr. Harris added a French harp, stationery, tablets, apples, and a coconut to his bill.

Perhaps the most poignant entry in the ledgers is the account of an old man who purchased cotton seed in anticipation of making a crop that year. The man was poor with no way to pay until the crop came in.

Several weeks after the purchase, the old man died, leaving no family or money. The next day someone, in old-fashioned, meticulous handwriting, had carefully entered "Paid" to his account.

Made in the USA
Coppell, TX
14 November 2020